The Cultural Transformation of a Native American Family and Its Tribe   1763–1995
A Basket of Apples

Sociocultural, Political, and Historical Studies in Education

Joel Spring, Editor

Non-Western Educational Traditions:
Alternative Approaches to Educational Thought and Practice

Timothy Reagan

The Cultural Transformation of a
Native American Family and Its Tribe 1763–1995
A Basket of Apples

Joel Spring

The Cultural Transformation
of a Native American Family
and Its Tribe   1763–1995
A Basket of Apples

Joel Spring

LEA LAWRENCE ERLBAUM ASSOCIATES, PUBLISHERS
1996 Mahwah, New Jersey

Lawrence Erlbaum Associates, Inc., Publishers
10 Industrial Avenue
Mahwah, New Jersey 07430

Cover design by Gail Silverman

Library of Congress Cataloging-in-Publication Data

Spring, Joel H.
    The cultural transformation of a Native American family
    and its tribe 1763–1995 : a basket of apples / Joel Spring.
        p. cm.
    Includes bibliographical references and index.
        ISBN 0-8058-2303-4 (cloth : alk paper). — ISBN
    0-8058-2247-X (pbk. : alk. paper)
        1.   Choctaw   Indians—History.   2.   Choctaw
    Indians—Relocation.   3.   Choctaw   Indians—Cultural
    assimilation. 4. Cherokee Indians—History. 5. Cherokee
    Indians—Relocation.   6.   Cherokee   Indians—Cultural
    assimilation. 7. Indians of North America—Southern
    States—Mixed descent. 8. Blacks—Relations with Indians.
    I. Title.
    E99.C8S67 1996
    305.897'3—dc20   96-12504
                                                             CIP

Books published by Lawrence Erlbaum Associates are printed
on acid-free paper, and their bindings are chosen for strength
and durability.

Printed in the United States of America
10 9 8 7 6 5 4 3 2 1

Contents

Preface

While engaged in a personal quest for my family's roots in Choctaw tribal history, I discovered a direct relationship between federal "civilization" programs and changes in my family and tribe from the 18th to the early 20th century. Educated as an historian of ideas with a primary focus on the history of educational ideas and institutions, I quickly became interested in the effect of government policies on the cultural transformation of both the Choctaws and my family.

I am not very proud of my family's leadership role in the cultural transformation of the Choctaws. During this period of cultural change, my family mirrored, at least from my perspective, some of the worst qualities of European-American society. For the Choctaws, civilization policies resulted in the development of social classes in what had been an essentially egalitarian society, the use of educational institutions to maintain political and economic power, the ownership of enslaved Africans, and, after fighting on the side of the Confederacy, the establishment of a racially segregated Choctaw school system.

My story begins with the cultural differences that existed between Native Americans and European colonists. Federal civilization policies were designed to eliminate these cultural differences. The civilization policies of the federal government were essentially educational policies designed to change Native Americans into model European Americans. The discussion of civilization policies begins with the 1790s, when President George Washington began and Thomas Jefferson continued to search for a means of gaining the lands occupied by the southern tribes, including the Choctaws.

Of course, Native Americans did not believe that European Americans had a superior lifestyle and they tried to change federal policies to meet their needs. Of particular importance to my family history are those European Americans who, deciding Native American values were superior, abandoned European culture and joined Native American tribes as "white Indians." In addition, the educators, primarily missionaries, had their own agenda. Therefore, my story involves a complicated interaction between the policies of the government, the agenda of White educators, and the desires of Native Americans. At each stage of my story, a family member plays an important and often infamous role in the cultural evolution of the tribe.

What makes this story both infamous and interesting as an attempt at planned cultural change and ideological management was that the final solution to gaining southern tribal lands was the forced removal of the so-called five civilized tribes from lands extending from North Carolina to Louisiana to lands west of the Mississippi. These western lands became Indian Territory where one of the most important attempts in world history at planned cultural transformation took place. In Indian Territory, as part of this social experiment, tribes organized into dependent constitutional republics with their own school systems.

In a broader context, my story is a study of the evolution of an American family from the extended support of the community and clan of the past to the present world of single parents adrift without community or family safety nets. In the 18th century, everyone in the large extended clan of my family was taken care of by other clan members. After two centuries of federal policies designed to "civilize" Native Americans, I grew up in a single parent household with no support from an extended family, no family history, and with an absent alcoholic father. This is the price I paid for the policies initiated by President George Washington. We are our history.

PART I

CHOCTAWS, CHEROKEES, AND A MIXED-BLOOD FAMILY PRIOR TO REMOVAL

1

A Basket of Apples

On January 23, 1896, a fire swept through the white-framed buildings of the Spencer Academy, killing my uncle, Pat (Samuel Guy) Spring, who was 10 years old at the time. Sometimes referred to as the National School of the Choctaw Nation, Indian Territory, the Spencer Academy offered college preparatory studies to the children primarily of wealthy Choctaw citizens. When the fire started, the children were hurried from the main building as clouds of smoke filled the classrooms and hallways. Wanting to save a basket of apples his father had sent him, Pat ran back into the building just as the fire was spreading. As he returned, the stairway collapsed, causing him to be badly burned. After hurrying to the school with horses and a wagon, my grandfather, Joel S. Spring, gently laid his son on the floor of the wagon. Racing to Paris, Texas for medical help, my grandfather ran the horses to death and Pat died a few days later. My grandfather probably agonized over whether or not he was responsible for the tragedy by sending his son the gift of apples. On Pat Spring's tombstone in the Spring Chapel Cemetery near Hugo, Oklahoma is carved a basket of apples.

Ironically, by the middle of the 20th century, "apple" came to mean a person who is Red on the outside but White on the inside. And that was precisely the educational goal of the Spencer Academy—to transform the minds and manners of Choctaw citizens into well-educated European Americans. Opened in 1844 by the Choctaw Nation, the Spencer Academy was the elite school within a whole system of schooling created by the Choctaw Nation after their removal from Mississippi to Indian Territory (now Oklahoma) in the 1830s. Along with the Cherokees, who were removed from areas in Tennessee, North Carolina, Georgia, and Alabama, the Choctaws were the largest and most acculturated of the so-called five "civilized" tribes to European-American ways. In the 1830s, these five tribes (the others being the Creeks, Chickasaws, and Seminoles) were removed by the United States government from the southeastern part of the United States to provide land for White settlers.

In the early 19th century, the removal of the five civilized tribes played an important role in the economic development of the United States. It opened lands for the growth of cotton and an expanded cotton economy, and it contributed to the continuation and expansion of slavery and, ultimately, to the onset of the Civil War.

Besides wanting to open land for White settlers, U.S. government officials hoped that isolating Choctaws from the worst elements of White frontier society and establishing school systems would "civilize" them. Civilizing southern tribes, as I explain later, was first made a goal by President George Washington.

Imagine the audacity of the U.S. government's plan to change the cultures of the five civilized tribes: Removal policies involved transporting entire nations of people across the continent on the Trail of Tears (as the trail to Indian Territory was called as a result of the psychological and physical suffering experienced during removal) for the purpose of conversion to a new way of living and thinking by eradicating cultural values, religions, family structures, governments, and economic relationships and replacing them with values and institutions compatible with the goals of the U.S. government. This was one of the largest attempts at planned cultural change in human history. Then after over seventy years of this experiment, in the late 19th and early 20th centuries, U.S. officials decided to take back the land, abolish the newly organized tribal governments, and change Indian Territory into the state of Oklahoma.

The school system operated by the Choctaw government in Indian Territory was highlighted in a 1969 Congressional report: "In the 1800s, for example, the Choctaw Indians of . . . Oklahoma [Indian Territory] operated about 200 schools and academies and sent numerous graduates to eastern colleges."[1] The report goes on to praise the Cherokee schools: "Using bilingual teachers and Cherokee texts, the Cherokees, during the same period, controlled a school system which produced a tribe almost 100% literate.[2] The report concludes, "Anthropologists have determined that as a result of this school system, the literacy level in English of western Oklahoma Cherokees was higher than the White populations of either Texas or Arkansas."[3]

The takeover by the state and federal governments had a disastrous effect on the education of future generations of the Indians of the five civilized tribes:

> Now, after almost 70 years of Federal and State controlled education, the Cherokees have the following educational record: 40 percent of adult Cherokees are functionally illiterate in English; only 39 percent have completed the eighth grade; the median educational level of the tribe's adult population is only 5.5 years; dropout rates of Indians students are often as high as 75 percent.[4]

One statistic in the 1969 report highlights the tragic decline of education in what had once been Indian Territory: "The statistical data speak for themselves: 87 percent dropout by the 6th grade at an all-Indian public elementary school near Ponca, Okla."[5]

CULTURAL TRANSFORMATION AND THE USE OF SCHOOLING

My purpose in studying the effect of formal schools on the Choctaws is twofold. First, I want to analyze the efforts by European Americans to exert cultural control over a conquered people, and the attempt of Native Americans to adjust to the presence of Europeans. Second, I want to highlight the emerging concerns of governments in using public schools to manage populations. Throughout the 19th and 20th centuries, governments have attempted to use schools and mass media to control the actions of their citizens. In Western society in the 19th century, the rise of the public school represented one important attempt to educate "good" citizens. In the 20th century, governments expanded their interests to include other forms of media, such as radio, movies, and television.[6]

I maintain that the attempt to transform the culture of an entire people is an important example of the use of schooling as an instrument of ideological management. And, as is often the case, the subjects, Native Americans, did not react passively. Many Indian leaders welcomed some form of schooling as necessary for national survival.

MULTIPLE PERSPECTIVES ON CIVILIZATION AND SCHOOLING

The Choctaws were not simply victims of federal civilization policies. Certain Choctaws welcomed these policies because they strengthened their economic and political position in the tribe. On the other hand, missionaries who implemented many of the civilization policies sometimes sided with the Choctaws in opposition to the U.S. government. Federal officials wanted schools to turn Choctaws into domesticated housewives and farmers so that they would not need extensive lands for hunting. This would provide more land for White settlers. Schooling, these officials believed, would make tribal members understand and conform to government laws designed to "civilize" them. State government officials, on the other hand, tended to oppose the federal policies on civilizing Indians because they worried that education might create resistance among Native Americans to the takeover of their lands.

Missionaries wanted to convert Indians to Christianity. Their goal was not in conflict with the federal government's goals, as most political leaders after the Revolutionary war believed that only good Protestants could be good Republicans. The Protestant ethic that reigned at the time supported the idea that a person should work hard to accumulate property and that wealth was a sign of God's blessings. To accomplish the goal of turning Indians into model European farmers, government officials believed that the values of Christianity needed to be instilled.

On the other hand, missionaries were primarily concerned with saving souls and not necessarily with turning Native Americans into farmers so that their lands would be available to White settlers. Consequently, there was a debate among missionary societies as to whether or not Indians should be "civilized" before conversion. Missionaries who were primarily concerned with conversion were often in conflict with federal officials and tribal leaders, who were primarily concerned with Indians receiving a general education. Some missionary educators did not support the goal of taking away Indian lands. Consequently, state governments often objected to missionary schools operating on tribal lands.

In contrast to missionaries and government officials, tribal leaders wanted schools to be a means of protecting the tribe against the onslaught of federal and state governments and White settlers. These Native Americans believed that literacy was necessary for understanding U.S. government laws and establishing formal governments among the tribes. Some Indians believed that acculturation to White ways would save tribal lands and governments. Other Native Americans believed that White racism made it impossible for Whites and Indians to coexist within the same communities.

Within the tribes, formal schooling supported the evolution of distinct social classes and the centralization of political power. After the Civil War, Choctaws were forced to free their enslaved Africans, and, consequently, the tribe established segregated schools. This reinforced Choctaw racism regarding African Americans. In addition, schools consciously worked to change gender roles to transform the Choctaws from a matrilineal clan system to a patrilineal nuclear family. This transition would make it possible for male tribal leaders to protect their wealth and pass it on to their sons.

Not all tribal members supported the introduction of European-American-style schooling. Some believed that the missionaries were primarily interested in tribal lands. Others did not want to give up their culture and religion. Some Indians believed their culture was superior to that of Europeans. Others argued that the existence of separate civilizations was an intended part of creation, and, therefore, acculturation should be avoided. Others believed that problems faced by the tribes were a result of attempts to acculturate.

TRIBAL AND FAMILY HISTORY

There are two distinct phases to the controlled cultural transformation of the Choctaws. The first phase occured between the 1790s and the removal period of the early 1830s, and its distinctive characteristic was the U.S. government's use of civilization policies to gain tribal lands. In the second phase, after removal to Indian Territory, the Choctaw government assumed control over its civilization policies through the operation of a Choctaw school system. These two phases correspond to the first and second parts of this book.

In addition to the history of the tribe, I am using my family history as an example of the effect of cultural changes. As I discuss, my family represents the effects of White men joining the tribe and of the growth of a mixed-blood class who make key decisions about the future of the tribe. My family also represents a social class within the tribe that welcomes the U.S. government's civilization policies and, upon arrival in Indian Territory, assumes control of the Choctaw school system.

In the first part of the book, which corresponds to the period prior to removal, I discuss both the Choctaws and Cherokees. In the second part, I focus on the Choctaw government and school system in Indian Territory. Because the Cherokees were the first target of U.S. government civilization policies in the 1790s and early 1800s, and because missionaries, who began their work with U.S. government support, moved from the Cherokees to the Choctaws, it is important to include both tribes in the discussion of the early Indian policies of the U.S. government. During the removal period, the Cherokees were involved in important decisions made by the U.S. Supreme Court which defined the legal status of Native Americans.

In chapters 2, 3, and 4, I contrast the goals of government civilization policies and missionary goals with the desires and social organization of the Choctaws and Cherokees. The intersection of government, missionary, and tribal goals resulted in social changes in the tribes that, ironically, defeated the U.S. government's major purpose of gaining tribal lands. Recognizing the failure of civilization policies in his First Annual Address to Congress in 1828, President Jackson advocated taking over Indian lands in the south by the removal of the tribes to an isolated area west of the Mississippi. Chapter 5 is devoted to the educational implications of the removal process.

The second part of the book focuses on the educational history of the Choctaws in Indian Territory from the early 1830s to 1907. Chapters 6 and 7 analyze the development of the Choctaw government and school system and the relationship among race, gender, and social class. Chapter 8 discusses the Choctaw alliance with the Confederacy during the Civil War and the growth of a segregated school system. The end of the Choctaw Nation and school system is discussed in Chapter 9.

My family was involved or was touched by most of the important events in tribal history in the 19th century. As I discuss, my great-great-great grandfather on my grandmother's side of the family, Louis Leflore, was a Frenchman who entered a polygamous relationship with two Choctaw sisters in the late 18th century, ran flatboats on the major rivers of the Nation, and opened a trading post on the present site of the original capitol building in Jackson, Mississippi. Eventually, he opened an inn, called French Camp, that still operates on the Natchez Trace. His mixed-blood children assumed important roles in the tribe and influenced its destiny immediately before and after removal.

My great-great grandfather on my grandfather's side of the family, Christopher Spring (Sprang), was born a Swiss-German and served as a commissioned officer in the Army of Napoleon at the Battle of Waterloo in 1815. After Napoleon's defeat, he immigrated to New Orleans and drifted into Mississippi, where he wed Susan Bohannan, a mixed-blood of French and Indian ancestry. While he was in Mississippi, the spelling of "Sprang" was changed to "Spring." Their mixed-blood son, Samuel Spring, married Elizabeth Leflore. Both the Leflore and Spring families played important roles in shaping the culture of the Choctaw Nation.

The last chapter of the book analyzes the consequences of the experiment in Indian Territory on the tribe and the personal results on my family. In part, this is not only a history of a Native American tribe but also a social history of a mixed-blood Native American family. The story demonstrates the complexity of the evolution of the modern American family.

CULTURAL PREFERENCE

I feel it is important for me to state my own cultural preferences. When I began my initial research, I was concerned with the actual transformation in cultural values that took place among the Choctaws. This required me to explore their traditional cultural values and compare them with those of the European settlers, particularly the English. In comparing cultural differences, I found myself admiring the values of the two tribes in comparison with those of the English. I found myself applauding Native American concepts of the clan, gender roles, child rearing, the sharing of wealth, government, and nature. In contrast, I found myself at odds with English concepts of the nuclear family, male domination, the breaking the will of the child, capitalism, authoritarian government, and the belief that nature exists for the benefit of humans.

My affinity for Native American values might emerge when I discuss cultural differences and cultural transformation. The danger, of course, is that I might seem to romanticize Native American cultures. So let me say at the beginning that there are certain things that I object to in these

Native cultures. I do not consider war a sport, nor do I consider killing another person a sign of manhood. I do not believe in the torture of other human beings. I do not believe in the infanticide of those born with birth defects. I do not believe in the ownership of slaves. These were tribal practices that keep me from concluding that the Choctaws lived in an ideal world before the arrival of Europeans. But, I believe in hindsight, that many of the basic values of Native Americans were preferable to those brought by Europeans.

THE END OF A DREAM

The creation of Oklahoma in 1907 ended the dream of separate but dependent Indian Nations with their own constitutions, economies, and school systems existing within a territory of the United States. What would have happened if the Choctaw Nation were allowed to continue? It would be difficult to answer this question. The Choctaws were not perfect in their organization and social structure. On the other hand, they might have held out as a real hope for the preservation of Indian tribes after they were conquered by European Americans.

I remember the sadness that swept over me in 1993 when I visited the abandoned buildings of the Wheelock Academy, the elite school for Choctaw girls. Founded shortly after removal at the Wheelock Mission in 1832, it evolved into a school attended by the children of many leading Choctaws, including Carrie Gooding, the second wife of my great-great grandfather, Basil Leflore. The beautiful two-story building with its wide front porch still remains standing. I was surprised by the size of the building as I counted eight pillars supporting the front porch with 10 windows on the front of each floor and 17 or 18 windows on the side of the building. Many of the outbuildings still remain standing.

When I entered the Wheelock Academy grounds, I encountered a recently hand-lettered sign with the Great Seal of the Choctaw Nation in its center. The sign identified the site of the Wheelock Mission and welcomed tourists to visit the grounds between 8 a.m. and 8 p.m. I thought of my uncle's basket of apples, my father's alcoholism, and my broken home as I read on the left side of the sign:

> HOME OF THE
> CHOCTAW NATION
> RECOVERY CENTER
> THE REDMAN'S ROAD
> TO RECOVERY: A NEW
> BEGINNING

FIG. 1.1. Basket of apples on the tombstone of Pat (Samuel Guy) Spring who died in the Spencer Academy fire in 1896. The tombstone is located in the Spring Chapel Cemetery, Hugo, Oklahoma.

FIG. 1.2. Current sign at the entrance to the grounds of the Wheelock Academy. As indicated on the sign a mission was first established at this site in 1832.

How different the lives of Choctaws might be if the Wheelock Academy remained as a girls' school, and the U.S. government honored the removal treaties that gave the land to the tribes with the guarantee of ownership "as long as grass should grow and water run."[7]

NOTES

[1] *Indian Education: A National Tragedy—A National Challenge 1969 Report of the Committee on Labor and Public Welfare U.S. Senate, 91st Congress, 1st Session* (Washington, D.C.: U.S. Government Printing Office, 1969), p. 25.

[2] Ibid., p. 25.

[3] Ibid., p. 25.

[4] Ibid., p. 25.

[5] Ibid., p. 29.

[6] See Joel Spring, *Images of American Life: A History of Ideological Management in Schools, Movies, Radio and Television*. (Albany: State University of New York Press, 1993).

[7] Angie Debo, *And Still the Waters Run: The Betrayal of the Five Civilized Tribes* (Princeton: Princeton University Press, 1940), p. 152.

2

Indian Policy as Ideological Management

"To conciliate the powerful tribes of Indians in the southern District [which included the Choctaw, Cherokee, Chickasaw, and Creek tribes] amounting probably to fourteen thousand fighting Men,"[1] President George Washington and Secretary of War Henry Knox warned the Senate in 1789, "and to attach them firmly to the United States, may be regarded as highly worthy of the serious attention of government."[2] By the late 1820s, Commissioner of Indian Affairs Thomas L. McKenney was advocating the removal of the same southern tribes to lands west of the Mississippi for their protection and "civilization." After negotiating in 1827 with the Chickasaw Indians for their removal west of the Mississippi, McKenney wrote Secretary of War James Barbour that, after removal, the southern Indians should be guaranteed their lands in the west and "schools should be distributed over all their country. The children should be taken into these, and instructed . . . [in] reading, writing and arithmetic, in mechanics and the arts; and the girls in all the business of the domestic duties."[3]

After the American Revolution, civilization policies were a pragmatic solution to the problems posed by the continued existence of well-organized Indian tribes. In the 1780s, federal officials believed that the government could not afford the cost of fighting an Indian war. Confronted with the possibility of fighting 14,000 warriors from the southern tribes, the prudent course was to follow a policy of peace. But a policy of peace was difficult because of the continuing expansion of White settlers. Therefore, by the time of Thomas Jefferson's administration (1801–1809), the argument shifted to that of civilizing the southern Indians so that they would live on small farms and, therefore, make available their hunting grounds to White settlers.

With the appointment of McKenney as superintendent of Indian trade in 1816, attention was focused on the use of schools to carry out civilization policies. By this time, there was also a concern by some government leaders that Native Americans were on the road to extinc-

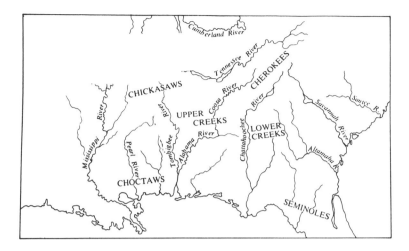

FIG. 2.1.   Map of the Southern Tribes 1780s–1830s. Reprinted from Thurman Wilkins, *Cherokee Tragedy* (Norman: University of Oklahoma Press, 1983), p. 2.

tion. Commissioner McKenney and others believed extinction was inevitable unless the tribes were civilized by being removed to lands west of Mississippi. The pressure and influence of White settlers, it was argued, were destroying the southern Indians in the same manner that Indians tribes on the east coast were earlier decimated by White settlers. Of course, removal made Indian lands available for the expansion of White settlement in the south and solved the problem of maintaining peace between the settlers and Native Americans. For McKenney, removal provided the opportunity for completion of the civilization project and, consequently, salvation of the southern tribes in an isolated and protected territory under federal control.

Thus, ideological management[4] as a policy of the federal government emerged as a pragmatic solution and rationale for obtaining Indian lands. In hindsight, the logic of destroying Native American culture and taking away Indian lands as a means of saving Indians seems rather twisted. But, I believe, it was a logical consequence of a population imbued with a belief in the superiority of European civilization—in the manifest destiny of Europeans' populating North America—and the growing belief in the ability and desirability of government control through peaceful management of the population by controlling values and ideas through public schools.

In the remainder of this chapter, I first explore the concept of cultural superiority and the meaning of "civilizing" and "civilization." I then examine the evolution of civilization policies from the presidency of Washington to McKenney's leadership of the Bureau of Indian Affairs in the 1820s. In addition, I compare civilization policies with the development of common schools as a method of social control. Again, I would like to remind the reader that later chapters show that Native Americans were not passive receptors of these federal policies.

CULTURAL AND RACIAL SUPERIORITY

On the surface, it appears to be the height of arrogance to think that Native Americans would have been better off if they were transformed into model European Americans. The English sense of cultural superiority, according to historian Takaki, originated with the invasion of Ireland in the 16th century. According to Takaki, the English considered the Irish inferior savages who could be redeemed only by adopting English culture. Eventually, English opinion was divided between the possibility of civilizing the Irish and a belief in their innate savagery. The latter position became part of a generalized belief that some groups of people were racially inferior to the English.[5]

When the English arrived in North America, many compared their experiences with Indians to their experiences with the Irish. Takaki found many written comparisons during colonial times between the "wild Irish" and the "wild Indians." As with the Irish, English opinion was divided over the possibility of civilizing Native Americans.[6] Extreme racist opinions led to the conclusion that the only solution to the Indian problem was genocide. This attitude is captured in General Philip Sheridan's comment in 1867 after defeating the Cheyennes: "The only good Indians I ever saw were dead." This statement was refined by one of Sheridan's officers to the famous saying, "The only good Indian is a dead Indian."[7]

Also, many European Americans envisioned North America to be a land that would be primarily inhabited by Whites. Benjamin Franklin worried about the larger number of Africans and Asians in the world than European Whites. He considered expansion into North America an opportunity to increase the White race. Shortly before the Revolution, as Takaki pointed out, Franklin argued that the English were the "principle body of white People" that should populate North America. The clearing of the forests, Franklin noted, would serve to make room for more Whites. "Why," he asked, "increase the Sons of Africa, by Planting them in America, where we have so fair an opportunity, by excluding all Blacks and Tawnys, of increasing the lovely White . . . ?"[8]

Congressional approval of the Naturalization Act of 1790 highlights the attitude of early government leaders that North America should be populated primarily by Europeans. The Naturalization Act excluded from citizenship all Nonwhites, including Indians. Indians were considered domestic foreigners and, therefore, ineligible for citizenship.[9] Although Native Americans in Indian Territory were granted citizenship in 1901, and citizenship was granted to other Indians in 1924 with the passage of the Indian Citizenship Act, the other racial restrictions of the 1790 Naturalization Act were not repealed until 1952.[10]

Concepts of cultural superiority and racism served as justifications for economic exploitation and for expropriating land of both the Irish and the Native Americans. For many European Americans, Indians were an obstacle to the spread of White Europeans from coast to coast. To make room for the expansion of Whites, the options were genocide, containment on small farms, or reservations. In Takaki's words, "This social construction of race occurred within the economic context of competition over land."[11]

Therefore, justifying their expropriation of Native American lands by claims of cultural and racial superiority, U.S. government leaders embarked on one of the most extensive campaigns of ideological management in human history. Their primary focus, as I demonstrate in the next section, was changing Native American ideas about the family, work, gender roles, child rearing, nature, accumulation of wealth, and political structures.

WHAT IT MEANT TO "CIVILIZE"
NATIVE AMERICANS

When government officials referred to "civilizing" Native Americans, they were including a large number of cultural changes including values, family structure, gender roles, child rearing practices, sexuality, economic relationships, and government. Later in this chapter, I discuss the plans of Thomas Jefferson and McKenney for the "civilization" of Native Americans. In this context, "civilization" refers to this broad sweep of changes in values and institutions. When Jefferson advocated teaching Indians to be good farmers, he believed it would result in completely changing Native American institutions and relationships. "Civilizing" as a form of cultural transformation would affect all aspects of Native American life.

To understand what advocates of "civilizing" meant requires an understanding of the cultural differences between European Americans and Native Americans. While many European Americans wanted to eliminate these cultural differences by changing Native Americans, others were attracted to the values and lifestyle of Indians and found becoming a "White Indian" a welcome relief from the sexual and economic oppression of white society.

One focus of civilization programs was on family organization and gender roles. The Choctaws and Cherokees were organized into matrilineal clans.[12] In marriage, the male left his clan and joined his mate's clan. If the couple separated, the male returned to his clan, leaving children and family property with the female's clan. The gender roles were clearly divided by work roles. Women took care of domestic and agricultural work, and men did the hunting. The major responsibility for childrearing was not with the father, but with the mother and her relations within the clan.

Many European-American men were offended by the power of women in the clan structure. On the other hand, Axtell found that many colonial women captured by Indians preferred to remain with the tribe because in Indian society women enjoyed higher status than in colonial society. Captured by Indians at the age of fifteen, Mary Jemison described female Indian work as being not as severe or hard as that done by White women. "In the summer season," she wrote, "we planted, tended and harvested our corn, and generally had all our children with us; *but had not master to oversee or drive us, so that we could work as leisurely as we pleased.*" Axtell concludes, "Unless Jemison was correct, it would be virtually impossible to understand why so many women and girls chose to become Indians."[13]

Often, Native American women exercised political power. The Cherokees, in particular, were noted for having female leaders and, frequently, female warriors. White male settlers often spoke despairingly of the "petticoat" government of the Cherokees. Cherokee women decided the fate of captives; they made decisions in Women's Council that were relayed to the general tribe by the War Woman or Pretty Woman. Clan-mothers had the right to wage war. War Women, among the Cherokees, were called Beloved Women and had the power to free victims from the punishment prescribed by the general council.[14]

In addition, those advocating civilization policies wanted to change the permissive childrearing practices of Native Americans. Indian children were seldom disciplined and ran around, in the minds of Whites, like "wild Indians." John Edwards, superintendent of the Wheelock Academy in the Choctaw Nation from 1851 to 1861, complained in a speech to the student body of the University of California in 1880 that among the Choctaws, "there is very little order or discipline in the family. Each does what is pleasing in his own eyes. A parent may beat a child in anger, but seldom does he chastise him with coolness and in love."[15]

The freedom allowed Indian children starkly contrasted with the rigid discipline of Puritan families. The most popular colonial textbook, The New England Primer, admonished children:

Good Children Must

Fear God all Day,	Love Christ Always,
Parents Obey,	In Secret Pray,
No False Thing Say,	Mind Little Play,
By no Sin Stray,	Make no delay,

In doing Good.[16]

Although many European Americans believed in the necessity of breaking a child's will, Indians let their children follow their own will. Edwards expressed his wish to impose a nuclear family structure and authoritarian childrearing practices on the Choctaws in his 1880 speech: "One serious difficulty with the [clan] system is that it takes from the father his proper place at the head of his family and leaves him comparatively little control of his children. With that Christianity has to contend, and it is gradually overcoming it."[17]

Allen forcefully described the consequences for women with these changes in gender roles and childrearing practices. Allen described these changes as "the replacing of a peaceful, nonpunitive, nonauthoritarian social system wherein women wield power by making social life easy and gentle with one based on child terrorization, male dominance, and submission of women to male authority."[18]

In addition, advocates of civilizing Indians believed that a patrilineal family would change economic practices. The Protestant ethic ascribed to by many Whites emphasizes the importance of hard work and the accumulation of property. Work, among many White Americans, was assumed to be a good activity that provided protection against sin. Time devoted to work kept the mind from wandering down the path of evil. "Idle hands are the Devil's tools." The Protestant ethic also valued the accumulation of wealth as a sign of God's blessing. In other words, hard work and the accumulation of wealth were considered outward signs of a Godly life.

Many Whites believed that the matrilineal clan structure kept men from accumulating wealth because they could not pass it on to their children. For example, Edwards stated in his 1880 speech regarding the Choctaws, "Col. Folsom, the first elected chief . . . once remarked that he had but little encouragement to make property, as it would not go to his family at his death . . . but would fall into the hands of his brothers."[19]

In contrast, Native Americans believed in the sharing of property. If another tribal member needed food or assistance, others gladly gave their time and food. Most North American tribes did not value the accumulation of property. In addition, there was no concept that work was a good in and of itself. In fact, before the introduction of the fur trade, there was no reason for a hunter to kill more animals than was needed by the clan. Time not spent hunting or in agricultural pursuits was considered important for celebrations and rituals that linked tribal members to nature and the cosmos. Rather then rushing to work to accumulate property as did most European Americans, Indians appeared to many settlers to be lazy.

Edwards argued that Choctaw attitudes about accumulating property and sharing wealth were a major obstacle in their being civilized. "One result of this [sharing wealth]," Edwards admitted in recounting his work with the Choctaws, is that they have no need of poorhouses . . . . In fact this unstinted hospitality on one side degenerates into spunging [sic] on the other, the lazy living upon the industrious.

You perceive that this militates very strongly against accumulation of property . . . . To refuse it savors strongly of meanness. But people are learning that it is necessary to refuse, and there is danger that some may go to the opposite extreme.[20]

Religious differences between Europeans and Indians were reflected in these opposing attitudes toward work and the accumulation of property. Many Europeans coming to North America assumed that Native Americans lacked religions because of the apparent absence of religious buildings and a priestly caste. Spiritual practices were often dismissed by European Americans as pagan. Edwards, in his speech at the University of California in 1880, expressed his belief that Choctaws originally lacked any type of religion.

As to religion, they had none. Other Indian tribes talk of the Great Spirit, of the great Being above, the Creator and Preserver of all; but the Choctaws had no term for Him. Some other tribes are idolaters; the Choctaws had no form of worship. As completely, almost, as possible, they were a people without a god. Still they had some notion of supernatural things. Some of them pretend to believe that man has no future state, that death ends his being. This is held by them in opposition to the gospel.[21]

It was not until 1978 that the U.S. Congress officially recognized the existence of Native American religions with the passage of the "American Indian Religious Freedom" resolution. The resolution admitted that "Federal policy has often resulted in the abridgement of religious freedom for traditional American Indians."[22]

The relationship between humans and the rest of nature was another concern of civilization programs. For Christians, nature exists to support humans. Humans are at the center of God's purpose in creating Earth. With the development of science, a major goal of Christians from the 16th century to the present is to control nature for the benefit of humans. Those involved in civilizing Native Americans in the early 19th century were distressed by the fact that Native Americans did not clear the forest land for cultivation. In fact, Europeans claimed a right to the land because Indians did not bring it under cultivation. In addition, the English claimed a right to Native American lands because Indians were not Christians. The Puritans often quoted Psalms 2:8: "Ask of me, And I shall give thee, the heathen for thine inheritance, and the uttermost parts of the earth for thy possession."[23]

On the other hand, Native Americans considered themselves part of the "sacred hoop of nature." Humans were of the same value as birds, deer, and other living things. Apologies were made to animals when they were killed for food. Most religious ceremonies focused on some aspect of the human relationship to the chain of the living. Consequently, the goal of most Native Americans in North America was to learn to live within the sacred hoop of nature.[24]

The result was that most Native Americans believed it was important to devote time to ceremony and ritual to express their relationship to the cosmos. In contrast, many Christians, particularly Calvinists, believed it was important to work hard and accumulate property to receive the blessing of God. Religious rituals for Christians were often relegated to Sunday or a particular part of the day. In the name of hard work and property, Christians felt compelled to tame nature by clearing land, killing animals wantonly, reshaping mountains, and changing the course of rivers.

Within this context, civilization meant trying to bring nature under the control of humans in contrast with the belief that humans must learn to live as just one part of nature. In 1634, William Wood of Boston captured the complaints among early colonists that Indians were lazy and did nothing to tame nature. "Fettered on the chains of idleness," he wrote, Indians let the land rot "for want of manuring, gathering, ordering, etc." For Wood, Indians were similar to animals that only "run over the grass."[25]

Since the Christian concept of sin was absent from traditional Indian cultures, tribal members were not driven to work and accumulate property by a fear of hell. In addition, the lack of a Christian concept of sin regarding sexuality was in sharp contrast with the sexual repression evident among many European Americans. Axtell provides, as an example of differing attitudes regarding sexuality, the laughter by Hurons when Father Le Caron tried to explain the Sixth Commandment regarding adultery. The Hurons simply stated, "It was impossible to keep that one."[26]

English colonists often called Native Americans "filthy." Originally, I was perplexed by this comment because of the English abhorrence of bathing in contrast to the daily plunge by most Indians into a river or other body of water. From the 16th to the 19th century, Europeans labeled Indians as "filthy" because of their seemingly unrepressed sexuality and not for their inattention to bathing.[27]

Consequently, many Europeans, particularly males, were attracted to the lifestyle of Indian tribes. The nonrepressive attitudes regarding work and sexuality among Native Americans resulted in many Whites marrying into the Choctaw and Cherokee tribes. These Whites and their mixed-blood children, as I explain in the next chapter, eventually formed the upper economic class in these tribes, and they were important as initiators of cultural changes.

Another focus of civilization programs was on government organizations. Traditional government structures among the Choctaws and
Cherokees depended on consensus and tradition. Crimes were avenged
by clan members on the principle of an eye for an eye and a tooth for a
tooth. For instance, if a clan member were killed by a member of another
tribe or clan, the death would be avenged by killing any member of the
other clan or tribe. The "civilizing" of the Choctaws and Cherokees
resulted in the tribes' eventual adoption of a constitutional form of
government modeled on that of the U.S. government, with written laws
protecting property and inheritance within a patrilineal family structure. One of the major consequences of tribal constitutions was the
disenfranchisement of women and their loss of power over clan property.[28]

In summary, what most U.S. government leaders meant by "civilizing" Native Americans was transforming clan structures into nuclear
families, reducing the power of women, instilling the economic ideals of
the Protestant ethic, changing concepts about the relation of humans to
nature, and establishing rule by law. Although a major purpose of
civilizing Native Americans was freeing their lands for White settlers,
there was a belief held by many White Americans that European
civilization, particularly English civilization, was superior to that of
Native Americans.

THE NOBLE YEOMAN: THOMAS JEFFERSON
AND THE CIVILIZING OF NATIVE AMERICANS

Thomas Jefferson's concept of civilizing Native Americans reflects most
of the attitudes discussed above. By the time he became president in
1801, the U.S. government was embarked on civilization policies designed to maintain peace with what was considered a potentially strong
enemy. There was a continuing desire for Indian lands, but the safest
route according to many government leaders was to acquire land
through purchase and treaties as opposed to conquest. Jefferson concluded that civilization policies would be the best method for gaining
tribal lands.

Initially, Jefferson's approach to the Indian issue used policies already
established by George Washington. These policies were outlined by
Washington in a 1783 letter to James Duane, who served as head of a
select committee on Indian Affairs in the Continental Congress. Washington wanted a boundary separating White settlers from Indian lands.
This boundary, he believed, would serve to reduce the potential for
warfare. In addition, he urged the purchase of Indian lands instead of
expropriation. "In a word," Washington wrote, "there is nothing to be

obtained by an Indian War but the Soil they live on and this can be had by purchase at less expense, and without bloodshed . . . ."[29]

By the 20th century, Washington's policy of conducting relations with Native Americans through the negotiation of treaties would be referred to by many Indians as "The Trail of Broken Treaties." The Treaty of Hopewell with the Cherokees in 1785 was one of the first in this tradition. The treaty established the boundaries for Cherokee lands and, reflecting the concern that the Cherokees might form an alliance with a European power, such as the British, the treaty "acknowledged all the Cherokees to be under the protection of the United States of America, and of no other sovereign whosoever." Articles of the treaty, which were difficult to enforce, promised that the United States would protect Cherokee lands from White settlers.[30]

The famous Northwest Ordinance of 1787 held out the same promise of peace and negotiation for Indian lands. The Ordinance states: "The utmost good faith shall always be observed towards the Indians, their lands and property shall never be taken from them without their consent; and in their property, rights and liberty, they never shall be invaded or disturbed.[31]

And, in what would later be used by Jefferson as a means of civilizing Native Americans, Washington proposed the establishment of official U.S. government trading houses on tribal lands as a means of "render[ing] tranquility with the savages permanent by creating ties of interest."[32] The legislation assigned an Indian agent to each trading house.[33] When Jefferson entered office, he hoped that trading houses and Indian agents would be the means for civilizing Native Americans and gaining their lands. The major flaw in these policies was the assumption that Indians would be willing to sell their lands. As Jefferson noted in a message to Congress in 1803, "the policy has long been gaining strength with them [Native Americans] of refusing absolutely all further sale on any conditions."[34] Faced with this resistance, Jefferson's problem was persuading tribes to relinquish their lands.

For Jefferson, the solution to breaking down resistance to selling land involved transforming Native Americans into yeoman farmers who, living on farms and no longer dependent on hunting, would not need vast tracts of wilderness for hunting. In his first annual message to Congress in 1801, he informed the members that "efforts to introduce among them [Indians] the implements and practice of husbandry, and of the household arts" was successful. "They are becoming more and more sensible," he stated, "of the superiority of this dependence for clothing and subsistence over the precarious resources of hunting and fishing." He was pleased to report that as a result of learning European-American methods of husbandry and agriculture, tribes "begin to experience an increase of population."[35]

The changes that had already taken place in Native American tribes as a result of contact with Europeans highlights the meaning of Jefferson's concept of "civilizing." By the late 18th century, the southern tribes were already engaged in an extensive trade in furs with European Americans. This trade revolutionized tribal economies. Prior to the fur trade, subsistence hunting did not cause a depletion of available game. On the other hand, commercial hunting resulted in a rapid depletion of game stocks and required hunters to travel greater distances to gather both food and furs for trade. In fact, Jefferson was probably correct that it was becoming more difficult for Native Americans to rely on hunting because of the damage caused by the fur trade.[36]

When Jefferson advocated turning southern Indians into farmers, he was primarily referring to, as he stated in his first annual message to Congress, "implements and practice of husbandry, and of the household arts." Prior to contact with Europeans, tribes on the east coast and in the south did engage in agriculture. In fact, these tribes produced a surplus of agricultural products that early colonists depended on for their survival. According to Jennings, the real difference between European and Native American agricultural concepts "was not farming but herding."[37] This difference, Jennings argued, had important implications for textiles. Native Americans depended on making furs and weaving reeds as opposed to using looms to create cloth from the wool of herded sheep. One of the major changes introduced into the economy of southern Indians during Jefferson's administration was the growing and weaving of cotton. Jefferson's reference to introducing "household arts" primarily meant the introduction of the loom.

Jefferson's willingness to entertain the idea of civilizing Native Americans was based on his assumption that all humans shared basic common sense regarding moral decisions. Therefore, an uncivilized people could be relied on to exercise good moral judgment. In fact, he believed that, often, the uneducated person was more capable of making good moral judgments than a highly educated person, whose mind might be clouded by a whirl of contradictory ideas.

In *Notes on the State of Virginia*, written in 1781, Jefferson argued that moral common sense was the basis of Indian governments. "Their only controls," Jefferson wrote in reference to the lack of written laws, "are their manners, and that moral sense of right and wrong, which, like the sense of tasting and feeling in every man, makes a part of his nature." Although tribes relied only on contempt, exclusion, and revenge as punishments, Jefferson noted, "crimes are very rare among them." In comparing the lack of law among the Indians to the burdensome laws of Europeans, he declared the primitive situation of Native Americans to be preferable because "the sheep are happier of themselves, than under care of the wolves."[38]

Although Jefferson claimed admiration for Indian governments, he recommended the creation of written laws among the tribes as a means of protecting property. Similar to other arguments for civilization of Native Americans, Jefferson linked the creation of the nuclear family with a desire to acquire property and the establishment of a formal government. Writing to the chiefs of the Cherokee Nation in 1806, he congratulated the tribe for beginning a transition from a lifestyle of hunting to one of husbandry and farming. The nuclear family structure resulting from farming, he argued, would create a desire to accumulate and pass on property. "When a man has enclosed and improved his farm," Jefferson wrote, "builds a good house on it and raised plentiful stocks of animals, he will wish when he dies that *these things shall go to his wife and children, who he loves more than he does his other relations, and for whom he will work with pleasure during his life* [italics added]."[39]

The accumulation of property, Jefferson warned the Cherokees, requires the establishment of laws and courts. "When a man has property," Jefferson wrote, "earned by his own labor, he will not like to see another come and take it from him because he happens to be stronger, or else to defend it by spilling blood. You will find it necessary then to appoint good men, as judges, to decide rules you shall establish."[40]

Jefferson used the Trade and Intercourse Act of 1793 to provide tools and domestic animals to Indians "in order to promote civilization among the friendly Indian tribes, and to secure the continuance of their friendship."[41] The legislation was originally intended to give federal control over trade with the tribes. New legislation during Jefferson's administration, the Trade and Intercourse Act of 1802, gave the President the power "to promote civilization" among the Indians by providing "domestic animals, and implements of husbandry, and with goods or money."[42]

By creating a desire in Native Americans for manufactured goods put on display at trading houses, Jefferson believed, Indians would be willing to sell their lands to gain cash for purchases. In this manner, Native Americans would become part of a cash economy and would become dependent on manufactured goods. In a special message to Congress urging the continuation of trading houses, he wrote that to counteract tribal resistance to selling land "and to provide an extension of territory which *the rapid increase of our numbers will call for* [italics added], two measures are deemed expedient." The first, he argued, was to encourage Indians to abandon hunting for agriculture and husbandry. "The extensive forests necessary in the hunting life," he told Congress, "will then become useless, and they will see advantage in exchanging them for the means of improving their farms and of increasing their domestic comfort." Second, he argued, the trading houses will make the Indians aware of what they can purchase with the money earned from the sale of lands. Consequently, Jefferson asked Congress, "To multiply trading houses among them, and place within their reach those things *which will contribute more to their domestic comfort than the possession of extensive but uncultivated wilds* [italics added]."[43]

Trading houses and Indian agents established by Jefferson did provide aid for the early establishment of schools among the Cherokees. In 1803, the Cherokee agent erected a schoolhouse and provided financial aid to a missionary teacher. After Jefferson's administration, similar aid was provided through Indian Agents to missionary Cyrus Kingsbury to operate a school among the Cherokees. These schools were to become a major part of the civilization project.[44]

It is important to emphasize what Jefferson was advocating. He not only wanted to change the economy, government, family relations, and values regarding property, but he also wanted to manipulate desires regarding consumption of goods. Similar to a 20th-century advertising firm, Jefferson hoped that the display of European-American goods in trading houses would create consumer desires that could be met only by the sale of lands and the accumulation of wealth on European-style farms. Civilizing Native Americans, in this case, meant completely wedding them to an economy of increasing production and demand for new goods. "In leading them thus to agriculture, to manufactures, and civilization," Jefferson told Congress, "in bringing together their and our sentiments, and in preparing them ultimately to participate in the benefits of our Government, I trust and believe we are acting for their greatest good."[45]

One could cynically discount Jefferson's allusion to "their greatest good" as simply a rationalization for acquiring Native American lands. Ironically, there does appear throughout the writings of advocates of civilization a belief that Native Americans were rapidly being wiped out by the onslaught of White civilization. Certainly, any reflection of the rapid disappearance of members of Eastern tribes during colonial times would lead to that conclusion. Jefferson frequently stated his belief that the only hope for stemming the tide of destruction was cultural transformation.

In his Second Inaugural Address in 1805, Jefferson declared that Indians had the right to continue to exist because they are endowed "with the faculties and the rights of men." But, he warned, "the endeavors to enlighten them on the fate [extinction] which awaits their present course of life . . . have powerful obstacles to encounter." The major obstacle, he told the crowd, was resistance to the civilizing attempts of the government and others. "They, too, have their anti-philosophers," Jefferson complained, "who find an interest in keeping things in their present state, who dread reformation, and exert all their faculties to maintain the ascendancy of habit over the duty of improving our reason, and obeying its mandates."[46]

Indian agents were to be the principle means for instituting Jefferson's civilization policies. Among the Cherokees, Indian Agents were instructed to establish schools to teach women how to spin and sew and to teach men the use of farm implements and methods of husbandry. Indian Agents acted as teachers and advertisers of manufactured goods. They were to begin the cultural transformation of Native Americans that would change Native American ideas about farming, families, government, and economic relations. At the end of his term, according to historian Prucha, Jefferson felt vindicated by his policies of civilization. "The southern tribes, especially," Prucha writes, "were far ahead of the others in agriculture and the household arts and in proportion to this advancement identified their views with those of the United States."[47]

Benjamin Hawkins was sent by President Washington in 1796 as the chief Indian Agent to the southern tribes, where he served for 20 years. During that time, he was convinced that Jefferson's agrarian ideals held out the only hope for saving the tribes from extinction. He carried out Jefferson's plans for providing Indians with the tools and knowledge for farming and the raising of domestic animals. Of particular importance for the future of the Choctaws and Cherokees, he introduced the methods of raising cotton and producing cloth.[48]

The cotton culture introduced by Hawkins contributed to the creation of a wealthy planter class among the Indians. As I discuss in chapter 3, the first Cherokee family, the Ridges, to be instructed by Hawkins in cotton farming became a powerful economic and political influence in the tribe. One of the major consequences of Hawkins' activities was the creation of social classes among the Choctaws and Cherokees, with the planter and trader class taking control of the tribes. Hawkins introduced cotton culture by teaching Native American women how to use the spinning wheel and loom, and by instructing men in the use of plows, hoes, and fertilizers. Of course, cotton culture contributed to the domestication of Indian women. But, as I stated earlier, Hawkins's efforts only changed the culture of a few members of the tribe.[49]

Hawkins also carried out Jefferson's plan to make Indians dependent on manufactured goods. Young warriors complained that Hawkins made the tribes lose their self-sufficiency by creating desires for coffee, cane sugar, and whiskey. In the words of his biographer, "Hawkins's personal goal in dealing with the Indians was to reconcile them to a more restrained way of life, a pastoral, cottage-industry way of life not too different from that of most white Americans . . . and [to] *prepare their minds 'to accommodate the wishes of our fellow citizens'* [italics added]."[50]

Unlike many White Americans who believed the key to cultural change among the Indians was teaching a love of wealth, Hawkins believed the most important change was replacing tribal governments with governments modeled on an Anglo-Saxon system. Peace on the frontier, he argued, required Indian governments with centralized authority, a judicial system, and a system of punishments. By the time of their removal to Indian Territory in the 1830s and 1840s, the Choctaw and Cherokee leaders were willing to organize governments based on these principles.[51]

For Jefferson and Hawkins, civilization of Native Americans included abandonment of hunting for small farms with the clan system being replaced by the nuclear family. And in abandoning the traditional belief in sharing property for a desire to accumulate property, Jefferson reasoned, Indians would want to protect their property by establishing governments based on written laws and judges.

It is important to emphasize, as I discuss in the next chapter, that certain Indians during the Jefferson administration welcomed these changes. Despite Jefferson's concerns about resistance to civilization, a very important group of Choctaws and Cherokees embraced the prospect of cultural transformation.

THOMAS L. MCKENNEY: THE GREAT EXPERIMENT

Born into a strong Quaker family on March 21, 1785, Thomas L. McKenney's religious values were reflected in policies stressing peace and Christianity during the 14 years of his service as superintendent of Indian trade and, after the office was abolished in 1823, as head of the newly created Office of Indian Affairs from 1824 to 1830.[52] Throughout his years of government service, McKenney was convinced that under the right conditions, Indians could be civilized. In 1827, while traveling as head of the Bureau of Indian Affairs through the Great Lakes region, he awoke one Sunday morning to hear the singing of Christian Indians. As he heard their songs, he reflected on the importance of converting Native Americans to Christianity and, also, the destructive power of White civilization. "Notes of thrush and nightingale sound sweeter when poured forth amidst the grove," he wrote, "so sounded those of these forest warblers, in the midst of the green foliage, and in the stillness of the woods . . . I felt humbled, and ashamed of my country, in view of the wrongs it had inflicted . . . upon these desolate and destitute children of the forest."[53]

Conceptualizing Indians as children, McKenney believed the key to civilizing them was schooling. Reflecting on the singing in the forest grove, he rhapsodized:

> There were flowers and gems there which needed only to be cultivated and polished, to insure from the one, the emission of as sweet odors as ever regaled the circles of the civilized; and from the other, a brilliance as dazzling as ever sparkled in the diadem of queenly beauty.[54]

McKenney believed throughout his career that civilizing Indians would be possible only if they were protected from the vices of White settlers. McKenney, as superintendent of Indian trade, considered trading houses and their agents to be an important means of maintaining peace with Indians. Similar to many reformers of this time, including common school reformer Horace Mann, McKenney supported the temperance movement, particularly among Native Americans. The control of Indian trade made it possible to assure, he wrote, that "not a drop of brandy, rum, or whiskey . . . [was] permitted to pass through the factories [trading houses]."[55]

Besides alcohol and other vices that Indians might be exposed to through contact with White settlers, he believed isolation was essential because of feelings of inferiority. In a 1829 letter to J. Evarts of the Board for the Emigration, Preservation, and Improvement of the Aborigines, McKenney asked: "And where we see one absolutely superior, and another absolutely inferior, does not the consciousness of that inferiority in the person feeling it depress his energies, and paralyze his efforts?" In answer, he argued that this was the present condition of Indians. Surrounded by the superiority of whites, Indians felt inferior, which made them unable to embrace civilization. McKenney emphasized:

Can a human heart beat free when oppressed by such degradation? . . . But the Indian has to endure one more thought. It is the total impracticability of his ever participating in those refinements of the social state, which are the necessary result of the white man's superiority over him in intellectual, moral, and political advantages."[56]

McKenney's belief that contact with White settlers resulted in the spread of vices and a feeling of inferiority led him to the conclusion that the civilizing process required isolation of the tribes. As superintendent of Indian trade, he tried to control trade relations with the Indians. Later, as head of the Bureau of Indians Affairs, he concluded that isolation from White settlers could only be accomplished by moving the tribes to a region west of the Mississippi. Thinking of Indians as children who only needed to be protected from evil and sent to school he concluded that, under the conditions of isolation and education, Indians could be civilized in one generation. "Now can any one doubt," McKenney wrote, "that this system [schools in Indian Territory], would not lift them in a single generation to a level with ourselves?"[57]

Consequently, shortly after being appointed superintendent of Indian trade in 1816, McKenney's interests shifted from trade as a means of cultural transformation to the use of schools. By 1819, McKenney was able to convince Congress to pass the Civilization Fund Act to provide money for the support of schools among Indian tribes. Reflecting on his effort to gain approval of the legislation, McKenney wrote, "I did not doubt then, nor do I now, the capacity of the Indian for the highest attainments in civilization, in the arts and religion, but I was satisfied that no adequate plan had ever been adopted for this great reformation."[58]

Just prior to the adoption of the Civilization Fund Act, McKenney recounts, it appeared "to me to be propitious for the making of the experiment."[59] It is important to emphasize that McKenney considered the introduction of schools into Indian tribes as an experiment in what I call ideological management. Could schools civilize Native Americans? Could schools bring about a cultural transformation? At the time, McKenney didn't consider the possibility that some tribal members might resent and resist this attempt at cultural transformation. He believed that the time was right for the experiment because of relative peace with the tribes and, besides, "there were now several missionary stations already in operation, though on a small scale, all of them furnishing proof that a plan commensurate to the object, would reform and save, and bless this long neglected, and downtrodden people."[60]

The Civilization Fund Act of 1819 authorized the president to "employ capable persons of good moral character, to instruct them [Indians] in the mode of agriculture suited to their situation; and for teaching their children in reading, writing, and arithmetic." The legislation provided an annual sum of $10,000 to be used by the president to hire teachers. The legislation specifically indicated that the funds were to be used with tribes "adjoining the frontier settlements of the United States." In practice, a large percentage of the money funded missionaries to set up schools among the Choctaws and Cherokees.[61]

SCHOOLS AS AN INSTRUMENT OF CULTURAL TRANSFORMATION AND CONTROL

McKenney was in tune with his times by focusing on schools as the means of cultural transformation. This was a period of growing belief that education, as a function of public policy, could rid society of crime, poverty, social and religious tensions, and political upheavals. By the 20th century, public schools were such a common part of life in the United States that many people have forgotten that at one time they constituted a major revolution in social thought. The idea that a government could control society by controlling the education of children was a significant change in public policy.

The concept of school evolving during McKenney's time extended the notion of learning beyond books to the social world of the school. Moral, social, political, and economic improvement were to result from book learning and, more importantly, from the habits and attitudes developed by the methods of instruction, the rules of the school, and the social contact with other students.[62]

For instance, many of the missionary teachers sponsored by the Civilization Fund Act established schools among the Choctaws and Cherokees using Lancasterian methods of instruction. Developed by Joseph Lancaster for charity schools in England, the two most important qualities of the method were its cheapness and its supposed ability to inculcate the social habits required by business and factories. In fact, it was often referred to as a factory of learning for children. Certainly, those calling for the civilization of Indians would not object to these qualities being taught in the Lancasterian classrooms of missionary schools.

Lancasterian methods were introduced into the United States by the New York Free School Society in 1805. Schools established under the auspices of the Free School Society were to combat urban crime. DeWitt Clinton, president of the Society, warned in 1809 in language that McKenney might have used to describe the results of contact between White settlers and Indians: "Great cities are, at all times, the nurseries and hotbeds of crimes . . . And the dreadful examples of vice which are presented to youth, and the alluring forms in which it is arrayed . . . cannot fail of augmenting the mass of moral depravity." In answer to the problem of urban crime, Clinton declared in the same 1809 speech with regard to the Lancasterian system, "I consider his [Joseph Lancaster's] system as creating a new era in education, as a blessing sent down from heaven to redeem the poor."[63]

The common school movement from the 1820s to the 1850s popularized the idea that education could be used to reform society. It was during the early period of the common school movement that McKenney concluded civilizing Indians required their isolation and exposure to a common school system.

As Kaestle argued in *Pillars of the Republic: Common Schools and American Society, 1780–1860*, the common school movement, which was responsible for establishing public schools as a common element of U.S. society, was primarily interested in "creating cultural and political values centering on Protestantism, republicanism, and capitalism."[64] In broader terms, Mann, one of the major leaders of the common school movement, argued that public schools, by instilling these values, would spur economic growth, provide equality of opportunity, end poverty and crime, reduce friction between social classes, and reduce political tensions.[65]

The specific values that common school reformers of the period wanted instilled, according to Kaestle, matched those advocated for the civilizing of Native Americans. For instance, common school advocates wanted the schools to teach the basic attitudes of capitalism: to desire and to respect property—the very foundations of the Protestant ethic.

Besides teaching morality, the common school was supposed to instill a respect for the nuclear family as the key to a moral society. In this context, women were assigned the role of creating a haven for the hard-working husband, managing domestic chores, and nurturing children. Applied to Native Americans, this meant an abandonment of the clan system. In addition, according to Kaestle, the form of Protestant culture to be instilled through the school was combined with a belief in America's unique destiny to "suggest to Americans that their nation was destined to reach the peak of human civilization."[66]

During McKenney's tenure as head of the Bureau of Indian Affairs, the lack of any objection to the use of government money to support religious missionaries to educate Native Americans highlights the assumption that instilling religious values was part of the process of schooling. From the perspective of some individuals in the late 20th century, the economic support of missionaries would appear to be a clear violation of the Establishment Clause of the First Amendment, which was used in the 20th century by the Supreme Court to ban school prayers, Bible reading, and prayers at public school graduations. Obviously, in the minds of most Whites of McKenney's generation, the financial support of religious missionaries by the Civilization Fund Act did not involve a violation of the Establishment Clause, but was considered a necessary part of public schooling and the civilization of Indians.

CONCLUSION: ISOLATION AND CIVILIZATION

After the passage of the Civilization Fund Act, the major problem McKenney encountered in his great experiment was keeping the tribes isolated from White settlers while they underwent cultural transformation. The federal government's control of trade and guarantees to evict settlers from Indian lands was one method for keeping tribes from being contaminated by the vices of frontier whites. But enforcement of these policies proved extremely difficult. For instance, McKenney and missionaries considered the worst form of corruption to be the sale of alcohol to Indians. In practice, even licensed government traders illegally supplied alcohol to Native Americans. In addition, unlicensed traders roamed tribal lands trading alcohol for furs.[67] Also, McKenney was faced with the shutdown of the trading houses when scandals about illegal fur trading caused Congress to end the system in 1822 and to substitute legislation requiring high bonds for licensed traders and restriction of trade in alcohol.[68]

The major stumbling block to stopping White encroachment was the growing demand by state governments for tribal lands. According to the Constitution and government practices, Indian tribes fell under the jurisdiction of the federal government. Although Supreme Court rulings supported federal jurisdiction, state governments openly defied their rulings. Eventually, the Choctaws and Cherokees found themselves at the mercy of state governments.

Wanting to take over Indian lands, state governments objected to McKenney's civilization program. State officials worried that education of Native Americans would result in strengthening tribal power and creating greater resistance to the relinquishment of tribal lands. State encroachment on Indian lands convinced McKenney that the only hope for the civilization project was removal of tribes to a federal territory west of the Mississippi where they would be under the complete protection of the U.S. government. To achieve this protection, the land would be designated as "Indian Territory" and would not fall within the boundaries of any state. As an official Territory, the federal government could regulate trade and Indian affairs without any interference from state governments. In addition, McKenney hoped the tribes could be isolated from the vices of White settlers.

Under the protection of the federal government, the tribes removed to Indian Territory could establish school systems that, McKenney argued, would civilize them in one generation. "It is proposed," McKenney told Board for the Emigration, Preservation, and Improvement of the Aborigines of America, "to give them a country, and to secure it to them by the most ample and solemn sanctions, suitable in all respects, in exchange for theirs; to pay them for all their improvements—and see them, free of cost, to their new homes—to aid them after their arrival there,—and protect them."[69]

The removal of an estimated 70,000 Indians to Indian Territory would, according to McKenney's vision, result in Native Americans' attaining

> an elevation, to which in their present relations, they can never aspire. And thus would new influences be created, ennobling in their tendencies . . . Under these, the Indian would rise into the distinction to which he has always been a stranger; and live and act with reference to the corresponding honors and benefits of such a state.[70]

The grandeur of McKenney's proposed experiment in social engineering cannot be overemphasized. To remove 70,000 people to an isolated area for their planned cultural transformation is unique in the history of humanity. The resulting tragedy of the Trail of Tears, the psychological trauma of being uprooted and moved, and, what I would call the genocide of many of these 70,000 Native Americans must be considered one of the most infamous chapters in human history.

NOTES

[1]Washington's and Knox's estimate of 14,000 soldiers provides a means of determining their conception of the total size of these tribes

and an estimate of the original size of these tribes before contact with Europeans. According to Francis Jennings in *The Invasion of America: Indians, Colonialism, and the Cant of Conquest* (New York: Norton. 1975, pp. 15–31), there were at least four other members of the tribe (wives, children, and elders) for every warrior. Therefore, the total population of these Southern tribes in the 1790s was about 70,000. Jennings also argued that the catastrophic effect of diseases introduced by Europeans reduced tribal populations by 90%. It should be remembered that some tribes on the east coast actually disappeared as a result of European contact. Therefore, using Jennings' figures, the population of these southern tribes before contact with Europeans was about 700,000.

[2]Quoted in Francis Paul Prucha, *The Great Father: The United States Government and the American Indians* (Lincoln: University of Nebraska Press, 1984), p. 53.

[3]"Thomas L. McKenney to Department of War, May 1, 1829," in *Thomas L. McKenney: Memoirs, Official and Personal*, edited by Hermann J. Viola (Lincoln: University of Nebraska Press, 1973), p. 335.

[4]As I am using the term, *ideological management* refers to the conscious attempt to control ideas and values to achieve policy objectives. In this case, ideological management involves the attempt to deculturalize the southern Indians and replace their culture with one similar to that of European Americans. This effort toward ideological management occurred during the same historical period as the development of education as an instrument of public policy. Educators were arguing that public schools, by instilling particular ideas and values, could end poverty, crime, and political conflict. And, in fact, there is a close parallel in time to the development of the common school and the establishment of school systems in Indian Territory.

[5]Ronald Takaki, *A Different Mirror: A History of Multicultural America* (Boston: Little, Brown and Company), p. 28.

[6]Ibid, pp. 28–29.

[7]Dee Brown, *Bury My Heart At Wounded Knee: An Indian History of the American West* (New York: Henry Holt and Company, 1970), pp. 171–172.

[8]Takaki, p. 79.

[9]Takaki, pp. 79–80.

[10]See "Citizenship for Indians in the Indian Territory. March 3, 1901." and "Indian Citizenship Act. June 2, 1924." in *Documents of United States Indian Policy, Second Edition*, edited by Frances Paul Prucha (Lincoln: University of Nebraska Press, 1990), pp. 199, 215.

[11]Takaki, p 39.

[12]See Alexander Spoehr, "Changing Kinship Systems: A Study in the Acculturation of the Creeks, Cherokee, and Choctaw," *Publications of*

the Field Museum of Natural History Anthropological Series Vol. 33. (New York: Kraus Reprint Co., 1968).

[13]James Axtell, *The Invasion Within: The Contest of Cultures in Colonial North America* (New York: Oxford University Press, 1985), p. 324.

[14]Paula Gunn Allen, *The Sacred Hoop: Recovering the Feminine in American Indian Traditions,* (Boston: Beacon Press, 1992), pp. 36–37.

[15]John Edwards, "The Choctaw Indians in the Middle of the Nineteenth Century" *Chronicles of Oklahoma* (1932):10, p. 410.

[16]*The New-England Primer* edited by Paul Leicester Ford (New York: Teachers College Press, 1962). Pages are unnumbered in the reproduction of the original work contained herein.

[17]Edwards, p. 402.

[18]Allen, pp. 40–41.

[19]Edwards, p. 402.

[20]Ibid, pp. 403–404.

[21]Ibid, p. 420.

[22]"American Indian Religious Freedom. August 11, 1978." Prucha, *Documents of the United States Indian Policy...,* pp. 288–289.

[23]Francis Jennings, *The Invasion of America: Indians, Colonialism, and the Cant of Conquest* (New York: W. W. Norton, 1975), p. 83.

[24]See Allen, pp. 54–76, for a beautiful discussion of the sacred hoop and Native American relationship to the cosmos.

[25]As quoted by Takaki, p. 39.

[26]Axtell, p. 123.

[27]Jennings, pp. 49–50.

[28]Allen, p. 37.

[29]"George Washington to James Duane. September 7, 1783." Prucha, *Documents of United States Indian Policy...,* pp. 1–2.

[30]"Treaty of Hopewell with the Cherokees. November 28, 1785." Ibid, pp. 6–8.

[31]"Northwest Ordinance. July 13, 1787." Ibid., pp. 9–10.

[32]"President Washington on Government Trading Houses. December 3, 1973." Ibid., p. 16.

[33]"Establishment of Government Trading houses. April 18, 1796." Ibid., pp. 16–17.

[34]"President Jefferson on Indian Trading Houses." Ibid, p. 21.

[35]"First Annual Message. December 8, 1801," *The Life and Selected Writings of Thomas Jefferson* edited by Adrienne Koch and William Peden (New York: The Modern Library, 1944), p. 324.

[36]Jennings, pp. 71–72.

[37]Ibid., p. 63.

[38]Thomas Jefferson, *Notes on the State of Virginia* (New York: Harper Torchbooks, 1964), p. 90.

[39]Jefferson, "To The Chiefs of the Cherokee Nation. Washington, January 10, 1806." In Koch and Peden, p. 578.

[40]Ibid., p. 579.

[41]Ibid., p. 140.

[42]"Trade and Intercourse Act. March 30, 1802." In Prucha, *Documents of United States Indian Policy...*, p. 19.

[43]"President Jefferson on Indian Trading Houses. January 18, 1803," Prucha, *Documents of United States Indian Policy...*, pp. 21–22.

[44]I discuss these schools in more detail in the next chapter.

[45]Ibid., p. 22.

[46]Jefferson, "Second Inaugural Address. March 4, 1805." In Koch and Peden, p. 342.

[47]Prucha, *The Great Father...*, p. 143.

[48]Florette Henri, *The Southern Indians and Benjamin Hawkins 1796–1816* (Norman: University of Oklahoma Press, 1986), pp. 94–111.

[49]Ibid., p. 95.

[50]Ibid., pp. 95–96.

[51]Ibid., pp. 97–98.

[52]Viola, "Introduction," In McKenney, pp. vii–xxvii.

[53]Thomas L. McKenney, "Memoirs, Official and Personal," Ibid., p. 81.

[54]Ibid., p. 81.

[55]Ibid., p. 19.

[56]*Documents and Proceedings Relating to the Formation and Progress of A Board in the City of New York for the Emigration, Preservation, and Improvement of the Aborigines of America, July 22, 1829* (New York: Vanderpool & Cole, Printers, 1829), pp. 13–14.

[57]Ibid., p. 18.

[58]McKenney, p. 34.

[59]Ibid., p. 34.

[60]Ibid., p. 35.

[61]"Civilization Fund Act. March 3, 1819." In Prucha, *Documents of United States Indian Policy...*, p. 33.

[62]This discussion of the growing importance of schools as an instrument of public policy is based on my book, Joel Spring, *The American School 1642–1993, Second Edition* (New York: McGraw Hill, 1994), pp. 32–96.

[63]Quoted in William O. Bourne, *History of the Public School Society of the City of New York* (New York: Wood, 1870), p. 17–19.

[64]Carl F. Kaestle, *Pillars of the Republic: Common Schools and American Society, 1780–1860* (New York: Hill and Wang, 1983), p. 103.

[65]See Spring, pp. 62–94.

[66]Kaestle, p. 90

[67]Prucha, *The Great Father...*, pp. 98–102.

[68]Ibid., p. 97.

[69]"Address," *Documents and Proceedings Relating to the Formation and Progress...*, p. 41.

[70]Ibid., p. 41.

3

The Ghost Dance, Schools, and Social Classes

In the late 18th and early 19th centuries, a new planter and trader class emerged among the Choctaws and Cherokees, who, eager to protect and increase their wealth, supported schooling and civilization policies. The new planter and trader class was composed primarily of mixed-blood Indians of Native American and European ancestry and Whites who joined the tribes. Education, the new planter and trader class believed, would enhance the ability of the tribe to trade and deal in contracts with Whites. Historian Kidwell wrote about the effect of Choctaw concerns with formal schooling as opposed to missionary focus on religious conversion: "The missionaries soon found that they themselves were subject to the molding forces of Choctaw leaders, who demanded that they teach Choctaw children to read and write and do mathematics (an important consideration in an increasingly market-oriented economy)." According to Kidwell, "Choctaw leaders saw missionaries as a means of gaining an education in the white man's way so that they could learn to deal with the forces infringing on their lives."[1]

In contrast, many full-blood Indians resisted formal schooling because they wanted to protect their traditional culture. And, contrary to the expectations of missionaries, only a few full-blood Indians were interested in conversion to Christianity. For example, in 1799, when Moravians asked the Cherokee Nation Council to open a mission, the council refused to let them preach the Gospel but accepted their request to open a school.[2] Missionaries constantly confessed frustration at the difficulty of converting Indians as opposed to educating them. Reverend Cyrus Kingsbury commented on the reception of his mission among the Choctaws: "We wish we could say that as much has been done to enlighten & save the souls of these perishing people as to make preparations for the instruction of their children."[3]

Despite resistance, conversions did take place. Although Choctaws and Cherokees initially focused on schooling, it was almost inevitable that religious efforts would eventually have some effect. Cushman's description of Kingsbury's first conversion of a full blood Choctaw, Tun-a pin a-chuffa, exemplifies the early conversion experience. Reflecting the literal and symbolical quality of his conversion, he dictated in a letter, "The black and dirty clothes I used to wear I have taken off and cast away. Clean and good clothes I now put on. My heart, I hope, had been made new."[4]

THE GHOST DANCE VISIONS

The Cherokee ghost dance of 1811 and 1812 symbolically resisted the influence of White culture but supported the idea of literacy. The dance expressed a longing for a world that existed prior to the arrival of Europeans. This theme would characterize ghost dances throughout the 19th century. But, unlike most ghost dances in the late 19th century, which involved the annihilation of the White population, this ghost dance envisioned a few select Whites helping the tribe maintain its independence by teaching reading and writing.

The Cherokee ghost dance was preceded by visions depicting White people as teachers. In 1799, Arcowee, former chief of the upper towns of the Cherokees, related a vision to the Moravians at the time they were requesting permission to open a mission. Explaining the differences between White and Indian civilizations, Arcowee said, "When the Great Father in the beginning created men, he had a great book. This he first extended to red men and bade them speak to it [that is, read from it] but they were unable to do so. Then he offered it to the white people . . . they were able to speak to the book at once, and thus it has come about that the White people know so much that is not known to the red."[5]

In January, 1811, another vision depicted Whites in the role of teachers. The vision was experienced by a Cherokee man and two Cherokee women while they were walking in the dusk on a mountain in northwest Georgia. After a large clap of thunder, they saw a band of Indians descend from the sky on horses, beating drums. The riders told the three Indians that the Great Spirit was upset that the tribe had let both "good" and "bad" White people onto their lands and the tribe had abandoned the traditional method of grinding corn by mortar and pestles for the large milling stones of the Whites. The Mother of the Nation had forsaken them, the Great Spirit said, but she would return to them and restore the game to the forests if they rid themselves of bad White people and returned to traditional ways.

The Great Spirit warned that it was impossible for Indians and Whites to overcome their differences. The Great Spirit said: "You yourselves can see that the White people are entirely different beings from us; we are made from red clay: they, out of white sand." It is possible, the Great Spirit said for Indians to "keep good neighborly relations with them [Whites]." Good neighborly relations could only be maintained, the Great Spirit advised, if Whites lived outside of tribal boundaries.[6]

The Great Spirit then passed on his blessing to the White teachers who were instructing the tribe in reading and writing. Four white houses descended from the sky in a beautiful white light. The Great Spirit told the three recipients of the vision to build these houses for Whites "who can be useful to them with writing."[7]

The implicit message of the visions was that White schoolmasters would provide tools to protect the tribe from exploitive treaties and contracts. If the tribe heeded the vision, then they would learn to read and write the White persons' language so that they could enforce treaty terms. This would allow them to expel Whites from tribal lands and to maintain tribal boundaries. The vision also made the idea of removal to a remote area tempting because of the possibility of isolation from White influence and of maintaining traditional ways of living.

Therefore, there were three major factions among the Choctaws and Cherokees regarding civilization policies. The planter and trader class, composed primarily of Whites and mixed-bloods, wanted schools as a means of enhancing and protecting their wealth. Traditionalists, most of whom were full-bloods, rejected schooling and civilization policies. And another group of full-bloods wanted literacy as a means of protection against White aggression.

PLANTER AND TRADER CLASS:
AN EXAMPLE OF A MIXED BLOOD FAMILY

My great-great-great grandfather Louis Leflore was typical of the new planter and trader class who welcomed civilization policies and whose mixed-blood children assumed economic and political leadership of the tribe. He was born in Mobile on June 19, 1762. Later, he joined the Choctaws as a trader and he played an active role in introducing schools sponsored by the Civilization Fund Act. Anthropologist Spoehr wrote about the effect of White Indians similar to Louis Leflore on the Choctaw and Cherokee tribes: ". . . from the point of view of kinship, the White settler's greatest influence probably was exerted by the fact that he so frequently had an Indian wife and passed on to his mixed-blood children many of the contemporary attitudes and usages of white society. Furthermore, the mixed-blood children in turn had considerable influence in Indian society."[8]

Louis Leflore's father and mother, Jean Baptiste LeFlau (the spelling of LeFlau was later changed in the Mississippi Territory by Louis to LeFleur and finally Leflore) and Marie Girard were part of a contingent of French citizens sent to North America to secure French interests. The French entered the Mississippi Valley in 1682 under the leadership of

Rene-Robert Cavalier, Sieur de La Salle. La Salle's, chief lieutenant, Henri de Tonti, opened trade with the Choctaws and founded Mobile (1702) and New Orleans (1718). Jean Baptiste LeFlau arrived in the early 18th century as a member of the French colonial army stationed at Fort Conde on Mobile Bay. After the death of his first wife, whom he married in Mobile in 1735, he married Marie Girard in 1753 and Louis was born on June 29, 1762.[9]

In 1763, one year after Louis' birth, the Peace of Paris was signed, bringing to a conclusion the French and Indian Wars. The treaty gave the British control of the area. The French government provided the option for troops serving in America to remain or return to France. After deciding to remain, Louis' father was granted a pension from the French government and in 1764 took an oath of allegiance to the British government.

With the onset of the Revolutionary War, the British found themselves fighting both the Americans in the northeast and the Spanish in the southeast. In 1781, the British surrendered West Florida to the Spanish. Choctaws living around Mobile and New Orleans became part of the Spanish colonial empire, while Choctaws living north of Mobile resided in the Mississippi Territory of the United States.[10] Sometime around 1780, my great-great-great grandfather began trading with the Choctaws and operating flat-boats on the Amite and Pearl rivers. One historian of the period, James D. Clayton, wrote that Louis Leflore "operated with handsome profits the main boat shuttle to Pensacola, carrying produce and commodities."[11] The shuttle also carried pelts from Indian tribes.

Louis Leflore, similar to many White traders who followed Choctaw customs, joined in a polygamous relationship with two mixed-blood sisters, Rebecca and Nancy Cravat. The relationship gave Leflore a certain status in the tribe because the two sisters were nieces of the famed Choctaw chief Pushmataha. The chief had been made a general in the U.S. Army by Andrew Jackson in the War of 1812 and who was later buried with full honors in the Congressional Cemetery in Washington, D. C.

So that he would be close to the Choctaw trading agency, Louis Leflore moved his family to the high bluffs on the west side of the Pearl River. Officially called LeFleur's Bluff, Pearl River, Choctaw Nation, Mississippi Territory, this was where my great-great grandfather, Basil Leflore, was born in 1810. When Jackson, Mississippi was made the state capital, the original capital building was built on the site of Leflore's house on the bluffs. In 1801, Louis Leflore opened an inn on the Natchez Trace, which had just opened as stage road between Nashville, Tennessee and Jackson, Mississippi. The inn was called French Camp, and it still exists as a tourist stop for those traveling on the Natchez Trace.[12] On the grounds of French Camp, Leflore helped Presbyterian missionaries establish one of the early schools sponsored by the Civilization Fund Act in the Choctaw Nation.

Louis Leflore changed the economy of the tribe by introducing cattle raising. By 1810, the combination of cattle raising, the operation of trading boats, and business at the inn made Leflore one of the wealthiest members of the tribe. In 1812, Leflore joined the U.S. Army and served, along with his relative Pushmataha, as a major in the War of 1812. Leflore's pocketbook was probably fattened when Andrew Jackson stationed his troops for several months at French Camp months prior to the Battle of New Orleans.[13]

Breaking with the Choctaw tradition that uncles and aunts guide the education of children, Leflore assumed responsibility for the education of his children. Greenwood Leflore, born on June 2, 1800, was sent by his father in 1812 to live in the home of Major John Donley in Nashville. Donley was a frequent guest at the French Camp inn while transporting the mail along the Natchez Trace. Since there were no available missionary schools within the nation at this time, Leflore took advantage of Major Donley's invitation to provide his mixed-blood son with an "American education."[14]

When Greenwood returned from Nashville in 1819, after marrying Major Donley's daughter, Rosa, he urged his father to establish a school for the tribe. Using $1,000 provided by the Secretary of War under the provisions of the Civilization Fund Act, the first Presbyterian day school, in contrast to the boarding schools that had already been established in the nation, was built at French Camp. When a church was added, the French Camp school was renamed the Bethel Mission and School.[15]

Although Louis Leflore rejected traditional tribal childrearing practices, there is some speculation that my great-great-great grandmother Nancy Leflore received a traditional Choctaw funeral after her death in 1817. The possibility of a traditional funeral indicates the cultural transitions occurring within the tribe. Although converted to Methodism by missionaries, she probably received a traditional funeral because she was Pushmataha's niece.[16]

The traditional funeral practice, which was completely abandoned by the next generation of the trader and planter class, placed the body on a raised platform for six months so that a combination of rot, birds, vermin, and weather would remove most of the flesh from the bones. Then an honored member of the tribe—who was known as a bone-picker, and who had distinctive tattoos and overgrown fingernails—would mount the platform and pick off any remaining flesh. The skull was then painted vermillion, and the bones were removed and placed in the village bone house.[17]

The next generation of Leflores abandoned most of the tribal practices that were objected to by Christian missionaries, including polygamous relationships, clan organization, funeral practices, and non-Christian

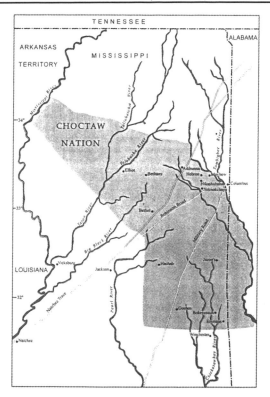

FIG. 3.1. American Board of Missions and Schools 1818–1830. Reprinted from Clara Sue Kidwell, *Choctaws and Missionaries in Mississippi 1818–1918* (Norman: University of Oklahoma Press, 1995), p. 125.

wedding ceremonies. In addition, similar to other mixed-bloods, many of Louis Leflore's nine children rose to prominence in the tribe. Greenwood Leflore became a chief in 1822 and signed the removal Treaty of Dancing Rabbit Creek on May 30, 1830, exchanging Choctaw land in Mississippi for land in Indian Territory. As a mixed-blood chief, he contributed to the cultural transformation of the tribe by suppressing numerous tribal customs and prohibiting the use of charms by medicine men. As chief, he advocated Christianity and the expansion of education. The town of Greenwood, Mississippi is named after him. My great-great grandfather, Basil Leflore, became a Principal Chief of the Choctaw Nation after the tribe was removed to Indian Territory.[18]

THE PLANTER AND TRADER CLASS
AMONG THE CHOCTAWS

One of the unintended effects on the Choctaws and Cherokees of McKenney's civilization policies was to help concentrate economic and political

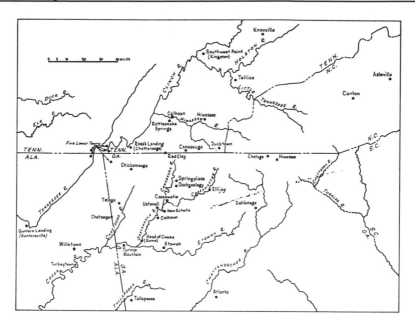

FIG. 3.2. Cherokee towns and settlements in the federal period, 1785–1838. Reprinted from Grace Steels Woodward, *The Cherokees* (Norman: University of Oklahoma Press, 1963), p. 111.

power in the hands of the new planter and trader class. Education and literacy were a major source of this power. Louis Leflore was concerned about the education of his children, as were many White traders who joined the Choctaw and Cherokee tribes. In itself, this paternalistic concern marked a break with the clan system, in which the father played a minor role in childrearing and the mother's brother and sisters played a major role.

Many of the Whites and their children accumulated large amounts of wealth. Frequently, they were traders when they joined the tribes, and, in opposition to tribal values, they became interested in cultivating lands and owning enslaved Africans. The result was mixed-bloods forming an upper economic class within the tribes. These social-class differences within the tribes were well developed by the time of removal. Traveling in Indian Territory in 1842 to investigate corruption in allotment payments, General Ethan Allen Hitchcock noted in his journal: "Indians have classes as well as white men; some are prudent and turn their annuity to a good account, others are improvident . . . . I must say a good deal about the half-breeds, the true civilizers after all. It is mostly those who are in power and wealth . . . among the Choctaws."[19]

By the time of removal to Indian Territory in the 1830s, wealth and political power in both the Choctaw and Cherokee tribes was concentrated in the planter and trader class. Cotton was a major source of wealth. Choctaw land included the prime cotton-growing area in the delta region of Mississippi. Obviously, White settlers coveted the lands for their own use and wanted the Indians removed.

As the cotton culture spread through the South, Whites and mixed-breeds in the Choctaw and Cherokee tribes bought slaves, built plantation homes, and cultivated cotton. By 1824, John Pitchlynn, a White who joined the tribe, and Greenwood Leflore were the two wealthiest men in the Choctaw tribe. John Pitchlynn could boast of ownership of 50 slaves and the cultivation of 250 acres, while Greenwood Leflore owned 32 slaves and cultivated 250 acres. John Pitchlynn's mixed-blood son, Peter, owned 10 slaves and cultivated 90 acres. Mixed-breed David Folsom, a leading promoter of schools, owned 10 slaves and cultivated 150 acres. Of this group, Greenwood Leflore would eventually be one of the wealthiest plantation owners in Mississippi after receiving a large bribe from the U.S. government for signing the removal treaty and then refusing to move to Indian Territory. The only full-blood Choctaw leader to own a significant number of slaves was Chief Mingo Mushulatubbee, who owned 10 slaves and cultivated 30 acres.[20]

In the Choctaw tribe, the Folsoms, the Pitchlynns, and the Leflores became the leading families in wealth, political power, and education. Nathaniel Folsom, John Pitchlynn, and Louis Leflore were the founders of these Choctaw families. Nathaniel Folsom's son David and John Pitchlynn, the two Choctaws who played a leading role in establishing the first school in the Choctaw Nation, were a mixed-blood and a White respectively. The descendants of these three families were active in the government and educational system in Mississippi Territory and, after removal, in Indian Territory.

An estimate of the wealth of family members can be made by calculating the value of slaves. During the period 1824 to 1825, Cyrus Kingsbury, head Presbyterian missionary among the Choctaws, considered purchasing slaves to erect churches and mission schools. At the time, he estimated, "They could be bought for $1,000."[21] This was the price for a skilled enslaved African. Field hands cost $400 or $500. In the 1820s, based on these prices, John Pitchlynn, Greenwood Leflore, Peter Pitchlynn, and David Folsom had $20,000 to $50,000, $12,000 to $32,000, $4,000 to $10,000, and $4,000 to $10,000 invested, respectively, in enslaved Africans. This was a considerable amount of money for the time. As a total in 1826, members of the tribe owned approximately 487 slaves worth from $160,000 to $487,000.[22]

The primary reason Whites joined the Choctaw tribe was for wealth. "My father had a great desire to go to Mississippi to get money," Nathaniel Folsom recalled in conversation with missionary Byington in 1823. "[t]hey said money grew on bushes! We got off [sic] and came into the Choctaw Nation."[23] Nathaniel Folsom was born in North Carolina in 1756 after his family moved from Massachusetts. In about 1775, his father decided to seek wealth in the Mississippi Territory. Nathaniel remained in the Choctaw Nation after his father moved on to the Chickasaw Nation. Similar to Louis Leflore, he married two Choctaw sisters and had 25 children. Marrying into the tribe, Nathaniel became a successful trader and, in his words, "I traded a long time in the Nation [Choctaw], sometimes taking up three or four thousand dollars' worth of goods. I followed trading about thirty years."[24]

David Folsom's letter to the *Niles' Register* in 1819 is indicative of the influence of mixed-bloods on cultural change. The letter was written shortly after the opening of the first school in Choctaw territory financed by the Civilization Fund Act, and his comments were consistent with the objectives of the legislation. The letter opened with Folsom apologizing for his poor English and his limited school attendance of six months. Then he declared that education was now vital to the tribe because of the decline in importance of hunting. He wrote: "I have been talking to my people, and have advised them for the best, turn their attention to industry and farming, and lay our hunting aside. And here is one point of great work, is just come [sic] to hand, before us which is the establishment of a school; and the Choctaws appear to be well pleased."[25]

John Pitchlynn also played an important role in establishing the first schools in the Choctaw Nation. Pitchlynn was born around 1756 on a British ship off the coast of the Caribbean Island of St. Thomas. At the age of 18, he accompanied his father to the Choctaw Nation, where his father died, and John joined the tribe. Following the Choctaw custom of polygamy by marrying sisters, he married two of Nathaniel Folsom's 25 children, Rhoda and Sophia Folsom. This polygamous relationship, of course, made him David Folsom's brother-in-law.[26]

Similar to Nathaniel Folsom, Pitchlynn became a successful trader. With his profits, he invested in cattle, bought slaves, and started a cotton plantation. He became part-owner of a stagecoach line that connected Columbus and Jackson, Mississippi. His financial interests extended into banking, and he became a major lender in the Mississippi region.[27]

The oldest son of Pitchlynn's wife Sophia, Peter Pitchlynn, was born at one of his father's early trading posts on January 30, 1806. As the son of a wealthy White trader and member of the Choctaw Nation, Peter played an important role in the cultural transformation of the tribe. At the age of 14, in 1820, he attended school for 1 year at Charity Hall, a Chickasaw missionary school and in 1821 for 1 year at the Columbia Academy in Tennessee. This brief education was supplemented by the contacts made with travelers at his father's house. By his late teens, he had accumulated a library consisting of moral philosophy, Shakespeare, history, and biography. According to his biographer, "Altogether his training reinforced him even farther from the traditional Indian pattern." Peter Pitchlynn played an important role in the establishment of the Choctaw Academy in Kentucky in 1825 and the Spencer Academy in Indian Territory in 1844.[28]

Peter Pitchlynn made a point of renouncing polygamous relationships when he married Rhoda Folsom, a half-blood daughter of Nathaniel and the half-sister of his mother, in a Christian ceremony conducted by missionary Kingsbury. His biographer wrote that Peter claimed that his marriage "killed the practice of polygamy among the Indians. He exaggerated his contribution, however; the institution still existed some fifty years later."[29]

The conflict over the education of the children of the mixed-breed McCurtain family is an example of the changes in childrearing patterns. As anthropologist Spoehr wrote, "Educational functions tended to be shifted to the mission schools and out of the hands of the mother's brother and the clan elders."[30] By tradition, the responsibility for the education of the McCurtain children was in the hands of their maternal uncle, Robert Cole. But, when missionary educator Kingsbury accepted only five of the six McCurtain children at his school at Mayhew because of overcrowding, McCurtain removed his five children and demanded that they all be accepted. Immediately, Cole wrote a letter to Kingsbury asking for the reinstatement of the children and apologized for their father's actions. Eight other Choctaws appended marks to the letter indicating their unhappiness with the acceptance of the decision of the father over that of the maternal uncle.[31]

Therefore, the mixed-blood children of white Indians contributed to cultural changes by maintaining monogamous relationships, assuming complete responsibility for the education of their children, and passing property on to their children. Another important change, according to anthropologist Spoehr, reflected the movement to a patrilineal family structure from a clan structure: "English surnames were adopted and were passed down in the male line, with a wife taking her husband's name at marriage."[32] According to Choctaw custom, names were not passed on from generation to generation, and children were classified with their mother's uncle. The adoption of English surnames, according to Spoehr, was related to another cultural change: "Personal property, although usually never very extensive, began to be inherited by a man's children rather than by his sister's children."[33]

Besides contributing to these cultural changes, the planter and trader class supported government civilization policies and the establishment of missionary schools. But, unlike missionary educators, the planter class wanted schools to provide their children with an education that would aid in the further accumulation of wealth and protection of property. At times, they were frustrated by the missionary focus on Christian conversion rather than teaching just reading and writing.

THE PLANTER AND TRADER CLASS
OF THE CHEROKEES

In the Cherokee tribe, similar to the Choctaws, wealth was concentrated in a few mixed-blood families who had an important role in welcoming civilization policies. The major political and economic leaders of the Cherokees in the early 19th century were members of the McDonald, Ross, Ridge, and Vann families. McLoughlin estimates that, in the 1820s, about 25 percent of the tribe were mixed-bloods, with only 6 percent owning one or more slaves, and less than 1 percent owning more than 10 slaves. Because land was held in common by the tribe, wealth was measured according to the number of slaves, wagons, plows, looms, and land under cultivation. The vast majority of Cherokees owned no slaves or wagons and cultivated less than 40 acres. In the 1820s, McLoughlin concludes, "Over three-quarters of the Cherokees were full-bloods who spoke no English. They preferred the steady routine of life and the extended kinship system of their clans."[34]

About a decade before the Choctaws, some Cherokees were influenced by civilization policies and began to accumulate wealth. By 1809, certain families were already accumulating large numbers of slaves and livestock. In 1809, it was reported that Joseph Vann, a mixed-blood and at the time the wealthiest tribe member, owned 115 slaves, 1,000 head of cattle, and 250 horses. During the same period, 94 students were enrolled in various missionary schools in the Cherokee nation.[35]

John Ross is a good example of a political and economic leader who resisted removal to Indian Territory. In fact, he was the major leader of the faction resisting removal. By the middle of the 1820s, Ross was identified as one of the wealthiest members of the tribe. He built a two-storied house with a slate roof, 20 glass windows to light the interior, a 10-foot-high porch running the 70-foot length of the house, and two tall brick chimneys and four fireplaces. The outbuildings housed his 20 slaves, a blacksmith shop, and workhouses. He had 175 acres under cultivation.[36]

Similar to many mixed-bloods, Ross's ancestral connection to the tribe was through his mother. His father, Daniel Ross, was born in Scotland around 1760 and was left an orphan in Baltimore, Maryland at the end of the Revolutionary War. Around 1785, he became a trader and was captured by the Cherokees while traveling on the Tennessee River. His future father-in-law, John McDonald, secured his release, and Ross married McDonald's daughter, Mollie, within a year. Mollie was a mixed-blood through her mother Anne Shorey.

John McDonald was born about 1747 in Scotland, and at an early age he traveled to the colonies in search of wealth as a trader. He served as an ensign in the Revolutionary War and he was appointed by the U.S. government to be an agent to the Lower Cherokees. In 1769, John

McDonald married a mixed-blood Cherokee, Anne Shorey. Anne Shorey's mother, Ghigooie, was a full-blood Cherokee, and her father was a White interpreter for the British.[37]

After marrying Mollie McDonald, Daniel Ross established a trading post in Cherokee Territory. By 1809, Ross was listed as owning 13 slaves and 90 head of cattle, and his father-in-law, John McDonald, is listed as owning 16 slaves and 100 head of cattle, in addition to money earned through trading.[38]

John Ross was born on October 3, 1790. According to the blood quantum standards of the 19th century, John Ross was only one-eighth Cherokee through his mother, Mollie. As a major chief and political leader among the Cherokees for over 50 years, he represents the importance of mixed-bloods in the history of the Choctaws and Cherokees. Given the influence of his father and grandfather, it is not surprising that he was educated by a private tutor, George Barbee and that his house was filled with English and American newspapers and books. In addition, his father sent him to study at the mission of Reverend Gideon Blackburn of the Presbyterian church near Chickamauga.[39]

Blackburn's mission school existed because of Jefferson's Indian policies. In the 1790s, Gideon Blackburn worked as a Presbyterian minister in Tennessee just north of the Cherokee border. When he decided to devote his life to the salvation and civilization of the Cherokees, he went directly to President Jefferson with a request for money for his civilization project. Jefferson provided him with $300 worth of supplies to be deducted from the budget of the Cherokee agency. With Jefferson's endorsement, he toured eastern churches collecting money for his mission. In 1804, with supplies from the Cherokee trading house, he built a boarding school for 25 students. In 1806, he opened a day school. Historian McLoughlin believes that Blackburn's claim to have taught 300 to 400 Cherokees to speak English over a 7-year period is inflated. In fact, most of Blackburn's students were similar to John Ross. They were mixed-bloods who came from families where English was spoken.[40]

Similar to the Folsom, Pitchlynn, and Leflore families among the Choctaws, the McDonald and Ross families played a major role in welcoming missionary educators. In 1816, prior to the government funding his mission among the Choctaws, Kingsbury bought 25 acres of McDonald's land to build the Brainerd mission. The U.S. government provided $500 for the land and furnished the school with farm equipment.[41] On this site, Kingsbury built four log cabins for boarding students and a schoolhouse designed to teach 100 students using the Lancasterian method.[42]

In opposition to John Ross's antiremoval faction, mixed-blood John Ridge supported removal to land west of the Mississippi. Ridge believed that removal would be the only way to save the tribe from extinction.

Ridge's father, The Ridge, was an important tribal chief born in 1770 or 1771.

The origin of the name "The Ridge" and the surname Ridge reflects the acculturation process occurring in the tribe. The Ridge's mother was a half-breed whose father was a Scots frontiersman, and The Ridge's father was probably a full-blood. The Ridge's birth name was Nung-noh-hut-tar-hee (he who slays the enemy in the path, or The Pathkiller). As a youthful hunter, he would frequently return to camp by walking along mountain tops. Because of this practice, the tribe gave him a new name, Kah-nung-da-tla-geh (the man who walks on the mountaintop). In English, this name was shortened to The Ridge and later generations adopted Ridge as their last names.[43]

The Ridge's wife, Susan Wickett, a full-blood Cherokee whose Indian name was Sehoya, was initially responsible for the wealth the family gained by growing cotton and the family's acceptance of the civilization policies of Jefferson's administration. During the fall of 1796, while the men were out hunting, Indian agent Hawkins taught a group of Chero-kee women, including Sehoya, how to spin and weave. Hawkins prom-ised that the U.S. government would supply spinning wheels and looms if they were interested in making cloth. On The Ridge's return, he found his wife producing more wealth through making cotton cloth than he had made through hunting. Encouraged by his wife's success, and by Benjamin Hawkin's advice, The Ridge was the first Cherokee male to abandon hunting for farming.[44]

Sehoya and The Ridge established a successful farm at Oothcaloga, where all their children were born, including John Ridge in 1803. In the 1820s, with money accumulated from farming, The Ridge built a large house that still stands in Rome, Georgia and that is known as the "Chieftain." In the 1820s, head of the Indian Bureau McKenney de-scribed the house: "[it] resembled in no respect the wigwam of an Indian, it was the home of the patriarch, the scene of plenty and hospitality."[45] The house is two stories high with dimensions of 54 by 29 feet. There are verandas in front and back, and there is a balcony supported by two twisted columns over the front door. The interior is paneled in hardwood with 30 glass windows providing light.[46]

Both Sehoya and The Ridge remained illiterate, and they knew almost no English. As a mixed-blood, John Ridge grew up on an Euro-pean-American style farm strongly influenced by Indian customs. Ridge's elder son, Yellow Bird, later wrote, "My father grew up . . . as an untutored Indian, and he used to remember the time when his greatest delight was to strip himself of his Indian costume, and with aboriginal cane gig in hand . . . wading up and down creeks in search of crawfish."[47]

Although illiterate, Sehoya and The Ridge welcomed missionary educators into the Cherokee tribe and in 1810 sent 7-year-old John to a Moravian missionary school at Spring Place. This missionary school was a result of the original Moravian request in 1799 to enter Cherokee lands. In granting their request, the National Council asked them "to instruct us and our children and improve our and their minds in the Nation."[48] John Ridge arrived at school speaking no English and dressed in tribal clothing. The Moravian teachers taught John to speak and write in English and, similar to most European-American children of the time, he learned grammar and spelling from the most popular textbook of the time, Noah Webster's spelling book. In 1814, John left Spring Place to return home to take care of his ill mother.[49]

In 1817, when Kingsbury opened the missionary school at Brainerd, The Ridge rode 60 miles to enroll his two oldest children, Nancy and John. A diarist at Brainerd noted that the two children "have rich clothing, many garments, & some knowledge of letters."[50] Disappointed that Brainerd was not teaching his son any more than he had learned at Spring Place, The Ridge decided to send John to the Foreign Mission School in Cornwall, Connecticut.[51] The experiences of John Ridge and his cousin Elias Boudinot at Cornwall would contribute to their support of removal.

Elias Boudinot (ne Buck Watie) also attended the Spring Place mission school, where he and John Ridge were the school's prized scholars. Elias Boudinot was the first of the two cousins to reach the Foreign Mission School at Cornwall in 1818. He left in the spring, traveling with one member of the Choctaw's Folsom family, who was also planning to attend the school. Stopping in Burlington, New Jersey to meet Elias Boudinot, the head of the American Bible Society and former president of the Continental Congress, he decided to change his name from Buck Watie to Elias Boudinot. Buck Watie enrolled in Cornwall as Elias Boudinot.[52] John Ridge enrolled the next fall. Indicative of the cultural transformation and the accumulation of wealth by The Ridge since the days of hunting along the tops of mountains was his appearance at Cornwall in 1821 to check on his son John's health. He arrived in town in a coach-and-four dressed in a "coat trimmed with gold [braid]." The Ridge's carriage was described as "the most splendid . . . that ever entered town."[53]

Most citizens of Cornwall, and most European Americans, had little knowledge of the wealth being accumulated and the cultural changes occurring among the mixed-blood leaders of the Choctaws and Cherokees. Through trading, the development of cotton plantations, and the use of slaves, these mixed bloods were creating a new social class in the tribes. But one of the important things learned by John Ridge and Elias Boudinot at Cornwall, as I discuss later, was that racism would keep European Americans from welcoming into their society these newly "civilized" Indians.

THE EDUCATION TREATIES

With the increasing wealth and political power of mixed-bloods, the two tribes began to demand treaty provisions that encouraged the expansion of formal education. After all, schooling held out the promise to some traditionalists that it would provide the tools for resistance and, to the planter and trader class, a means of increasing their wealth and political status. Ironically, the more educated the tribal leadership became, the more difficult it was for U.S. officials to bargain for Indian lands. As Indian resistance to loss of land and removal increased, so did the federal government's use of force and bribery increase.

The series of treaties signed by the southern tribes in 1785 and 1786, including the Treaty of Hopewell with the Choctaws and Cherokees in 1785 reflects the initial naivete of Indians when dealing with the newly formed U.S. government. The Indians agreed to recognize the United States government, to establish boundaries to tribal lands, and to accept the protection of the U.S. government. In turn, the U.S. government gave the Indians the right to expel White intruders on Indian land. The Treaty of Hopewell promised: "That the Indians may have full confidence in the justice of the United States . . . The hatchet shall be forever buried . . . ."[54] Reflecting on the important place of women in the affairs of the Cherokees', the Beloved Woman, Nancy Ward, said at the signing of the treaty, "I have a pipe and a little tobacco . . . to smoke in friendship . . . I am now old, but hope yet to bear children who will grow up and people our Nation, as we are now under the protection of Congress and have no more disturbances."[55]

The constant violation by White settlers of the Treaty of Hopewell resulted in the first educational provisions to be included in a treaty. Worried that the violations of the Hopewell Treaty would weaken U.S. control of the Cherokees, Secretary of War Knox wrote to President Washington in 1790, "The disgraceful violation of the Treaty of Hopewell . . . [shall cause] Indian tribes [to] have no faith . . . and . . . [shall cause] lawless whites [to] ridicule a government which shall, on paper only, make Indian treaties and regulate Indian boundaries.[56] In response to Knox's warning, President Washington called for a new treaty with the Cherokees that was signed on July 2, 1791. In the Treaty of Holston, as it was called, the Cherokees gave up claims to the Cumberland Valley and gained assurances of U.S. protection against White settlers.

The Treaty of Holston also promised to help the tribe become "civilized." "The Cherokee Nation may be led to a greater degree of civilization," the treaty states in Article XIV, "and to become herdsmen and cultivators, instead of remaining in a state of hunters, the United States will from time to time furnish gratuitously the said nation with useful implements of husbandry."[57] In addition, the treaty called for the U.S.

government to send four interpreters to the tribe who would be furnished with land for cultivation.

For some Cherokees, the promise of assistance in husbandry was considered important. Cherokee Chief Bloody Fellow complained to Secretary of War Knox in 1792 about the lack of attention by his office to the promise of assistance to start farms. "The treaty mentions plows, hoes, cattle, and other things for farming; this is what we want; game is going fast away among us. We must plant corn and raise cattle, and we desire you to assist us . . . ."[58] In addition, Jefferson used the Treaty of Holston to justify the provision of goods given to Reverend Gideon Blackburn to start his school among the Cherokees in 1804.

Treaties with the Choctaws also contained provisions for the U.S. government to supply farm implements. One of the major provisions for education was included in Treaty of Doaks Stand in 1820 and 1825. In 1825, the Treaty of Doaks Stand paved the way for Choctaw removal to Indian Territory. The treaty exchanged Choctaw land for a wilderness area west of the Mississippi. After removal in the 1830s, part of this land would be inhabited by the Choctaw Nation. One problem with the treaty was that part of the land given to the Choctaws was heavily occupied by White settlers. Later, this portion of land would be incorporated into Arkansas.

The seventh article of the Treaty of Doaks Stand provided that 54 sections of land would be sold to create a school fund. This provision of the treaty might have resulted from missionary Kingsbury telling the U.S. negotiators that Choctaws would only be interested in giving up land for schools. The negotiators later reported that they believed the only reason the Choctaws finally signed the treaty was because of the provision for a school fund.

To resolve the problem of the western land that was already inhabited by White settlers, a contingent of Choctaws went to Washington in 1824, where, it is sometimes claimed, federal officials bribed the delegation by paying the delegation's bar bill of $2,149.50, their room and board bill of $2,029, and their bill for oysters and liquor of $349.75. In addition, more than $1,000 were spent on suits for each delegate.[59]

One result of the renegotiation of the Doaks Stand Treaty was a $6,000 annuity for 16 years to be spent on education. The annuity was compensation for the land that was already settled by whites that the Choctaws ceded back to the U.S. government. Also, the boundary between what would be Indian Territory and Arkansas was established. This is still the boundary between Oklahoma and Arkansas. The annuity from the Doaks Stand Treaty was used to fund the Choctaw Academy in Kentucky, and, subsequently, it provided the basis for the creation of the Spencer Academy in Indian Territory.

The educational provisions of these treaties reflects the interests of the leaders of the Choctaws and Cherokees in schools and civilization projects. But, their educational experiences helped to raise suspicions of the racist intentions of Whites. Two examples of the consequences of Choctaw and Cherokee interests in education, and the government's civilization projects, were the racial conflicts experienced by John Ridge and Elias Boudinot at school in Cornwall and the role of the Choctaw Academy in solidifying the power of mixed-bloods in the Choctaw tribe.

LOVE AND RACE IN THE LITCHFIELD HILLS

Elias Boudinot and John Ridge didn't realize when they set off for the Foreign Mission School nestled in the Litchfield hills of Connecticut that the most important part of their educational experience would be living in a town of White inhabitants. The Ridge and his brother, David Watie, decided to send their sons to the Foreign Mission School after Reverend Cornelius rode through the south in search of pupils. He arrived on horseback in September, 1817 in Cherokee territory where he recalled telling a group of chiefs, including The Ridge, "I had been sent to them by a society of great and good men at the North who loved them . . . it was their belief that in no way could they do the Cherokee so much good as by sending wise and good men . . . to instruct them in the arts of agriculture; and in the knowledge of their great Creator; by means of which they might be made happy and useful in this life . . . ."[60] In turn, The Ridge praised Cornelius' words because he believed, "It will also promote our children's good to labor for their living when they come to years of manhood. I am sensible the hunting life is not to be depended on."[61]

The Foreign Mission School was established in 1817 by the American Board of Commissioners for Foreign Missions for the education of "foreigners." In this case, "foreigner" obviously meant anyone who was not of European descent, rather than meaning someone who didn't reside in the United States. Therefore, Native Americans were placed in the same category by the school as Asians and Pacific Islanders, who also attended. Arriving in the spring of 1818, Elias Boudinot may have witnessed the Governor of Connecticut installing Reverend Herman Daggett as principal of the school. Also, probably in attendance at the service were Benjamin Gold and his daughter, Boudinot's future wife, Harriet. Benjamin Gold was a leading man of the community and one of the founders of the Foreign Mission School.[62]

John Ridge arrived at the Foreign Mission school in the fall of 1818. Three years later, John's and Elias' hearts would turn from books to love, causing turmoil in the Cornwall community. In 1821, The Ridge arrived in Cornwall to take his sick son home. At first, John refused to go because he was still ill, and, consequently, his father returned alone. John had fallen in love with 14-year-old old Sarah Northrup, the daughter of the steward of the school. After finding out about the romance from John, Sarah's mother immediately confronted her and she confessed her love for John. Although Mrs. Northrup expressed her disapproval, she did describe John as "a noble youth, beautiful in appearance, very graceful, a perfect gentleman everywhere." Fearing further contact between the two lovers, the Northrups immediately whisked Sarah away to her grandparents in New Haven with instructions for them to introduce her to other young men.[63]

The Ridge was equally horrified by the possibility of the match after a White minister in the Cherokee Nation told him "that a white woman would be apt to feel above the common Cherokees . . . ."[64] The Ridge also wanted John to marry the daughter of an important tribal chief. But the real decision about marriage rested in the hands of John's mother, Sehoya, who finally relented to John's pleading letters and gave him permission to marry. The Northrups finally agreed to the marriage if John went home for a year and waited until the leg problem that was bothering him was cured.

The community uproar over the marriage began a year later when John and The Ridge appeared in a carriage driven by a liveried enslaved African. The town was shocked when it was realized that John and Sarah were actually going to be married. After the marriage ceremony was completed at the Northrups' house by a Congregationalist minister, The Ridge and the couple faced an angry crowd outside the house. Fearing the townspeople, The Ridge and the newly married couple quickly departed for the comfort of a southern plantation. One wonders what Sarah thought about leaving a stuffy, puritanical New England village for life in the Cherokee Nation.

Public criticism of the marriage appeared in the local newspaper, *The American Eagle*. The editor of the newspaper, Isaiah Bunce, wrote in an editorial: "This subject of INTERMARRIAGES with the Indians and blacks of the missionary school at Cornwall . . . [is] not a subject for irony. The affliction, mortification and disgrace, of the relatives of the young woman, who is only about 16 years old, are too great for that . . . ."[65] Fearing further humiliation of the family, Bunce did not mention the family's name. He went on to blame the "missionary machinery" for creating the opportunity for contact between young women and men of different races. Blaming missionaries, Bunce wrote, would be more appropriate than "some of whom have said that the girl ought to be publicly whipped, the Indian hung, and the mother drown'd."[66]

A month later, Bunce reprinted the article on "Intermarriages" and he warned that young ladies of the town were spending time with students of the school while the "young men of the town, poor White boys, were often cast into the shade by their colored and tawny rivals . . . ." In response to Bunce, a meeting was held by the Bachelors of Cornwall Valley, where the membership passed a resolution criticizing

Bunce for insinuating "that we are thus cast in the shade, and eclipsed by the intervention of these our tawny rivals. . . ."[67]

It was against this background of controversy that Harriet Gold, about 8 months after the marriage of John and Sarah, asked her parents if she could marry Elias Boudinot. Since returning to the Cherokee Nation 3 years before, Boudinot had maintained a romantic correspondence with Harriet. Harriet's parents were infuriated and Benjamin Gold quickly sent off a letter to Elias refusing the marriage. Consequently, Harriet became bedridden with some unexplainable illness that disappeared when her parents gave their consent to the marriage. They made Harriet promise to keep the news from the rest of the family.

Benjamin Gold feared that after the uproar over Sarah and John, the backlash from the marriage of Harriet and Elias would destroy the Foreign Mission School. A meeting of the agents of the school resulted in the issue of a public disclaimer of responsibility for the marriage. The disclaimer opened with a reminder that after the marriage of Sarah and John, the school promised that there would be no more marriages between students of the school and local females. But, the agents argued, they were unable to stop the romance because it was carried out in secrecy with a great deal of deception. The disclaimer closed with a plea to not blame the school for the marriage, and it reiterated that the agents of the school condemned these types of marriages. And, to reinforce their objections to interracial marriages, the agents wrote, "we regard those who have engaged in or accessory to this transaction, as criminal; as offering insult to the known feelings of the Christian community: and as sporting with the sacred interests of this charitable institution."[68]

On June 17, 1825, the disclaimer landed like a bombshell in the little community. The secrecy surrounding the marriage was broken. That night, Harriet was burned in effigy in the town's commons. Harriet's brother-in-law, Reverend Herman Vaill, wrote a 5,000-word letter trying to persuade Harriet not to go through with the marriage. He told her that the marriage would force the closing of the Foreign Mission School, that, he assured her, was not opened to create a mixture of races, but, "it was to civilize, and to Christianize the heathen. . . ."[69] Harriet was warned that the marriage might hurt the prospects for her unmarried sister in finding a suitable mate.

On March 28, 1826, Harriet and Elias were married in the home of her father, and the couple left immediately for Cherokee country. In the fall of 1826, the furor over the marriages caused the Foreign Mission School to close its doors.

Did the experiences in Cornwall contribute to John's and Elias' decision to support removal to Indian Territory and their eventual assassinations at the hands of opponents to removal? Obviously, it would be an oversimplification to attribute this course of events to the experience of racism in Cornwall. On the other hand, marriage under those conditions must have left a lifelong impression about the impossibilities of peaceful coexistence between White and Indian communities.

After his experience in Cornwall, John Ridge angrily denounced racism as "the ruling passion of the age, and an Indian is almost considered accursed." He realized that neither education nor civilization would ever, in the eyes of Whites, make them equal. "If an Indian is educated in the sciences, has a good knowledge of the classics, astronomy, mathematics, moral and natural philosophy, and his conduct equally modest and polite, yet he is an Indian," Ridge wrote bitterly, "and the most stupid and illiterate white man will disdain and triumph over this worthy individual."[70]

Ridge's reaction to the events in Cornwall seemed to confirm part of the vision that more than a decade before had resulted in the ghost dance. For Ridge, the sense of superiority and racism of Whites meant that no matter how much Native Americans adopted the ways of European civilization, there would still be no peace between the two groups.

Two months after his marriage to Harriet, the concern about racism and coexistence between Whites and Indians appeared in a speech Boudinot gave on May 16, 1826 at the First Presbyterian Church of Philadelphia. Boudinot was not interested in offending his audience, because he was raising money to support the *Cherokee Phoenix*, the first Native American newspaper, that he would edit proudly. While praising his tribe and the efforts it had made to learn about European civilization, he warned: "The prejudices in regard to them [Cherokees] are strong and lasting." And, with a theme that would echo through his speeches and writings and would provide justification for signing the removal treaty, he warned of the "evil effects of their [Cherokees] intercourse with their white neighbors." He sadly lamented at the close of his speech, "We have seen, I say, one family after another, one tribe after another, nation after nation pass away; until only a few solitary creatures are left to tell the sad story of extinction."[71]

Whereas the experience of John Ridge and Elias Boudinot in Cornwall confirmed the difficulty of living in the close presence of whites, the reaction by Indians to the Choctaw Academy confirmed the role of education in distinguishing social classes and in providing access to political power.

THE EDUCATION OF A SOCIAL ELITE:
THE CHOCTAW ACADEMY

Writing for his illiterate cousin Thomas Leflore to Agent Armstrong of the Choctaw Agency in Arkansas in 1840, my great-great grandfather Basil Leflore complained, "It appears from all accounts that the students [at the Choctaw Academy in Kentucky] are not fed with a sufficiency, and that they are badly clothed."[72] The complaint is indicative of several things. First, unlike his cousin, Basil was literate because he was sent to the Choctaw Academy in 1829.[73] Second, in 1840 Basil was working as Choctaw Clerk of the District in the newly formed Choctaw government created in Indian Territory after removal. Basil's position indicates the importance of literacy in the new government. And, last, the major complaint tribal leaders had about the Choctaw Academy was about the poor treatment of the students. Apparently, the European Americans operating the school did not appreciate that many of their students were coming from wealthy planter and trader families. The complaints about the social conditions at the Choctaw Academy were a major factor in the Choctaw government's decision to remove their children and establish their own Spencer Academy in Indian Territory.

Established in 1825, the Choctaw Academy was an important institution for the training of future politicians and government bureaucrats. The first group of 21 boys Peter Pitchlynn took to the Academy in 1825 were primarily mixed-breeds, including members of the mixed-blood Folsom, Wade, Nails, and Pitchlynn families.[74] According to Foreman, "The Choctaw Academy in Kentucky had educated many of the most intelligent men in the Indian country, and they were to be seen in their councils taking the deepest interest in the welfare and prosperity of their people."[75]

The elitist quality of the Academy is clearly indicated in the class distinctions made by tribal leaders between education at the Choctaw Academy and education received from missionaries working in the Nation. The 1825 revision of the Doaks Stand Treaty, which financed the Academy, clearly stated that the educational funds would be used to educate youth outside of the Nation. An 1825 letter by Peter Pitchlynn to the Secretary of War, James Barbour, reveals that the intention was to use the treaty money to educate the children of the tribal elite. Pitchlynn wrote that he had delivered the first group of 21 Choctaw students to the Academy and that: "It is my decided opinion that the promising youths of our nation should be educated in this method, leaving the mass of our population to the . . . missionaries who settled among us."[76]

In addition, many Choctaw leaders expressed dissatisfaction with the type of education being provided at missionary schools within the Nation. In a letter written in 1830 to President Jackson and signed by eight Choctaws, three of whom were illiterate in English as indicated by Xs for their signatures, the following reason is given for the establishment of the Choctaw Academy: " . . . we have employed and payed [sic] those Yankee missionarys [sic] for twelve years for which we have Recd. no compensation we have never Recd. a Scholar out of their Schools that was able to keep a grog shop Book." And, reflecting some satisfaction with the type of education being received at the Academy, the authors informed President Jackson, "when we found that we could get nothing from them [the missionaries] we established an academy in Kentucky . . . from which we have Recd. a great number of first Rate Scholars."[77]

The mixed-blood leaders of the Nation wanted to spare no expense in the establishment and maintenance of the school. In a letter to the Department of War, Greenwood Leflore defended the expense of the school: "And although it is probable that we could get our children taught something cheaper yet we do not wish to put out their education to the lowest bidder and if we were to do it we do not know that we should profit by it."[78]

The Choctaw Academy was a cooperative undertaking between the tribe and Colonel Richard Johnson. Johnson's interest in operating the school for the Choctaws resulted from activities in the Baptist Church. As a member of the Board of Directors of the Kentucky Baptist Society for Propagating the Gospel among the Heathen (founded in 1814), he participated in sending a letter to Indian agents suggesting that each tribe send several of their children to White settlements for their education and religious conversion. The organization offered to cover all expenses. In 1819, McKenney again notified agents of the Baptist offer and instructed them to contact Johnson's brother. From 1819 to 1824 several Indian children lived in Johnson's house.[79]

When money was made available for the education of Choctaws by the 1825 revisions of the Doaks Stand Treaty, Johnson wrote to Indian Agent Ward of the Choctaw Agency, proposing that the children be educated at his Blue Spring farm near Great Crossings, Kentucky. After interpreting the letter to the tribe, there was a general agreement to accept Johnson's offer. In a letter to the War Department of September 27, 1825, Johnson indicated the Choctaw acceptance of his proposal: "As I am better situated to take them than any other person in the country, they have consigned them to me to board and clothe, . . . the Indians will be here by 15th October. I am now preparing to receive them; my working men are fixing tables, benches, chairs."[80]

The Choctaw Nation did appear to invest a good deal of money in the future education of its leaders. First, the Academy had four enslaved Africans to attend to the personal needs of its students. Second, the school was furnished with the latest in educational equipment. The superintendent of the Academy, Reverend Thomas Ward, described in a letter to the War Department on November 1, 1825, "The school room is large and commodious, well furnished with maps, globes, books, etc." The school's equipment included two globes, five large maps, two surveying compasses with chains, and a telescope.[81]

The use of slaves at the Academy indicates the social status and growing racism of the Choctaw students. As an example of Choctaw attitudes toward enslaved Africans, Peter Pitchlynn, after he attended the school in 1827, was critical of the quality of food, the dirtiness of the four slaves serving the students, the quality of the hats given to the students, and the straw mattresses.[82] The Academy teacher, Thomas Henderson, responded to these charges in a letter to David Folsom. Henderson said that Pitchlynn's complaints contained lies, and, in a statement indicating attitudes regarding the social status of the slaves in relationship to the Choctaw students, he said, "I have heard of the Col. [Johnson] whipping some [slaves] very severely for insolence to the students but these are not those who wait on the table. . . ."[83]

Once in Indian Territory, tribal leaders began to question the wisdom of sending their children as far away as Kentucky. In addition, there were increased concerns about the conditions at the Choctaw Academy and the curriculum changes that took place at the Academy during the 1830s. In an action that would result in schools being organized to protect the power of the mixed-breed elite, the National Council of the Choctaw Nation informed the U.S. Agent to the Nation, William Armstrong, that they would no longer be sending students to the Choctaw Academy. They proposed to use the funds being spent on the Choctaw Academy for an advanced school for boys and an advanced school for girls.[84]

One of the reasons for withdrawing their children from the Choctaw Academy was the shift to a manual training curriculum. The mixed-breed leadership wanted to send their children to a school with a classical curriculum. Interestingly, when the Choctaw Nation organized their educational system, manual training schools were for the poorer full-bloods and the classical curriculum was for the elite. An example of the reasoning behind the manual training programs objected to by Choctaw leaders is in a letter written in 1832, by the head teacher at the Choctaw Academy, Thomas Henderson, to the Department of War requesting $500 for the erection of three workshops for training wheel-wrights, blacksmiths, and shoemakers.[85] Writing to the Secretary of War about the workshops, Henderson outlined the classic argument for manual and vocational education.

> It is very certain (were it even practicable to make scholars [sic] of every youth sent to the institution) that by their education alone, they cannot all hope to get employment and be supported in the nation, in its present uncultivated condition—and it is equally certain that nothing will tend more rapidly to promote civilized habits . . . than the encouragement of the mechanical arts—Every person is well apprised that it is not every sprightly boy among our own white children that is calculated to become a scholar [sic] . . . by proper management the greater part of the students in nearly the same time, now devoted at school, could be sent home with good trades & a sufficient education for mechanics and farmers.[86]

Although elite Choctaw leaders supported manual training for other members of their tribe, they were not interested in it for their children.

In addition, the leadership was disturbed by a 1839 letter signed by 33 students at the Choctaw Academy, complaining about conditions at the school. The letter demonstrates the genteel concerns and Christian morality of the mixed-breed students. Similar to Pitchlynn in the 1820s, the students complained about service, food, and clothing. The students wrote, "One drunken negro at the head of the table affairs, hardly any forks on the tables. No table-cloths on the two tables and but one on the monitors table. Our shirts are scarce, one for summer and one for winter. No suspenders. Our bed clothes are very indifferent. Our rooms we are constantly patching."[87]

Also, they complained about moral conditions. As a result of the letter, Chief Thomas Leflore complained to the U.S. Agent Armstrong that school students were learning "all the bad vices that can be, such as gambling, drinking and, I have heard this from different students that came from there . . . It appears from all accounts that the students are not fed with a sufficiency, and that they are badly clothed."[88]

Chief Leflore requested that his son be sent home from the Academy. And in 1839, Leflore refused to send any more students from the Nation to the Choctaw Academy. In 1840, Agent Armstrong wrote to Commander of Indian Affairs, Crawford, complaining about the difficulty of recruiting students for the school. Referring to the students' letter and Leflore's complaints, Armstrong wrote, "[I]t cannot therefore be wondered that there should be great feeling against the Choctaw Academy . . . it is now spoken among the *leading* [italics added] Choctaws to send for their children and bring them home."[89] The next step in providing an education for the elite members of the tribe was the establishment of the Spencer and Wheelock Academies.

CONCLUSION:
MOLDING NATIVE AMERICAN CHARACTER

Similar to the attitudes toward children held by common school advocates, U.S. government leaders assumed that Native Americans were lumps of clay that could be easily molded into any form. In the late 18th and early 19th centuries, many educators and government leaders assumed that human character could be shaped for the good of society. These attitudes are reflected in Mann's explanation of why he gave up the practice of law as a means of creating the good society in favor of the campaign to establish common schools. "Having found the present generation composed of materials almost unmalleable," Mann wrote in the 1830s, "I am about transferring my efforts to the next. Men are cast-iron; but children are wax."[90] Believing that Indians were like children, Washington, McKenney, and other government leaders gave up the practice of war as a means of gaining Indian lands in favor of civilization policies and schooling.

And similar to common school reformers, who discovered that they could not perfectly mold children to eliminate crime, poverty, class conflict, and other social problems, advocates of civilization policies discovered that education was not an easy answer for obtaining Native American lands. People are not malleable lumps of wax that can be shaped according to a government's agenda.

Despite the lack of a one-to-one relationship between the government's intentions and results, civilization policies did have an impact. This impact can be traced from decade to decade beginning in the 1790s. Government policies in the 1790s did provide the training and tools for Sehoya and The Ridge to give up hunting for the establishment of a farm for growing cotton, producing cloth, and raising domestic animals. The Ridge fulfilled Jefferson's dreams of turning Native Americans into farmers. The funding of schools under the Civilization Fund Act did educate a new generation of Indian leaders. Family organizations did begin to change from clan systems to patrilineal families. Women did begin to lose political and economic rights within the tribes. Values regarding wealth did begin to change from values of sharing to values of accumulation.

However, these changes had unexpected results for government leaders. First, civilization policies contributed to the creation of a small planter and trader class that came to dominate the economic and political life of the Choctaws and Cherokees. Second, the majority of full-bloods were not directly influenced by civilization policies. The majority of full-bloods were indirectly influenced by government policies through the growing power of the planter and trader class. Last, civilization policies did not result in Native Americans wanting to sell their tribal lands. The planter and trader class and the majority of full-bloods resisted in different ways the attempts by the federal government to take over tribal lands. In the end, the federal government could only obtain the tribal lands of southern Indians by forcing their removal to Indian Territory.

There are other dimensions to the story, which I explore in the next chapter, and they are the intentions and influence of the missionaries who carried out government civilization programs.

NOTES

[1]Clara Sue Kidwell, *Choctaws and Missionaries in Mississippi, 1818–1819* (Norman: University of Oklahoma Press, 1995), p. xiv.

[2]William G. McLoughlin, *Cherokees and Missionaries 1789–1839* (New Haven, CT: Yale University Press, 1984), p. 45.

[3]Quoted in Kidwell, p. 33.

[4]Quoted in Horatio Bardwell Cushman, *History of the Choctaw, Chickasaw, and Natchez Indians*, edited by Angie Debo (New York:

Russell & Russell, 1972), pp. 99, 103. Cushman's book, originally published in 1899, is an important primary source on the history and cultural traditions of the Choctaws in the 19th century. Cushman was born at the Mayhew missionary station in the Choctaw Nation where his parents were sent in 1820 by the American Board of Commissioner for Foreign Missions. Cushman's book is full of fond memories of growing up at Mayhew and participating in Choctaw life. He personally knew the Folsom, Pitchlynn, and Leflore families. See Angie Debo's foreword to the book.

[5]Quoted in McLoughlin, *Cherokees and Missionaries*, p. 39.

[6]William G. McLoughlin, *Cherokee Renascence in the New Republic* (Princeton: Princeton University Press, 1986), pp. 168–180.

[7]Ibid., p. 180.

[8]Alexander Spoehr, "Changing Kinships Systems: A Study in the Acculturation of the Creeks, Cherokee, and Choctaw," *Publications of Field Museum of Natural History Anthropoligical Series Vol. 33,* (New York: Kraus Reprint Co., 1968) p. 217.

[9]Ralph Folsom McBride and Alberta Patrick McBride, *A Family Makes Its Mark: The Leflores of Mississippi* (Jacksonville, FL: The Leflore Family Association, 1976), pp. 1–7.

[10]See Kidwell, pp. 3–19, and McBride and McBride, p. 8.

[11]Quoted in McBride and McBride, p. 8.

[12]N. D. Deupree, "Greenwood Le Flore," *Publications of the Mississippi Historical Society Vol. 7,* (Jackson, MI: Jackson, Mississippi Historical Society, 1903), p. 142 and Kidwell, p. 19.

[13]McBride and McBride, p. 19.

[14]Ibid., pp. 17–18.

[15]Kidwell, pp. 56–57.

[16]McBride and McBride, p. 20.

[17]Angie Debo, *The Rise and Fall of the Choctaw Republic* (Norman: University of Oklahoma Press, 1961), pp. 4–5.

[18]R. Halliburton, Jr., "Chief Greenwood Leflore and His Malmaison Plantation," in *After Removal: The Choctaw in Mississippi* edited by Samuel J. Wells and Roseanna Tubby (Jackson: University of Mississippi, 1986), pp. 56–57.

[19]*A Traveler in Indian Territory: The Journal of Ethan Allen Hitchcock, late Major-General in the United States Army*, edited and annotated by Grant Foreman (Cedar Rapids, IA: The Torch Press, 1930), 186–187.

[20]"Table I: Owners of Land and Slaves in the Choctaw Nation," in Clara Sue Kidwell, *Choctaws and Missionaries in Mississippi* (Norman: University of Oklahoma Press, 1995), pp. 108–109.

[21]Kidwell, p. 82.

[22]This estimate is based on figures provided in Kidwell, pp. 108–109.

[23]Cushman, p. 326.

[24]Ibid., p. 326.

[25]Debo, p. 42.

[26]Baird, p. 6.

[27]Ibid., p. 7.

[28]Ibid., pp. 20–21.

[29]Baird, p. 22.

[30]"Changing Kinship Systems: A Study in the Acculturation of the Creeks, Cherokee, and Choctaw," *Publications of the Field Museum of Natural History Anthropological Series Vol. 33* (New York: Kraus Reprint Co., 1968), p. 203.

[31]Debo, p. 43.

[32]Spoehr, p. 204.

[33]Spoehr, p. 204.

[34]McLoughlin, *Cherokee Renascence...*, pp. 328–329.

[35]"Table 5: Schools and Pupils in the Cherokee Nation, 1809" and "Table 6: Prosperous Cherokees in 1809" in McLoughlin, *Cherokee Renascence...*, p. 174.

[36]Gary E. Moulton, *John Ross: Cherokee Chief* (Athens, GA: University of Georgia Press, 1978), pp. 30–31.

[37]Ibid., pp. 3–5.

[38]McLoughlin, *Cherokee Renascence...*, p. 174.

[39]Moulton, pp. 6–7 and McLoughlin, *Cherokee Renascence...*, pp. 74–76.

[40]McLoughlin, *Cherokee Renascence...*, pp. 75–76.

[41]Moulton, p. 7.

[42]Thurman Wilkins, *Cherokee Tragedy: The Ridge Family and the Decimation of a People, Second Edition, Revised* (Norman: University of Oklahoma Press, 1986), p. 98.

[43]Ibid., pp. 6–7, 15.

[44]Ibid., p. 32.

[45]Quoted in Wilkins, p. 186.

[46]Ibid., pp. 186–187.

[47]Ibid., p. 34.

[48]McLoughlin, *Cherokees and Missionaries...*, pp. 46–47. [49]Wilkins, pp. 99–103.

[50]Ibid., p. 98.

[51]Ibid., pp. 110–188.

[52]Ibid., pp. 115–116.

[53]Ibid., p. 130.

[54]"Treaty of Hopewell with the Cherokees. November 28, 1785." In John Paul Prucha, *Documents in United States Indian Policy, Second Edition* (Lincoln: University of Nebraska, 1990), p. 8.

[55]Grace Steele Woodward, *The Cherokees* (Norman: University of Oklahoma Press, 1963), pp. 105–106.

[56]Ibid., pp. 11–12.

[57]Ibid., pp. 11–12.

[58]Ibid., p. 117.

[59]Debo, p. 50.

[60]Quoted in Wilkins, p. 111.

[61]Quoted in Ibid., p. 112.

[62]Ralph Henry Gabriel, *Elias Boudinot Cherokee & His America* (Norman: University of Oklahoma Press, 1941), pp. 43–48.

[63]Quoted in Wilkins, p. 133.

[64]Quoted in Ibid., p. 133.

[65]Quoted in Gabriel, p. 61.

[66]Quoted in Ibid., p. 62.

[67]Quoted in Ibid., pp. 63–64.

[68]Quoted in Gabriel, p. 77.

[69]Quoted in Ibid., p. 83.

[70]Quoted in Wilkins, p. 147.

[71]Quoted in Gabriel, pp. 106–109.

[72]Carolyn Thomas Foreman, "The Choctaw Academy," *The Chronicles of Oklahoma* (1932)10: 106.

[73]Basil Leflore was listed on the school's rolls in 1829 as reproduced by Carolyn Thomas Foreman in "The Choctaw Academy," *Chronicles of Oklahoma* (1928)6: 472.

[74]Ibid., pp. 454–455.

[75]Grant Foreman, *The Five Civilized Tribes* (Norman: University of Oklahoma Press, 1934), p. 33.

[76]Leland Winfield Meyer, *The Life and Times of Colonel Richard M. Johnson of Kentucky* (New York: Columbia University Press, 1932), p. 362.

[77]Quoted in Foreman, "The Choctaw Academy," (1928), p. 475.

[78]Ibid., p. 461.

[79]Meyer, pp. 343–352.

[80]Ibid., pp. 355–356.

[81]Foreman, "The Choctaw Academy," (1928), pp. 459–460.

[82]Ibid., pp. 464–465.

[83]Ibid., p. 467.

[84]Ibid., p. 57.

[85]Foreman, "The Choctaw Academy," (1928), pp. 477–478.

[86]Foreman, "The Choctaw Academy," *Chronicles of Oklahoma* (1931)9: 389.

[87]Ibid., p. 103.

[88]Foreman, "The Choctaw Academy," (1932) pp. 105–106.

[89]Ibid., pp. 105–106.

[90]Quoted in *Life of Horace Mann* (Washington, D.C.: National Education Association, 1907), edited by Mary Peabody Mann p. 83. Horace Mann's edited letters and journal are reprinted in this volume.

4

The Missionaries and Their Schools

In a photograph, I am standing next to the restored Presbyterian Church at Goodland, Oklahoma, holding a piece of timber that looks rough and dry from its crude manufacture and age. The wood is from the original church attended by many of my relatives in the 19th century. Today, the Goodland church and mission school are the oldest church and mission school in continuous existence in Oklahoma. The mission site was originally selected by Cyrus Kingsbury after he crossed on the Trail of Tears in 1835 to join the Choctaws in Indian Territory. His continuous work with the Choctaws in Mississippi and with the tribe after its removal to Indian Territory earned him the title of "The Apostle to the Choctaws."[1]

At the site of the now-restored church, a plaque indicates that the Goodland Mission was started in 1848 by Reverend John Lathrop of the Presbyterians' Board of Foreign Missions. In 1850, Reverend O.P. Stark built the church, and his wife opened a one-room school. Among those listed in service to the mission is my relative, Samuel Bailey Spring. A poster inside the offices of what is now the Goodland Presbyterian Children's Home indicates the evolution of the institution from a mission and day school to an Indian Industrial School, to the Goodland Indian Orphanage, and to its present role of "providing a Christian home, education and training for children and youth, with Presbyterian and private assistance."[2]

My great-great grandfather's second wife, Carrie Gooding Leflore, born in Indian Territory in 1836, began teaching at the mission school just before the beginning of the Civil War. She is listed as one of the founding members in 1894 of the Women's Aid and Missionary Society of the Goodland Presbyterian Church.[3] A plaque at the Goodland Cemetery reads: "THE PROPERTY FOR THIS CEMETERY WAS DONATED TO GOODLAND INDIAN ORPHANAGE BY MRS. BASIL (CARRIE GOODING) LEFLORE." An obelisk-shaped tombstone in the cemetery marks the burial place of my great-great grandfather. The epitaph on

64

the stone reads: "In memory of Ex. Gov. B.L. Leflore died at Goodland, C.N. [Choctaw Nation] Oct. 15, 1886 at the aged [sic.] 76 years." Basil Leflore was first elected Principal Chief[4] of the Choctaw Nation in 1859. Prior to that date, he served as Secretary and Treasurer of the Second District of the Choctaw Nation from 1834 to 1857 and Treasurer of the Choctaw Nation from 1866 to 1871.[5] Carrie Gooding Leflore died in 1909, 2 years after the end of the Choctaw Nation and Indian Territory and the establishment of Oklahoma.

On the grounds of the Goodland Mission stands a small museum made, according to the sign, of "Timbers from Old Home of 3 Times Choctaw Gov. Basil Leflore." My grandmother, Winnie Gooding, and my grandfather, Joel S. Spring, were married in the house in 1883. Basil Leflore, my great-great grandfather was born at Leflore's Bluff, Choctaw Nation, Mississippi Territory, educated at the mission school at French Camp and the Choctaw Academy in Kentucky, and laid to rest at the Goodland Mission, Choctaw Nation, Indian Territory; his life spanned the years of the major cultural transformation of the tribe. Presbyterian missionaries played an important role in this transformation.

THE MISSIONARIES AND SOCIAL CLASS

Although the Presbyterians were not the only missionaries to work among Choctaws and Cherokees, they had an important impact on the planter and trader class. Presbyterians believed that conversion of the tribal leadership would result in Christianity and civilization trickling down to other tribal members. In contrast, Baptists and Methodists believed that their work should begin with conversion of the common full-blood Indians. As a reflection of the strategy of these three missionary groups, the Presbyterians established schools to serve the planter and trader class, whereas the Baptist and Methodist focused on the schooling of the full-blood Indian.[6] For instance, in the Choctaw Nation, Indian Territory, the Presbyterians operated the academies serving primarily mixed-blood families, while the Methodist operated manual training schools serving primarily full-bloods.

As I discuss in chapter 3, the Moravians were allowed to enter the Cherokee Nation in 1800 because they promised to teach reading and writing. Initially, the Moravians struggled to raise enough money to establish a school that could provide room and board for students. They were interested in making their community self-supporting by organizing a Christian village and farm. They did not ask for a federal subsidy until 1809. They were offered land by leading White Cherokees John McDonald and James Vann. Putting slips of paper marked with these two names into a box, they chose the Vann site after holding a "spiritual lottery" to seek the advice of the Lord. On the Vann site they built a farm and christened it Springplace. It was to this site in the early 19th century that many of the leading mixed-blood families sent their children, including John Ridge and Elias Boudinot. One of the primary concerns of the Moravians was instilling a work ethic into what they considered to be a lazy culture.[7]

Presbyterians were also concerned with instilling a work ethic, but, in contrast to the Moravians, they put more emphasis on classroom instruction. Funded by the Presbyterian General Assembly and given supplies by Jefferson, Gideon Blackburn opened his first school among the Cherokees in 1804 with the help of Presbyterian layperson Jonathan Blacke, and in 1806, he started a second school with the help of schoolmaster Robert Denham.[8] Although he received funds from the Presbyterian General Assembly, Blackburn's achievements were mainly the result of his own missionary vision rather than of an organized plan of the Presbyterian church. A more organized effort by the Presbyterians began in 1810 with the founding of the American Board of Commissioners for Foreign Missions (ABCFM), which was an interdenominational and national organization of Presbyterians and Congregationalists with a global mission. In 1812, the ABCFM began to send missionaries abroad.

In 1817, in response to the successful conversion and "civilization" of Polynesian Henry Obookiah, the ABCFM opened the Foreign Mission School at Cornwall, Connecticut. Obookiah, who was born in the Hawaiian Islands, was one of many Polynesians who ended up in New England after joining the crews of sailing ships that toured the South Pacific. New Englanders hoped to save other heathen Polynesians similar to Obookiah and Native Americans through education and conversion at the Foreign Mission School.[9] During the period of the Foreign Mission School's existence, 10 students, including John Ridge, attended from the Kingsbury's mission at Brainerd in the Cherokee Nation. These Cherokee students mixed with other students from ABCFM missions around the world. In 1817, the ABCFM sent Reverend Kingsbury of the Presbyterian Church as a missionary to the Cherokees, where he opened a school at Brainerd, with two of his first students being John and Nancy Ridge. Within a few years of opening the Brainerd school, Kingsbury was asked by the Choctaws to open missions in their territory.[10]

Reverend Kingsbury eventually became known as the "Apostle to the Choctaws" because of his lifelong service to the Choctaws in Mississippi and in Indian Territory. In 1863, he performed the marriage of my great grandmother, Roseana Leflore, to my great grandfather, Henry Gooding, in Fort Towson, Indian Territory.

Kingsbury was born on November 22, 1786 at Alstead, New Hampshire. He graduated from Brown University in 1812. Missionary zeal gripped Brown students during his years at college, and another member of his graduating class, Adoniram Judson, became the first American missionary to India.[11]

While working as a missionary for the ABCFM, Kingsbury's goal was to transform Native Americans into idealized forms of Christians who worked hard, were pious, used their spare time to read the Bible and religious tracts, and lived in the world according to the moral principles of Christianity. "It is our intention," he wrote regarding the education of Choctaws,

> to embrace in their education, that practical industry, and that literary, moral and religious instruction, which may qualify them for useful members of society; and for the exercise of those moral principles, and that genuine piety, which for the basis of true happiness.[12]

Kingsbury's work among the Cherokees attracted the attention of the Choctaws, who sent an urgent message in 1818 to the ABCFM requesting missionary help.[13] In August 1818, with money allotted from the Civilization Fund Act, Kingsbury established a mission at Elliot in the Choctaw Nation. In August of 1819, Kingsbury met with the ruling council of the Choctaw Nation to discuss the development of schools. The council provided annuities of $3,000 a year and donated $1,800 and 80 cows to support the establishment of missionary schools. Kingsbury, aided by Choctaw leaders David Folsom and John Pitchlynn, selected a site for a mission school at Mayhew in 1820, and it opened in 1821.[14] John Pitchlynn personally gave $1,000 to the work of the school.[15]

In 1838, the General Assembly of the Presbyterian Church founded its own Board of Foreign Missions (BFM). From 1838 to 1893, the BFM sent more than 450 men and women to 19 different tribal groups, including the Choctaws in Indian Territory. In the words of historian Coleman, "These Presbyterians could accept nothing less than the total rejection of the tribal past, and the total transformation of each individual Indian, a cultural destruction and regeneration to be brought about by the Gospel of Jesus Christ."[16]

Whereas Presbyterians focused their efforts on the leadership of tribes as a strategy for civilization and conversion, Baptists directed their efforts at the full bloods. At first, Baptists were not interested in missionary work because of their belief in predestination. The doctrine of predestination led many Baptists to believe that God in His good time would save Native Americans. But, in 1814, the American Baptist Foreign Mission Society was founded for the purpose of establishing missions in other countries. In 1817, the BFMS expanded its efforts to Indian tribes and in 1819 voted to establish a school and mission among the Cherokees at Valley Towns under the direction of Humphrey Posey. In 1820, Lancasterian schoolteacher Thomas Dawson was hired.

Similar to both the Moravians and Presbyterians, the Baptists found the Cherokees more interested in learning English than in being converted. In general, they might have said, "We want our children to learn English so that the White man cannot cheat us."[17] Despite these concerns, the Baptists placed a strong emphasis on inculcating piety and moral standards. Whereas the early Baptist efforts among Indians emphasized civilization and education before conversion, this attitude changed after 1827 when the ABCFM shifted its focus to conversion.

Baptist influence among the Choctaws resulted from the work of graduates of the Choctaw Academy.[18] The Choctaw Academy deviated from the general pattern of Baptist concern with the common folk because Choctaw leaders specifically cooperated in its establishment for the purpose of educating the children of the elite members of the tribe. In Indian Territory, the Baptists would operate the Armstrong Academy serving primarily full-blood Choctaws.

Methodist circuit riders attracted traditional full-blood Cherokees and Choctaws because they were nondoctrinal and their camp meetings contained all the excitement of all night Indian religious ceremonies.[19] Rather than establishing missions and boarding students, Methodist missionaries rode circuits of 200 to 400 miles in length through the Cherokee Nation, holding camp meetings along the way. Other religious groups, particularly Presbyterians and Congregationalist, were appalled at the emotional outbursts, "jerks," and falling down of those possessed by the Spirit at the Methodist camp meetings. But Methodist efforts eventually touched the leadership of the Cherokees, when in October 1829, John Ross received the Spirit at a revival meeting. Interestingly, his conversion provided him with strong support from full-bloods in his attempt to resist removal efforts.[20]

In 1823, Presbyterian Kingsbury noted that the Methodists were having the same effect among the Choctaws as among the Cherokees. At the Mayhew mission, Kingsbury was surprised at the sudden religious interest of some of the students. It turned out that the religious interest was not the result of Kingsbury's work, but of the preaching of the Methodist circuit rider Wiley Ledbetter. Kingsbury described Ledbetter's revival at Mayhew as causing in the audience "an unusually great anxiety . . . for the salvation of their souls."[21] Of course, Kingsbury disdained the Methodist camp meetings. After their removal to Indian Territories, the Choctaws invited the Methodists to operate the New Hope and Fort Coffee Academies, which were boarding schools for teaching manual training to children from full-blood families.

Even in 1993, I could see the lasting relationship between the work of early missionaries and social classes in the tribe. It was evident in the invitation from the full-blood cemetery keeper to attend a camp meeting, and the continuing existence of the Presbyterian church attended by my mixed-blood ancestors. It is reflected in the 19th century

Spencer and Wheelock Academies where Presbyterians provided a classical curriculum for mixed-breed children while the Methodists at New Hope and Fort Coffee Academies provided a manual arts education for full-bloods.

TEACHING A WORK ETHIC AND GENDER ROLES

In the early days of missionary schools, teaching the value of work became a major source of conflict between teachers and parents. Considered lazy by missionaries, Native American children attending missionary schools experienced strict discipline, constant activity, and hard work. As I discussed in chapter 1, the difference in values attached to work was a major difference between Native American and English cultures. In addition, concepts of work were related to concepts of gender roles. In teaching the value of work, missionaries also hoped to train Indian men to be farmers, and Indian women to be housekeepers. At first, Choctaws and Cherokees objected to the value placed on work and discipline at the boarding schools. Indians were interested in sending their children to school to learn how to read and write and were often appalled at the work requirements of the missionaries. Despite the early objections of Choctaws and Cherokees, the first boarding schools placed a major emphasis on instilling Protestant notions of work through farming, discipline, and the instructional methods of the Lancasterian classroom.

In 1804, the Moravian boarding school opened with four boys boarding at their school, and three or four boys and girls boarding at James Vann's house. The primary emphasis of the school was on teaching farming and carpentry to boys and domestic arts to girls. The Moravians believed the primary problem with the Cherokees and other Native Americans was laziness, particularly among males. Consequently, the children were kept busy from sunrise to sunset to instill a work ethic. According to the Moravians' minister John Gambold, in 1809, "where the Indians are not cured from their idleness, which is admired in their nations and deeply ingrained in their nature, things must remain precarious for Christianity."[22]

In their attempt to instill a work ethic and to change gender roles to match the ideals of European Americans, the Moravians taught the girls to sew, clean, make butter and cheese, and raise vegetables and chickens. Boys learned to plow, cultivate, care for livestock, and do carpentry. This type of vocational training fit Jefferson's ideal of turning Cherokees into hard-working agrarians who sold their unused hunting lands to White settlers. For the Moravians, creating hard-working farm households was an essential step to conversion. As John Gambold wrote, "following Jesus and laziness are incompatible."[23]

Cherokee parents strongly objected to the manual work demanded of their children. They believed that the Moravians were just exploiting their children. One Cherokee family, believing that the Moravians were demanding work from their child because they were short of labor, offered a slave to the Moravians to do their child's work. Parents argued that they wanted to have their children learn to read and write, and they did not want them to spend time working.[24]

John Gambold wrote the following description of the daily routine of the school through which, he claimed, "we are seriously engaged to destroy . . . this pillow for Satan on which he lulls the people to sleep to their eternal destruction, namely, idleness." Every morning, he wrote, children were required to carry water to the house and to their dormitory and to gather vegetation to feed the pigs. The children were also required to carry water for the vegetable patch and for washing. The children shelled corn, helped with the harvest, and cut and gathered wood. Each student was assigned a plot of ground for growing vegetables. During the winter, children were assigned the task of removing seeds from cotton. Gambold argued that although they were interested in destroying a interest in hunting—"for their own good,"—they did send the boys to hunt for game. Added to these chores were school lessons, religious worship, Bible reading, and the singing of religious songs.[25]

Cherokee parents did not seem to understand that the Moravians believed that work was good for a child. In fact, instilling a work ethic, from the perspective of the Moravians' desire to achieve conversion, was more important than teaching reading and writing. From this standpoint, Moravians were primarily interested in socializing children to fit into the work patterns and gender roles of European-American farmers. Moravians believed that a Christian life for Native Americans required the abandonment of the clan structure and hunting economy.

The Presbyterians used vocational instruction to change gender roles and the economic relationships within the tribes. In addition, the Presbyterians used the Lancasterian method of instruction which, as I discussed in chapter 3, was designed to develop a work ethic. Kingsbury's first annual report in 1819 from the Elliot Mission, Choctaw Nation, Mississippi Territory describes the building of, "A school house 36 ft. x 34 hewed logs; and finished on the Lancasterian plan." In describing the activities of the new mission school, Kingsbury wrote:

In addition to the common rudiments of education, the boys are acquiring a practical knowledge of agriculture in its various branches, and the girls, while out of school, are employed under the direction of the female missionaries in different departments of domestic labor. We have also a full-blood Choctaw lad learning the blacksmith trade; and another, now in school, wishes to engage in the same employment, so soon as there is opportunity."[26]

Students at Kingsbury's school awoke at daybreak and did chores around the mission. They gathered at 7 o'clock for reading, prayers, and breakfast. Then the students attended school where they again prayed and read a chapter of the Bible. After being examined on the chapter studied the previous day, the students were instructed in reading, writing, and arithmetic. At the end of the school lessons, boys were engaged in agricultural tasks and girls learned sewing and other domestic arts.[27]

Horatio Cushman, the son of one of the Presbyterian missionaries in the Choctaw Nation, linked Christian conversion to economic change. He recorded: "After the conversion of Tun-a pin a-chuffa, a great and wonderful change for the better was soon seen. . . . The men soon began to acquire habits of industry, cultivating cotton and enlarging their corn fields."[28] In this context, teaching hard work and religious principles would, the missionaries believed, change the tribal economy to one resembling that of European Americans.

Similar to the Cherokees, the Choctaws objected to the discipline and manual training required at the missionary schools. On visiting the school at Elliot, Choctaw leader Robert Cole complained that they "made little boys work with heavy axes & when they had lame feet." Choctaws did not object to their children learning mechanical trades, but they did complain about forced labor on the farm. But, similar to the Moravians, the Presbyterians believed that hard work was essential for becoming a Christian.[29]

Of primary importance for instilling a work ethic was the Lancasterian method used in both Presbyterian and Baptist mission schools.Because of the Lancasterian system's supposed effect on the character of students, the ABCFM adopted it for its mission schools. Unlike most traditional methods of schooling among European Americans, the Lancasterian system was premised on the idea that the method of instruction was of primary importance in shaping the character of the child. In contrast, traditional approaches assumed that the primary way of shaping character was through the imparting of knowledge, such as religious maxims and Bible stories. The revolutionary approach of the Lancasterian system was the use of the structure and methods of the classroom to socialize the student to a given set of values.

The Lancasterian system was developed for charity schools, where it was assumed, just as missionaries assumed regarding Native Americans, that poverty could be overcome by instilling a work ethic. Within the framework of this argument, poverty was considered a product of laziness. Just teach people to have habits of industry, it was argued, and poverty would disappear.

Obviously, missionaries hoping to instill a work ethic were attracted to the Lancasterian system. The basic idea of the system was that the teacher would teach the best students, called monitors, who would in

turn instruct sections of large classes. One of the important requirements in educating children in these large classes was the maintenance
of orderliness and constant work. Lock step marches, humiliating punishments, rewards, and busywork were the hallmarks of the system.
Lancaster coined mottos for his system: "A place for everything and
everything in its place," and "Let every child at every moment have
something to do and a motive for doing it."[30]

Educators in England, in the United States, and in Canada hailed
the system for the habits developed in classroom work. When the Boston
School Committee investigated the New York Lancasterian schools in
1828, they declared that "its effects on the habits, character, and intelligence of youth are highly beneficial; disposing their minds to industry,
to readiness of attention, and to subordination, thereby creating in early
life a love of order, preparation for business."[31]

A combination of arduous work on the mission farm and in the mission
household and instruction in a Lancasterian classroom surrounded the
students at these early missions with a socializing environment designed to change the image of the "lazy Indian" to that of the "industrious
and hard-working Indian." However, this attempted cultural change
struck at the very heart of Cherokee and Choctaw values. Missionaries
wanted to change a system of beliefs based on sharing property, subsistence living, extended clan families, permissive childrearing, and maxi-
mizing time for ceremonies and celebrations into a belief system based
on Protestant values of hard work, accumulation of wealth, strict
childrearing methods, and nuclear families. The Protestant belief that
"Idle hands are the Devil's tools," and "A woman's place is in the kitchen"
were guiding principles of these early missionary educators.

LANGUAGE INSTRUCTION: ENGLISH OR NATIVE AMERICAN?

One thing that missionaries and students' parents agreed on was the
importance of learning English. Missionaries believed that teaching
English was necessary for the civilization of students. The planter and
trader classes of the Choctaws and Cherokees believed that learning
English was essential for economic and political reasons. Bilingualism
was important in commercial transactions and in dealing with the U.S.
government. Bilingualism provided the opportunity for Choctaw and
Cherokee leaders, such as Greenwood and Basil Leflore, John Ridge,
John Ross, and Elias Boudinot to play leading roles in the removal
debates of the 1820s and 1830s. In addition, bilingualism contributed to
the social class differences within the tribes. Given the opportunity to
act as mediators in economic and political affairs between the tribes and

the English-speaking White world, those who were bilingual could assure their own economic and political advantages.

An important part of the vision that sparked the Cherokee ghost dance was the role of Whites in teaching literacy. With the development of written Choctaw and Cherokee languages, the question occurred of whether or not Native Americans should be taught literacy in their own languages, in European languages, or in both. Literacy in tribal languages might have aided in the retention of traditional cultures because of the close relationship between language and culture. On the other hand, literacy in English appeared to enhance the power of mixed-bloods over full-bloods who spoke no English.[32]

Literacy in English as a source of political power was evident in 1817, when the Cherokee National Council passed a written law, in English, creating a National Committee to govern when the National Council was not in session. The law specified that the National Committee would have a clerk keep written records *in English*. As William McLoughlin noted, "it was assumed that most of the National Committee would be made up of those of mixed ancestry who could speak and write English."[33]

The importance given by the planter and trader class to literacy in English was recorded in the 1820s by an English traveler, Adam Hodgson, when he visited Kingsbury's school. There were 80 students in the school, with 70 of them being boarding students. Fifty of these students spoke only Choctaw when beginning their schooling. During Hodgson's visit, mixed-blood David Folsom told students to learn English and the Choctaw language so that they could function as translators of words and customs between the worlds of the Indians and European Americans. Folsom, who traveled 60 miles for the occasion, translated for the students from English to Choctaw a letter he received from some friends from the North. He then spoke to the students at great length in Choctaw.[34]

The teaching of English was a major objective of Kingsbury's mission school. He described this instruction:

> Thirty-one began the A.B.C.'s. Several of these can now read the Testament, and others in easy reading lessons. Most of them have also made considerable progress in writing.

> There have been instances of lads 14-to-16 years old, entirely ignorant of our language, who have perfectly learned the alphabet in three days, and on the fourth day could read and pronounce the abs [sic]. We have never seen the same number of children in any school, who appeared more promising. Since they commenced, their attention has been constant. No one has left the school, or manifested a wish to leave it.[35]

Ironically, one threat to the power derived by the planter and trader class from bilingualism and literacy was the creation of written Native American languages. Another interpretation of the ghost dance vision was that Whites brought knowledge of the possibility of a written language. Framed in this manner, literacy could mean the ability to read and write in Choctaw or Cherokee without knowledge of English or any other European language. Literacy in native languages would be an advantage for non-English-speaking full-bloods.

The revolutionary possibilities of a written Native American language were evident in 1821 when Sequoyah, a mixed-blood Cherokee whose English name was George Guess, returned to the Cherokee Nation from Arkansas with a Cherokee alphabet using 86 characters of his invention. Sequoyah was born in a small Cherokee village in Tennessee, served in the War of 1812, and joined a group of Cherokees in 1819 who immigrated to Arkansas. According to legend, Sequoyah worked 12 years on the development of his alphabet. An important thing to note about Sequoyah's work is that he was illiterate and he did not speak English. Consequently, his approach to developing a written language was different from that of a literate missionary using English or another European language to render the Cherokee language into a written form. Although he probably got the idea of having a written language from Europeans, Sequoyah's invention was based on his creation of characters to represent different sounds in the Cherokee language.[36]

The genius of Sequoyah's alphabet was that because each of the 86 characters matched a particular sound in the Cherokee language, it was possible for a Cherokee to quickly become literate in Cherokee. With diligence, a person speaking Cherokee could learn the alphabet in 1 day and learn to read Cherokee in 1 week. A Moravian missionary described the following changes resulting from Sequoyah's invention:

> The alphabet was soon recognized as an invaluable invention . . . in little over a year, thousands of hitherto illiterate Cherokees were able to read and write their own language, teaching each other in cabins or by the roadside. The whole nation became an academy for the study of the system. Letters were written back and forth between the Cherokees in the east and those who had emigrated to the lands in Arkansas.[37]

Elias Boudinot recognized the importance of Sequoyah's invention and decided to publish the first Native American newspaper in English and Cherokee. In requesting funds for his newspaper, Boudinot told the congregation at the First Presbyterian Church in Philadelphia in 1826 that one of the most important things to happen to the tribe was the "invention of letters." He pleaded for funds for a printing press "with the types . . . to be composed of English letters and Cherokee characters.

Those characters," he informed the congregation, "have now become extensively used in the nation; their religious songs are written in them; there is an astonishing eagerness in people of all classes and ages to acquire a knowledge of them. . . ."[38]

After his address in Philadelphia, Boudinot headed to Boston to collect the newly cast type in Sequoyah's symbols. He returned to the Cherokee Nation and on February 21, 1828, the first Native American newspaper ever to be published, the *Cherokee Phoenix,* appeared with columns written in English and Cherokee. Of primary importance for full-bloods, the newspaper published Cherokee laws in both English and Cherokee.

Despite the fact that missionaries had struggled for years to create a written Cherokee language, they were not very receptive to Sequoyah's invention. One important reason for their reluctance to embrace the new alphabet was that it required a knowledge of spoken Cherokee. None of the missionary educators had been able to learn Cherokee and, consequently, Sequoyah's symbols were of little use to them. In addition, many missionaries feared that if Cherokees learned to read and write in their own language, they would never learn English. In the minds of most missionaries, learning English was essential for the purpose of destroying traditional Cherokee culture. Moravian educator Gambold wrote, "It is indispensably necessary for their preservation that they should learn our Language and adopt our Laws and Holy Religion." With regard to Sequoyah's invention, he stated, "The study of their language would in a great measure prove but time and labor lost. . . . it seems desirable that their Language, Customs, Manner of Thinking should be forgotten."[39]

Therefore, although Sequoyah's invention proved a uniting force among full-blood Cherokees, it did not become a language of the missionary schools prior to removal. Because the missionary instructors did not speak Cherokee, the non-English-speaking students were taught by bilingual classroom monitors. In the Lancasterian system, the best students were selected as monitors and they received their education directly from the teacher. This meant that mixed-breed students, who spoke English, would receive their lessons from the English-speaking missionaries. In turn, they would teach these lessons using a combination of English and Cherokee to the other students. Consequently, one can assume that non-English-speaking students received a significantly poorer education in these missionary schools as compared to English-speaking students.

Among the Choctaws, missionaries proved more willing to tackle the language issue. The Choctaws did not have the benefit of a genius similar to Sequoyah to overcome the illiteracy of full bloods. The Choctaws depended on the leadership of missionary Cyrus Byington at the Mayhew mission in the 1820s, who, along with two other missionaries, Alfred Wright and Loring S. Williams, translated parts of the Bible and hymns into Choctaw. They were helped by Peter Pitchlynn and several members of the Folsom family.

In contrast to Sequoyah's motivation, missionaries, as I discuss in chapter 8, were primarily concerned with developing a written Choctaw language in order to destroy traditional Choctaw culture. Written materials in Choctaw were limited to Christian religious tracts, the Bible, the Choctaw Constitution, government laws, and a bilingual newspaper published in Indian Territory. Presbyterian missionaries were not interested in creating a written language as a means of preserving Choctaw culture.

English remained the preferred language of the planter and trader class. Written Choctaw and Cherokee did serve to unite the nations by making the full bloods aware of laws and other tribal affairs, but literacy in English remained the key to economic and political power. Knowledge of English served as another source of class divisions within the tribes.

THE BEGINNINGS OF AN ELITE EDUCATION

Prior to removal to Indian Territory, some members of the Choctaw and Cherokee tribes were taught at schools outside the Nations. For instance, Elias Boudinot, John Ridge, and a small number of other Cherokees and Choctaws attended the Foreign Mission School in Cornwall, Connecticut where they studied theology, Latin, Greek, and Hebrew. This curriculum was modeled on the traditional grammar school in which the study of Latin, Greek, and Hebrew served religious purposes and, it was believed, refined the moral and reasoning processes of the mind. Although these studies were not intended to be of practical value except in the study of theology, they were considered an essential part of the education of a gentlemen. During this period, the famous *Yale Report* of 1828 reiterated the basic principles of a classical education by claiming that the study of classical literature exercised the mental faculties that were essential for the proper development of good character.[40]

In this context, the education at the Foreign Mission School was a form of cultural capital that could be used to distinguish social groups. In other words, if you believed that the study of Greek, Latin, and Hebrew contributed to the education of a superior human being, then you might believe that those who studied these subjects were superior to those who did not. This was the central argument for the education of a gentleman in the 19th century and served as a form of cultural capital that distinguished social classes.

Of course, it is difficult to determine what full-blood Indians thought of this concept of cultural capital. Obviously, within the realm of traditional Native American practices, the classical curriculum of the grammar school and college was meaningless. On the other hand, those Native Americans who emulated European American culture might believe that this form of education made them superior to others. Certainly, those mixed-blood families that sent their boys to the Foreign Mission School felt they were providing them with a superior education.

Schooling that involved contact with other White students created another form of cultural capital. At the Foreign Mission School and other academies attended by Native Americans, Indians learned the manners, dress, and behavior of European Americans. Through these contacts, Choctaw and Cherokee leaders began to dress and act like European-American gentlewomen and gentlemen whereas most full bloods maintained traditional dress and manners.

As I discuss in chapter 3, Choctaw leaders supported the establishment of the Choctaw Academy "in," as Peter Pitchlynn stated, "the bosom of our white brethren," as the best means of educating children of the elite members of the tribe.[41] In turn, the founder of the Academy, Richard M. Johnson, and the superintendent, Reverend Thomas Henderson, supported mixing White and Indian youth as a means of civilizing Native Americans. In his quarterly report in 1826, Henderson praised the mixing of White and Indian youth because it caused Native Americans to emulate the learning of the Whites. He described the quality of White students and their relations with Native American students in the following words: "The youths of the neighborhood are the sons of the most respectable and wealth[y] families, of good morals, and they associate in the most friendly manner with the Indian boys."[42]

Henderson claimed that white students motivated the Indians to study. He wrote,

the sciences the white boys are studying have fired the Indian boys with an uncommon zeal to attain to similar knowledge; one class is studying surveying, and one geography, on the globes, maps. Since the white boys have commenced using the compass and plotting; and using the globes and drawing maps, some of the Indian boys will scarcely leave their studies during the hours of recess.[43]

In addition, it was believed that contact with White students aided in the teaching of English. Richard Johnson explained in a letter to the War Department written on September 27, 1825, "We shall have as many white children to be taught with them to learn them to speak the English Language as well as to learn them to read. . ."[44]

While attending the Choctaw Academy, my great-great grandfather, Basil Leflore, was instructed by the Lancasterian method in a broad range of studies. The quarterly report issued on May 1, 1829 indicated that all students were studying English grammar and geography and that 20 (of the now more than 60 students) were studying surveying, moral philosophy, and astronomy.[45] In contrast to the classical curriculum of the grammar school, this curriculum was similar to that of other academies being established around the country. Considered more practical than the traditional grammar school curriculum, the academies, in the words of Benjamin Franklin, were to teach the "Great End And Real Business of Living."[46]

To prepare Native American youth for interaction with White society, Richard Johnson instituted extracurricular programs. A Nepolian Society was organized for the teaching of manners. Reverend Thomas Henderson wrote, "The Nepolian Society is admirably calculated to benefit the Indian youths, as its principle object is to instruct the young men in all the peculiarities of etiquet [sic] observed in the polite circles of Society."[47]

In addition, Academy instructors introduced Native Americans to European-style justice through the organization of a "Lycurgus" student court consisting of a grand jury, a judge, a sheriff, two lawyers, and a clerk. The student court followed the procedures of U.S. common courts. Punishment for student misconduct was given by the court. Many of the Choctaw students who participated in the student court were later to participate in the courts established by the Choctaw Nation in Indian Territory.[48]

By introducing Indian students to European-American medicine, instructors at the Choctaw Academy tried to break tribal dependence on traditional Native American medicine. One of the major successes of the Academy, Johnson believed, was the medical education of Choctaw Adam Nail. Nail was instructed by the Academy's physician, Dr. H. T. N. Benedict. In an 1837 report, Benedict praised Nail and claimed his talents "bid fair to make him an ornament to the profession."[49] Two years later, a report from a board of inspectors indicated that "Dr. Adam Nail, who has become the resident physician lists '2 cases of Pleuracy, 1 Ague & Fever, 1 Chicken Pox, 2 Sore Throat' since his last report."[50]

As I discussed in chapter 3, Choctaw leaders accepted the educational work of the Choctaw Academy until the introduction of a manual training curriculum. In addition, tribal leadership constantly complained about the social conditions at the Academy. On the other hand, Reverend Henderson worried that the Academy was unsuccessful in civilizing many of the Indian youth. In response to Choctaw criticism of the Academy in 1839, he wrote, "We always expected that many . . . would make but little or no use of an education . . . & that others . . . would on their return home fall back into their Indian customs and habits and soon forget what they had learned." Henderson noted that critics of the Academy failed to recognize "the meritorious and the many who have done credit to the school and have been an honor to the nation and themselves." And, reflecting the real contribution the Academy made to the Choctaw Nation in Indian Territory, Henderson claimed, "this school can boast of having produced a greater numbers of the best schollars [sic], and mechanics; some of the best accountants and school teachers, as well as some of the best farmers and merchants, than any other institution of which I have any knowledge."[51] The one thing that Henderson apparently didn't understand was that Choctaw leaders wanted more from the institution than it could provide. For this reason, the Choctaws created their own national academy in Indian Territory.

CONCLUSION: CULTURAL DOMINATION AND THE DEVELOPMENT OF THE PATRILINEAL FAMILY

The process of cultural transformation I have described can be put into the following framework. I devised this framework as a general explanation of how one nation might pursue the control of the land of another nation without, at least initially, using armed force. In this framework, the government leaders of one nation decide they want, without the expense of using an armed force, to take over the lands of another nation. In other words, they want to colonize the other nation. The colonizer believes that the inhabitants of the other nation are racially and culturally inferior. The colonizer develops three strategies. The first strategy is to make the other nation dependent on the purchase of their manufactured goods. The second strategy is to change the economy of the other nation so that land is made available to the colonizer. The third strategy is to change the culture of the other nation so that it is similar to that of the colonizer. Implied in this process is that the colonized will be taught that the culture of colonizer is superior. Because the culture of the colonized can never be exactly like that of the colonizer, the colonized will always feel inferior to the colonizer. In addition, the colonizer's language becomes the language of trade.

To achieve these three objectives, the colonizer sends traders and teachers to the other nation. The role of the trader is to develop an interest in the purchase of the colonizer's manufactured goods. This begins the process of monetary exchange between the two nations, resulting in the creation of a new trader class in the colonized nation. Because teachers are to bring about the cultural transformation of the colonized, the colonizer decides that the best teachers will be their religious leaders, who can impart their moral values. The one group in the colonized nation that is particularly hospitable to these religious teachers is the new trader class that has become economically dependent on trade with the colonizer nation. And, because they have an economic interest in keeping close ties with the colonizer nation, the traders willingly support the expansion of the colonizer's schools. Through the influence of trade and schools, the culture of the colonized country becomes a blend of two cultures, with the culture of the colonizer being considered superior.

In the end, the colonizer discovers that the three strategies do not result in taking over the land of the colonized. Yes, the colonized became economically dependent on the colonizer. Yes, the culture and economy of the colonized does change. However, the new trader class is not interested in the colonizers taking over their nation. The traders want to protect their wealth by maintaining normal trading relations. The religious teachers are not interested in territorial expansion but in the conversion of souls. These three strategies having failed, the colonizer has only one option left, and that is to reconsider the use of armed force.

The original three strategies were developed at a time when the U.S. government could not afford the use of armed force against the southern Indians. However, by the 1830s, the threat and use of armed force was an economic possibility. This made it possible for the colonizer to use this option. And, to the dismay of the Choctaws and Cherokees, the U.S. government turned to the threat and use of armed force to drive the tribes off their land. This was the final solution for the territorial expansion of White settlers into southern lands.

The one point of agreement among these various forces for cultural transformation was the replacement of the matrilineal clan system with a patrilineal nuclear family based on a strong work ethic. The goal of the U.S. government's trade and civilization policies was the transformation of a hunting society organized around matrilineal clans into a farming society of patrilineal nuclear families. The planter and trader class abandoned the matrilineal clan for a patrilineal family for the protection of property. In the eyes of the missionaries, the clan system with polygamous relations was an abomination in the eyes of God. Also, missionaries believed idle hands were the devil's tools. One of the missionaries' major concerns was the introduction of Christian marriages and family relations. The result was an increased subservience of the female in Choctaw and Cherokee societies, the undermining of a clan system that assured aid and support to those in need and a work ethic that emphasized individual greed as opposed to sharing.

NOTES

[1]Sammy D. Hogue, *The Goodland Indian Orphanage: A Story of Christian Missions* (Goodland, OK: The Goodland Indian Orphanage, 1940), pp. 13–15.

[2]Quoted from the school's poster.

[3]*Reflections of Goodland Volume I* (Hugo, OK: Goodland Presbyterian Children's Home, 1992), no page numbers.

[4]The titles Principal Chief and Governor were both used to identify the highest elected office in the Choctaw Nation.

[5]Peter James Hudson, "A Story of Choctaw Chiefs," *Chronicles of Oklahoma* (June 1939), XVII, #2, p. 193.

[6]William G. McLoughlin, *Cherokees and Missionaries 1789–1839* (New Haven, CT: Yale University Press, 1984), pp. 135–151.

[7]Ibid., pp. 45–50.

[8]See chapter 3 for discussion of Gideon's school.

[9]Ralph Henry Gabriel, *Elias Boudinot: Cherokee & His America* (Norman: University of Oklahoma Press, 1941), pp. 33–43.

[10]McLoughlin, *Cherokees and Missionaries*, pp. 139–140.

[11]"Diary of Rev. Cyrus Kingsbury," *Chronicles of Oklahoma* (1925)3: 151–157.

[12]Quoted in Horatio Bardwell Cushman, *History of the Choctaw, Chickasaw, and Natchez Indians* edited by Angie Debo (New York: Russell & Russell, 1972), p. 99. Cushman's book, originally published in 1899, is an important primary source on the history and cultural traditions of the Choctaws in the 19th century. Cushman was born at the Mayhew missionary station in the Choctaw Nation, where his parents were sent in 1820 by the American Board of commissioner for Foreign Missions. Cushman's book is full of fond memories of growing up at Mayhew and participating in Choctaw life. He personally knew the Folsom, Pitchlynn, and Leflore families. See Angie Debo's foreword to the book.

[13]"Diary of Rev. Cyrus Kingsbury," pp. 151–153.

[14]Angie Debo, *The Rise and Fall of the Choctaw Republic* (Norman, OK: University of Oklahoma Press, 1961), p. 42.

[15]W. David Baird, *Peter Pitchlynn: Chief of the Choctaws* (Norman: University of Oklahoma Press, 1972), p. 17.

[16]Michael C. Coleman, *Presbyterian Attitudes Toward American Indians, 1837–1893* (Jackson: University Press of Mississippi, 1985), pp. 5–6.

[17]McLoughlin, *Cherokees and Missionaries*, p. 55.

[18]See chapter 3 for a discussion of the Choctaw Academy.

[19]When I visited my grandmother's and grandfather's graves in Hugo, Oklahoma in 1993, the full-blood Choctaw cemetery worker, who happened to be a distant relative of mine, invited me to one of these all-night camp meetings.

[20]Ibid., pp. 167–179.

[21]Clara Sue Kidwell, *Choctaws and Missionaries in Mississippi, 1818–1918* (Norman: University of Oklahoma Press, 1995), p. 75.

[22]Ibid.

[23]Ibid.

[24]Ibid.

[25]Ibid., p. 62.

[26]Kingsbury's first annual report is reprinted in Cushman, pp. 98–100.

[27]Ibid., pp. 43–44.

[28]Ibid., p. 105.

[29]Kidwell, pp. 54–55.

[30]David Salmon, *Joseph Lancaster* (London: McKay, 1904), p. 9.

[31]"Report on Monitorial Instruction to the Boston School Committee; Boston, 1828" in *Readings in public education in the United States: A collection of sources and readings to illustrate the history of educational practice and progress in the United States,* edited by Ellwood Cubberly (Cambridge, MA: Riverside Press, 1934), p. 137.

[32]In the late 20th century, there is a great deal of debate about the role of language in maintaining culture, the value of bilingual education, and the importance of maintaining traditional languages and cultures in public schools. For a discussion of this literature see Joel Spring, *The Intersection of Cultures: Multicultural Education in the United States* (New York: McGraw–Hill, 1995), pp. 117–135.

[33]William G. McLoughlin, *Cherokee Renascence in the New Republic* (Princeton: Princeton University Press, 1986), p. 225.

[34]Ibid., p. 44.

[35]As quoted in Cushman, p. 98.

[36]See Grant Foreman, *Sequoyah* (Norman: University of Oklahoma Press, 1938).

[37]Ibid., p. 11.

[38]Speech is reprinted in Gabriel, pp. 108–109.

[39]McLoughlin, *Cherokee Renascence in the New Republic*, pp. 354.

[40]See Joel Spring, *The American School 1642–1993, Third Edition* (New York: McGraw-Hill, 1994), pp. 10–'12, 51–54.

[41]Leland Winfield Meyer, *The Life and Times of Colonel Richard M. Johnson of Kentucky* (New York: Columbia University Press, 1932), p. 362.

[42]Carolyn Thomas Foreman, "The Choctaw Academy," *Chronicles of Oklahoma* (1928), p. 459.

[43]Ibid., p. 459.

[44]Ibid., p. 454.

[45]Ibid., p. 469.

[46]Spring, *The American School...*, p. 23.

[47]Carolyn Thomas Foreman, "The Choctaw Academy," *Chronicles of Oklahoma* (1931), p. 391.

[48]Ibid., p. 391.

[49]Carolyn Thomas Foreman, "The Choctaw Academy," *Chronicles of Oklahoma* (1932), p. 89.

[50]Ibid., p. 100.

[51]Ibid., pp. 101–102.

5

Removal, Betrayal, and Death

In the early 1830s, Basil and Narcissi Leflore and Samuel Spring and his future wife Elizabeth Leflore, my great-great grandparents and great grandparents respectively, traveled the Trail of Tears from Mississippi through parts of Louisiana and Arkansas to Indian Territory.[1] There is no record of their personal experiences on the Trail, but all Choctaws making the 350-mile trip faced the hardships of traveling through wilderness country, crossing swamps, cutting through dense canebrakes, and filling cramped quarters on boats navigating swollen and treacherous rivers. The U.S. government promised to provide provisions at certain locations on the Trail, but because of graft and inept officials, the provisions were either inadequate or spoiled. Dressed for summer and fall at the beginning of the trip, many Choctaws died from exposure in some of the worst blizzards in regional history. Adding to the horror of the trip were the devastating effects of a cholera epidemic. In a letter to a federal official, Peter Pitchlynn expressed the sentiments of many tribal members: "The privations of a whole nation before setting out, their turmoil and losses on the road, and settling their homes in a wild world, are all calculated to embitter the human heart."[2]

The migration to Indian Territory took a strong psychological toll on the Choctaws. Missionary William Goode wrote, "Melancholy and dejected with their compulsory removal, years elapsed without much effort for improvement."[3] He told the story of the drunken Choctaw who threw himself into the last boat leaving for Indian Territory shouting, "Farewell white man! Steal my Land!"[4] Near his home in 1832, Horatio Cushman recalled the sounds from the encampment of Choctaws waiting for removal: "...there came, borne upon the morn and evening breeze from every point of the vast encampment, faintly, yet distinctly, the plaintive sound of weeping."[5] After visiting the encampment, Cushman recorded this bleak portrait:

> The venerable old men . . . expressed the majesty of silent grief; yet there
> came now and then a sound that here and there swelled from a feeble

moan to a deep, sustained groan—rising and falling till it died away just as it began . . . while the women and children, seated upon the ground heads covered with shawls and blankets and bodies swinging forward and backward . . . sad tones of woe echoing far back from the surrounding but otherwise silent forests; while the young and middle-aged warriors, now subdued and standing around in silence profound, gazed into space . . . here and there was heard an inarticulate moan seeking expression in some snatch of song, which announced its leaving a broken heart.[6]

On September 27, 1830, Greenwood Leflore, Basil Leflore's brother, completed the negotiating of the Treaty of Dancing Rabbit Creek. The treaty resulted in the Leflore and Spring families' traveling on the Trail of Tears. This was the first treaty signed for the removal of a tribe of southern Indians to Indian Territory.[7] Failing to gain Indian lands through civilization programs and schooling, President Jackson reached the conclusion that the lands occupied by southern Indians could be opened to White settlers only by the forceful removal of the tribes to an area west of the Mississippi. After receiving the bribe for signing the treaty, Greenwood Leflore reportedly said, "Which is worse, for a great government to offer a bribe or a poor Indian to take one?"[8]

Basil made the trip over the Trail, but his brother Greenwood, after signing away Choctaw lands in Mississippi, remained in Mississippi. Before or immediately after traveling on the Trail of Tears, my great grandmother Elizabeth Leflore, a mixed-blood Choctaw and member of the extended Leflore family, married a mixed-blood Choctaw, Samuel Spring. Samuel Spring's father, Christian Spring, emigrated to the United States sometime after the defeat of the Napoleonic Army at the Battle of Waterloo in 1815 with his brother, Samuel Spring. Drifting to Mississippi, Christian married mixed-blood Susan Bohannan. While in Mississippi, he changed the spelling of his name from Sprang to Spring.[9]

THE EFFECT OF CIVILIZATION PROGRAMS ON THE REMOVAL DEBATE

The story of the negotiation of the Treaty of Dancing Rabbit Creek has been told many times. What I intend to do is analyze the Treaty and the removal from the perspective of schooling and other government civilization programs. I examine three major aspects of the removal process. First, I will analyze the actual changes in the civilization policies of the federal government that led to the decision to remove southern Indians to Indian Territory. Second, I examine the role of the educated elite among the Choctaws and Cherokees in the removal debate. And third,

I discuss the educational provisions of the Treaty of Dancing Rabbit Creek.

By the time Andrew Jackson entered the White House in March 1829, the demands for land in Mississippi had reached a fevered pitch. The succession of treaties leading to the removal of the Choctaws is representative of the advance of the cotton culture in Mississippi. In treaties signed between the Choctaws and the federal government between 1801 and 1816, the Choctaws relinquished land across the lower half of the Mississippi Territory, including the rich cotton-growing area around Natchez. After Mississippi adopted its state constitution in 1817, there was even greater pressure on the U.S. government to move Choctaws off other cotton-growing land. The Treaty of Doaks Stand in 1820, which in its 1825 revision provided money for the establishment of the Choctaw Academy, relinquished fertile land along the Mississippi from Vicksburg north to a point just east of present day Greenwood, Mississippi, named after Greenwood Leflore.

During the 1820s, with the only uncultivated cotton-growing areas left being held by the Choctaws, rumors spread across the nation of the fabulous wealth to be earned growing cotton in Mississippi. Several factors contributed to the cotton boom. One factor was the many rivers in Mississippi—including the Pearl River, on which Louis Leflore operated flatboats—that provided cheap and easy access to the ports at New Orleans and Mobile, for shipping cotton abroad. Transportation of large numbers of bales of cotton over rough dirt roads was expensive and slow. The second factor was the development of a cotton seed that resisted rot and produced a cotton plant that was easy to pick. An enslaved African could pick 200-300 pounds of cotton a day from the new breed of plants, as compared to 75 pounds a day with the previous breed. This improvement in cotton plants significantly reduced the costs of using enslaved African labor. The third factor was the continuous growth of the textile industries in the United States and Great Britain until 1839. Because of these important factors and the removal of the Choctaws, by the end of the 1830s, Mississippi eclipsed other states as the leading producer of cotton.[10]

With dollar bills floating in their heads, White Mississippians and other land speculators were pressuring President Jackson to do something about the southern Indians and in particular the Choctaws. Jackson was aware of the failure of the civilization and education projects to open Indian lands to White settlers. By the middle of the 1820s, even Commissioner of Indian Affairs McKenney, declared his civilization and schooling plans a failure because of the vices the Indians learned from Whites living on the frontier. Also, the interference of state governments with Indian tribes was, from McKenney's perspective, leading to the eventual annihilation of all southern Indians. The only hope, McKenney felt, was removing the Indians to an area—Indian

Territory—under the protection of the federal government, where Indians could be isolated from the evil effects of contact with Whites, protected from state governments, and civilized in one generation.[11]

Jackson did not share McKenney's vision of civilized Indian tribes. He wanted land cleared for White settlers. But Jackson used McKenney and the idea of civilization to gain support for his Indian removal policies. In hindsight, it is easy to understand Jackson's dilemma. In my perspective of the 20th century, the removal of tribes from their ancestral homes sounds somewhat like Hitler's Final Solution for Jews, Gypsies, and homosexuals. Even from the perspective of the 1830s, the removal proposal seemed awfully harsh, and many Whites raised their voices in protest.[12] However, by arguing that the purpose was to save and civilize the southern Indians, the removal argument gained a certain humanitarian tone. In the end, it also meant that to maintain a humanitarian facade federal officials would try to fulfill their promises to provide educational opportunities to the removed tribes.

In his First Annual Message to Congress in December 1829, Jackson devoted considerable space to outlining his arguments for Indian removal. In the message, Jackson argued that previous attempts to gain Indian land through civilization policies had failed. In addition, he argued, southern states were now encountering a conflict between the claims of tribal sovereignty and the sovereignty of state governments. And, echoing McKenney's argument for removal, Jackson declared:

> Surrounded by the Whites with their arts of civilization, which by destroying the resources of the savage doom him to weakness and decay, the fate of the Mohegan, the Narragansett, and the Delaware is fast overtaking the Choctaw, the Cherokee, and the Creek. . . . Humanity and national honor demand that every effort should be made to avert so great a calamity.[13]

One of the crucial parts of Jackson's argument was the right of White settlers to Indian lands. Previously, President Washington had argued that Indian lands should be acquired by treaties and purchases. Now, President Jackson proposed a combination of treaties and exchange of lands for land west of the Mississippi. In addition, Jackson maintained that White settlers had rights to Indian lands that were not cultivated. In other words, he only recognized as legitimate claims by Indians for land on which they had made improvements. Claims could *not* be made for land, in Jackson's words, "on which they have neither dwelt nor made improvements, merely because they have seen them from the mountain or passed them in the chase."[14]

Jackson's concept of land usage was heatedly contested in Congressional debates over the Indian Removal Act. In the Senate, Theodore Frelinghuysen of New Jersey argued:

. . . where the Indian always has been, he enjoys an absolute right still to
be, in the free exercise of his own modes of thought, government and
conduct. In the light of natural law, can a reason for a distinction exist in
the mode of enjoying that which is my own? If I use it for hunting, may
another take it because he needs it for agriculture?[15]

In proposing to set aside land west of the Mississippi for the relocation
of Indians, Jackson promised to give each tribe control over the land and
the right to establish their own form of government. The only role of the
U.S. government, Jackson argued, would be to preserve peace among
the tribes and on the frontier. In this territory, Jackson declared, the
"benevolent may endeavor to teach them the arts of civilization, and, by
promoting union and harmony among them, to raise up an interesting
commonwealth, destined to perpetuate the race and to attest the humanity and justice of this Government."[16] The key to fulfilling the
humanitarian goals of removal would be education. In its final version,
the Indian Removal Act of May 28, 1830 authorized the President to set
aside lands west of the Mississippi for the exchange of Indian lands east
of the Mississippi. In addition, the President was authorized to provide
assistance to the tribes for their removal and settlement on new lands.

Four months after the passage of the Indian Removal Act the first
treaty for removal was signed at Dancing Rabbit Creek. Under the
treaty, the final removal of the Choctaws was to be completed by the fall
of 1833. The reaction of White speculators and settlers after the Choctaw
lands were made available is expressed by Mississippi historian John
Hebron Moore:

> Stimulated by skyrocketing prices during the boom of 1833–1837, the
> immigrants swarmed into the hills of northern Mississippi, creating
> scenes similar to those of the California gold rush of 1849. With the aid of
> hordes of slaves . . . the new citizens of Mississippi placed the former
> domains of the Choctaws . . . under cultivation in less than half a decade
> . . .[17]

In the end, full-blood Choctaws were replaced in the racial hierarchy
of Mississippi by large numbers of enslaved Africans working on cotton
plantations.

SCHOOLING AND THE TREATY
OF DANCING RABBIT CREEK

There were clear divisions based on education and social class over the
issue of the signing of the Treaty of Dancing Rabbit Creek. Led by
Greenwood Leflore, those Choctaw leaders supporting the Treaty were
primarily educated, members of the trader and planter class, and
Christian. In opposition to the treaty were anti-Christian and full-blood

Choctaws. It is important to note that adoption of an anti-Christian position was tantamount to rejecting the whole civilization program of the federal government. The reasons for the introduction of Christianity were, among other things, to teach Indians the value of hard work, accumulating property, cultivating the land, and living within a patrilineal nuclear family. In the context of civilization programs, the anti-Christian position meant a rejection of Jefferson's ideal of turning Indians into noble yeomen and domesticated women.

There was also an important economic basis for the struggle over the treaty. First, both the Choctaws and Cherokees still practiced common ownership of land. In other words, the tribe officially owned all tribal lands. Private use of tribal lands was based on occupancy. If a Choctaw cleared a piece of tribal land, that was not being used by another Choctaw for cultivation or building a house, then that land was hers or his to use until she or he stopped using the land. Once usage of the land stopped, another tribal member could take it over; the user of the land never actually owned the land. This practice was carried over to the Choctaw Nation, Indian Territory. Historian Debo described the system in the following words:

> The entire structure of the Choctaws' economic life was based upon the ancient tribal system of common ownership of land. Any citizen was entitled "to open up a farm" in any portion of the public domain, provided he did not encroach upon the property of another citizen. He might construct improvements, and hold the land as long as he cared to use it for agricultural purposes; if he should abandon it the title would revert to the Nation.[18]

The common ownership of land meant that if the state of Mississippi took over Choctaw lands, then Choctaw planters would lose most of their wealth. The possibility of takeover by the Mississippi government was a reality, as recognized in the preamble to the Treaty of Dancing Rabbit Creek:

> Whereas the General Assembly of the State of Mississippi has extended the laws of the said State to persons and property within the chartered limits of the same, and the President of the United States has said that he cannot protect the Choctaw people from the operation of these laws.[19]

On the other hand, the Removal Treaty passed by Congress promised an exchange of lands and, most importantly, compensation for improvements on the land. This meant that the choice for Choctaw planters was losing almost all wealth by the takeover of lands by the Mississippi state government, or signing a treaty with the U.S. government that provided land and money for improvements. Although the land in Indian Territory was of poorer quality than Choctaw lands in Mississippi, and there were the hardships of removal, the planters were economically better off agreeing to the terms of the U.S. government.[20]

Consequently, when mixed-blood planters arrived in Indian Territory, they were in much better economic condition than traditional full-bloods. Members of the planter class arrived with ample supplies of money and slaves to begin a prosperous existence. Writing about his missionary experiences among the Choctaws in Indian Territory in a book published in 1864, William H. Goode described the arrival of Choctaws in Indian Territory, "Some were in better circumstances, especially mixed bloods, owning slaves . . . some of these had good farms, with comfortable improvements, and a few were the owners of considerable cotton plantations."[21]

The political and economic divisions in the tribe corresponded to the cultural divisions. Greenwood Leflore was chief of the Northwest District and leader of the protreaty group, and Mushulatubbe and Nitakechi were chiefs of the Northeastern and Southern Districts, respectively, and leaders of the antitreaty faction. Planters and "civilized" Indians in the Northeastern and Southern Districts shifted their allegiance from their district chiefs to Greenwood Leflore. For instance, David Folsom and John Garland withdrew their support from their district chiefs and declared Greenwood Leflore chief of the whole Nation. In turn, Leflore declared himself Chief of the Choctaw Nation, but the claim did not receive the support of the full-bloods.[22]

The burning of churches and books by the antitreaty faction was a clear expression of their anti-Christian and "anticivilization" position. The antitreaty faction took seriously the warning by Pushmataha never to elect or allow to participate in the Choctaw government anyone with a drop of White blood. An observer of the time wrote, "The inherent avarice of the white blood, he [Pushmataha] said, would prompt the owner to favor sale of their lands. His warning was unheeded, and to the influence of the mixed blood Greenwood Leflore, the Choctaws ascribe the loss of their lands."[23]

Of course, the agents for the U.S. government preferred to deal with Greenwood Leflore not only because of his willingness to negotiate a treaty but also because he acted very much like a European American. Greenwood was 12 years old when my great-great-great grandfather, Louis Leflore, put him in a stage coach in 1812 to ride up the Natchez Trace to the home of Major John Donley in Nashville. Greenwood lived in Major Donley's home for 6 years. The years between 12 and 18 are a very formative part of anyone's life. During his time at Major Donley's, Greenwood was taught to dress according to the latest style of European Americans in Nashville, to use "proper" table and social manners, to be a Christian, and to speak English. In addition, he attended school. The degree of his becoming "civilized" in Major Donley's household is attested to by the Major's willingness to let him marry his daughter, Rosa Donley.[24]

When Greenwood returned to the Choctaw Nation, his dress, manners, and religion set him well apart from traditional Choctaws. In fact, what he learned while living in the Donley household combined with the inheritance from his father and the bribe from the U.S. government allowed him to fit into the society of rich planters in Mississippi after the removal the Choctaws.[25]

In the end, Mushulatubbe and Nitakechi agreed to sign the treaty with Greenwood Leflore because of the threats from the Mississippi state government and because of the shrewdness of U.S. negotiators, who also gave them bribes. The Treaty provided four sections of land (1,000 acres) in Mississippi to Greenwood Leflore, Mushulatubbe, Nitakechi and, for his support of the treaty, David Folsom. The Treaty specified that two of these sections would adjoin existing improved land. Chiefs Leflore and Nitakechi were granted annual payments of $250, and Mushulatubbe was given $150. In addition, as an added inducement to other tribal leaders to agree to the Treaty, they were granted land and annual payments of varying amounts.[26]

There was an interesting educational aspect to the bribes. Greenwood Leflore and David Folsom were each given $100 to pay for tuition for one child each to attend academies in Georgia. Folsom also received an annual $210 to send his son Allen to Miami University in Oxford, Ohio and $300 annually to send his two daughters to a school in Columbus, Mississippi.[27]

The educational bribes received by Leflore and Folsom reflected the concern of the planter and trader class with the education of the children. Consequently, one of the important articles added to the treaty would later guarantee the sending of students from the Choctaw Nation, Indian Territory to colleges outside the Nation. Choctaws in Indian Territory would refer to this process as "sending students to the states." Article XX of the Treaty specified:

> The U.S. agree and stipulate as follows, that for the benefit and advantage of the Choctaw people, and to improve their condition, there shall be educated under the direction of the President and at the expense of the U.S. *forty Choctaw youths for twenty years. This number shall be kept at school, and as they finish their education others, to supply their places shall be received for the period stated* [italics added].[28]

THOSE WHO REMAINED

To satisfy Choctaws who wanted to remain in Mississippi, and to satisfy his own desire to stay, Leflore negotiated insertion of Article XIV in the Treaty of Dancing Rabbit Creek that granted 640 acres of land to each "Choctaw head of a family being desirous to remain and become a citizen of the States . . ." In other words, a Choctaw family that remained in Mississippi lost all claims to tribal annuities and gained U.S. citizenship. Furthermore, with his own property in mind, Leflore included a statement that the land granted "shall include the present improvement of the head of the family."[29]

In reality, this article primarily provided land for literate mixed-breeds similar to Greenwood Leflore. The full-bloods that remained behind were cheated out of their grant of land and forced into a state of homeless poverty. The land rush in Mississippi from 1833 to 1837 resulted in White squatters and speculators taking over most of the Choctaw lands. Aided by corrupt Indian agents, most Choctaws that remained behind lost their lands to Whites. In the words of Ronald N. Satz, "The Choctaw who remained in Mississippi after 1833 were victims of one of the most flagrant cases of fraud, intimidation, and speculation in American history."[30]

These remaining full-blood Choctaws existed on the margins of Mississippi society until a Congressional investigation in 1917 found that they owned little and primarily lived as sharecroppers indebted to White planters. Most of the full-bloods remained illiterate in English and they were ill-fed and poorly clothed. Also, similar to African Americans in Mississippi, they were disenfranchised by the poll tax.[31]

This situation was not corrected until 1944, when the U.S. government recognized that the terms of the Treaty of Dancing Rabbit Creek had been violated by denying these Choctaws grants of land. As restitution, a reservation was established near Philadelphia, Mississippi in 1944 and a tribal government was organized in 1945 as the Mississippi Band of Choctaw. When I visited the reservation in the early 1990s, the tribe proudly operated a modern-looking school system, including an up-to-date Head Start program. Located on the reservation were several industrial plants and a shopping mall, that, ironically, provided the major source of employment for Whites in the area. The most telling sign of economic changes in the tribe was the Federal Express box located at the end of a canopy that sheltered a sidewalk running to the Office of the Chief in the Tribal Council Building. Next to the sidewalk, where the canopy could provide protection from rain for anyone stepping out of a car, was a parking space marked "Reserved for the Chief."

Accused of being a traitor and despised by many Choctaws, Greenwood Leflore remained in Mississippi to become a legendary plantation owner of the antebellum South. Other mixed-breeds also remained in Mississippi and merged into the local White community. Most of these mixed-bloods, along with Leflore, settled in the rich delta section, where they expanded their land holdings and bought more enslaved Africans.[32]

Greenwood Leflore's plantation of 15,000 acres and 400 slaves was located 14 miles from present-day Greenwood, Mississippi. A reflection on his wealth and his character, he hired architect James Harris in 1854 to build a house modeled after a chateau 10 miles from Paris where Josephine Bonaparte lived the last 16 years of her life. Greenwood Leflore was a lifelong admirer of Napoleon Bonaparte and Josephine. The house was named "Malmaison," or the "House of Sorrow," after Josephine's chateau. The two-story house had six fireplaces and chimneys, 15 rooms, eight of which were 20 x 25 feet, and the ceilings were 15 feet high. He imported all the furnishings from France with the silver and glassware for the dining room costing $150,000. The house could accommodate and entertain 200 guests at a time. When his daughter, Rebecca, married James Harris, he gave the couple a plantation and 100 enslaved Africans. He remained loyal to the U.S. government during the Civil War and, as a result, lost most of his property and cotton. He died on August 21, 1865 at Malmaison. Malmaison remained as a model of antebellum architecture until its destruction by fire on March 31, 1942.[33]

THE FRUITS OF CIVILIZATION POLICIES: THE CHEROKEES

Were civilization and education policies too effective with the Cherokees? President Jackson complained, in proposing Indian removal in his First Annual Message to Congress on December 8, 1829, that the U.S. government defeated its own goals by creating an educated group of Indians who demanded their own independent government. "A portion," he stated in reference to the Cherokees, "of the Southern tribes, having mingled much with the whites and made some progress in the arts of civilized life, have lately attempted to erect an independent government within the limits of Georgia and Alabama."[34]

The irony of the situation was not lost on Cherokee leaders. On February 8, 1829, 8 months before Jackson's address to Congress, The Ridge told a meeting at Turkey Town, Cherokee Nation, that the U.S. government had changed its argument for taking over Cherokee land. The Ridge's speech, recorded by his son John, attacked the idea of removal. "We have noticed," said The Ridge, restating one of the arguments for taking over Indian lands, "the ancient ground of complaint, founded on the ignorance of our ancestors and their fondness for the chase, and for the purpose of agriculture as having in possession too much land for their numbers. What," he asked, "is the language of objection this time?"[35]

The Ridge, the first Cherokee farmer trained under Jefferson's civilization policies, noted that now the U.S. government was complaining because the Indians had become too civilized.

The case is reversed and we are now assaulted with menaces of expulsion, because we have unexpectedly become civilized, and because we have formed and organized a constituted government. It is too much for us now to be honest, and virtuous, and industrious, because then are we capable to aspiring to the rank of Christians and Politicians, which renders our attachment to the soil more strong, and therefore more difficult to defraud us of the possession.[36]

One of the arguments made by U.S. government leaders was that the land to be given west of the Mississippi was equivalent or better than that owned by the tribes. Astutely, The Ridge observed, the land was vacant because White settlers avoided settling in the area that would be Indian Territory and later Oklahoma. "If the country," The Ridge said, "to which we are directed to go is desirable and well watered, why is it so long a wilderness and a waste, and uninhabited by respectable white people. . ."[37]

In another ironic twist in history, the civilization and education policies designed to acquire Indian lands resulted in an educated class of Indians willing to use the legal instruments of the U.S. government to protect their lands. In his First Annual Address, Jackson was concerned about Cherokee resistance to the decision by the state of Georgia to expropriate Cherokee lands and gold mines. Cherokee leaders argued that according to the U.S. Constitution and the treaty process of the federal government, the Cherokees were an independent nation and, therefore, were not subject to the laws of Georgia. Jackson lashed out at this reasoning:

The Constitution declares that "no State shall be formed or erected within the Jurisdiction of any other State" without the consent of the legislature. If the General Government is not permitted to tolerate the erection of a confederate State within the territory of one of the members of this Union against her consent, much less could it allow a foreign and independent government to establish itself there.[38]

The issue of Cherokee sovereignty and freedom from state laws was argued before the U.S. Supreme Court in 1831. Although the Court did not recognize the right of the Cherokee Nation to sue, the Court did define their legal status. In the case, the Cherokee Nation brought suit against the state of Georgia for expropriating Cherokee land. Chief Justice John Marshall, in delivering the opinion of the Court, posed the basic question involved in the case: "Is the Cherokee nation a foreign state in the sense in which the term is used in the constitution?" The answer to this question hinged on the interpretation of the eighth section of the Third Article of the Constitution, which gave Congress the power to "regulate commerce with foreign nations, and among the several states, and with the Indian tribes."[39]

Indian tribes, Marshall wrote are: "domestic dependent nations. They occupy a territory to which we assert a title independent of their will, which must take effect in point of possession when their right of possession ceases. Meanwhile they are in a state of pupilage. Their relation to the United States resembles that of a ward to his guardian."[40]

Marshall's language reflected the general attitude of the White population toward Native Americans. He identified them as being "in a state of pupilage" and as being "a ward." In the language of civilization policies, the government was the father or teacher to Native Americans. And, as Marshall commented, Indians referred to the President "as their great father." As a teacher and father, the U.S. government had a responsibility to protect its wards and treat them with kindness.

Marshall's decision defined the Constitutional relationship of Native American tribes to the U.S. government and state governments. They were "dependent nations" under the protection of the U.S. government. They were distinct political entities.The concept of "dependent nation" was expanded on by Marshall after the state of Georgia arrested three missionaries for working in the Cherokee Nation without a state of Georgia license. Leaders in Georgia did not support the work of the missionaries because they believed education made it more difficult to take the land away from the Indians. Governor Gilmer of Georgia expressed his displeasure with the ministers in the following words: "[These missionaries] have exercised extensive influence over the Indians . . . [and] under the cloak of religious ministry, teach discord to our misguided Indian people and opposition to the rulers. . . ."[41] On July 5, 1831, the Georgia guards arrested ABCFM missionary Samuel Worcester and two Methodist ministers, James Trott and Dickson McLeod. Although the charge was trespassing on Indian lands without a license, the real reason for the arrest was the fact that missionaries were opposed to removal and state officials believed they were helping tribal leaders to pursue their grievances.

On September 16, 1831, the ministers were found guilty by a Georgia court and sentenced to 4 years of hard labor. A decision on the issue was immediately sought from the Supreme Court. Here was a real test of the independence of tribes from the power of state governments. Could states require licenses for entry into tribal lands? Could states exercise authority over tribal governments? Did state governments have the power to take over Indian lands?[42]

Andrew Jackson did not like the answer to these questions given by Chief Justice Marshall in his written opinion for the Court in *Worcester v. Georgia (1832)*. In declaring Georgia's actions unconstitutional, he expanded on his earlier declaration that Native Americans were dependent nations. Marshall argued, "The Cherokee nation, then is a distinct community, occupying its own territory, with boundaries accurately described, in which the laws of Georgia can have no force. . . The whole intercourse between the United States and this nation, is, by our Constitution and laws, vested in the government of the United States."[43]

On the surface, this decision was a severe blow to efforts to convince tribes to sign removal treaties because of the possibility that state governments might take over their lands. Threat of the Mississippi government taking over Choctaw lands was one of the major reasons the full-bloods capitulated to Greenwood Leflore's arguments. With this decision, Cherokee leaders thought they could simply ignore Jackson's demand that they sign a removal treaty. After all, a treaty required agreement on both sides. This argument was supported by Marshall's statement in the *Worcester* decision: "The Constitution, by declaring treaties already made, as well as those to be made, to be the supreme law of the land . . . and consequently admits their rank among those powers who are capable of making treaties."[44]

But, in the end, The Ridge was right when he declared, "Disappointment inflicts on the mind of the avaricious white man, the mortification or delay, or the probability of the intended victim's escape from the snares laid for its destruction."[45] From his perspective, even if it was declared unconstitutional for a state to take over Indian lands without a treaty, the greed of White women and men would prevail over the Constitution.

President Jackson, who swore to uphold the U.S. Constitution when he entered office, said about the *Worcester* decision: "John Marshall has rendered his decision; now let him enforce it."[46] Despite submitting to civilization programs, creating an educated class, and receiving favorable Supreme Court rulings, it now appeared inevitable that all southern Indians would be removed to Indian Territory.

CHEROKEE REMOVAL:
THE EDUCATED CLASS DEBATE THE DECISION

In 1832, after the *Worcester* decision, The Ridge gave his considered opinion that only educated Cherokees with White people's skills should govern. Illiterate, The Ridge, who had fulfilled the Jeffersonian ideal of the yeoman farmer, now stepped aside to allow his son, John Ridge, to lead the struggle over the removal treaty.[47] By this time, The Ridge decided that the only hope for the Cherokee Nation was to follow in the footsteps of the Choctaws and remove to Indian Territory. Shortly before the signing of the removal treaty, he sadly told the negotiators, it was recorded:

> I am one of the native sons of these wild woods . . . . [but] they are strong and we are weak. We are few, they are many. . . . I know we love the graves of our fathers...We can never forget our homes. . . . I would willingly die

to preserve them, but any forcible effort to keep them will cost us our lands, our lives and the lives of our children. . . . Make a treaty of cession. Give up these lands and go over beyond the great Father of Waters.[48]

As The Ridge wanted, the major debate over the removal treaty took place between members of the educated class of Cherokees. The leader of the antitreaty faction was Principal Chief John Ross, who had received his early education from Reverend Gideon Blackburn and had attended the Kingston Academy in Tennessee. In preparation for following in the career path of his father as a trader, John Ross studied merchandising in Tennessee with his father's friend Thomas Clark. Clark had many business ties with the Cherokees. After his schooling at the Academy, Ross worked as a clerk in the Tennessee trading firm of Neilson, King, and Smith. On returning to the Cherokee Nation, Ross joined Timothy Meigs, the son of Indian Agent Return J. Meigs, in the trading enterprise of Meigs and Ross. Using his father's contacts in Washington, Meigs was able to obtain many lucrative government contracts for the firm. During the Creek War, the firm supplied Cherokee warriors with government supplies. When Timothy Meigs died in 1815, Ross invited his brother Lewis to join in a partnership, John and Lewis Ross. Later, Lewis Ross was identified as one of the three richest Cherokees to be removed to Indian Territory. The government contracts continued, and, in addition, the two brothers were able to furnish goods at lower prices than other traders. They also capitalized on the fact that they were members of the tribe and, consequently, were trusted. Ross's Landing on the south bank of the Tennessee river became a frequent stopping place for Indians, government agents, and White travelers on the Federal Road between Nashville and Augusta.[49]

As one of the wealthiest men in the Cherokee Nation, Ross became active in tribal government. In 1826, Ross acted as president of a constitutional convention created to overhaul the Cherokee government. The resulting constitution provoked the debate about the independent political status of Indian tribes that culminated in the 1832 *Worcester* decision. The first articles of the constitution declared that the tribe would consider their lands to be inviolate against any encroachment by state or federal governments. The constitution created a bicameral system composed of a National Council and National Committee, with the executive power being invested in a single individual called the Principal Chief.[50]

The Cherokee constitution reflected the changed status of women in the tribe and the acceptance of a patrilineal family and male-dominated society. Modeled, in part, after the U.S. Constitution, the Cherokee constitution disenfranchised women. In the words of Paula Gunn Allen, ". . . Elias Boudinot, The Ridge, and John Ross . . . and others, drafted a constitution that disenfranchised women and blacks. . . No longer possessing a voice in the Nation's business, women became pawns in the struggle between white and Cherokee for possession of Cherokee lands."[51]

In 1827, Principal Chief Pathkiller, a cousin of The Ridge, died, leaving the office open for John Ross. Principal Chief Ross and The Ridge, the speaker of the National Council, who were among the wealthiest traders and planters, respectively, were now the leaders of the Cherokee Nation.

From a purely economic point of view, Ross had much to lose if the Cherokees were removed to Indian Territory. His whole business was built on trading with Whites and Indians in the area, and with travelers on the National Road. Ross's Landing was strategically located for trade on the Tennessee river. Although he would later gain wealth by handling government contracts during the removal process, the perspective from the 1820s was that removal would be disastrous for his business. From a political perspective, as Principal Chief, Ross was expected to uphold the first article of the constitution, which was to protect Cherokee lands from encroachment by state and federal governments.

Therefore, both economic and political reasons propelled Ross into the leadership of the antitreaty faction. In addition, there was Ross's loyalty to Indian nations and his outrage about the injustices against Native Americans. He expressed this outrage in a speech to Seneca Indians in 1834:

> We have been made to drink of the bitter cup of humiliation; treated like dogs; our lives, our liberties, the sport of white men. . . . we [are] vagrants and strangers in our own country, and look forward to the period when our descendants will perhaps be totally extinguished by wars. . . ."[52]

In the 1830s, Ross proposed as an alternative to removal a plan that might have caused the extinction of the Cherokee Nation. He argued that the Cherokees had advanced in "civilization" to the point where they could eventually merge with White communities. He suggested that they be treated similarly to European immigrants and eventually be given U.S. citizenship. He proposed that the Cherokee Nation sell large tracts of land in Georgia, Alabama, Tennessee, and North Carolina to the U.S. government. In return, the United States would guarantee protection for the remaining lands and provide the opportunity for U.S. citizenship. From an economic perspective, this proposal would protect Ross's Landing and Ross's trading interests.[53]

The leaders of the protreaty faction, Elias Boudinot and John Ridge, who experienced education and racism together in Cornwall, directly attacked Ross's focus on "dollars and cents" and claims that the Cherokees could easily merge into the White community. As the most important leader of the protreaty faction, Boudinot represented a new type of educated Indian who was neither a trader or a planter. It would seem appropriate, given Boudinot's interests, to classify him, along with Sequoyah, as representing an intellectual class of Indians, which could be placed in the tradition of the tribal wise person or medicine person. Of course, the important distinction between Boudinot and the traditional wise person is that Boudinot could quickly spread his ideas throughout the nation with the aid of his bilingual newspaper.

Boudinot used the pages of the *Cherokee Phoenix* to argue for removal until 1832, when John Ross, using the power of his position of Principal Chief, forced him to resign. Boudinot continued campaigning for removal and consolidated his arguments in 1837 in a pamphlet addressed to Ross and distributed to the American public. Reflecting the influence of his religious education, Boudinot castigated Ross for focusing on money and the value of gold mines and land in the Cherokee Nation. "Can it be possible," Boudinot said, addressing Ross, "that you consider the mere pains and privations of the body, and the loss of a paltry sum of money, of a paramount importance to the depression of the mind, and degradation and pollution of the soul?"[54]

In countering John Ross's argument that Cherokees were civilized enough to resist the vices of Whites and could easily merge in White society, Boudinot pointed out the class distinctions in the tribes. The description of Cherokees as civilized, Boudinot argued, could only be applied to "a portion of our people, confined mostly to whites intermarried among us, and the descendants of whites." On the other hand, Boudinot said: "But look at the mass—look at the entire population as it now is. . . can you see any indication of a progressing improvement?"[55]

Although this small group of mixed-bloods, Boudinot argued, might be able to melt into White society, the vast majority of Cherokees still lived according to traditional practices and, therefore, were susceptible to corruption from Whites. Contact with Whites would lead these full-bloods into a life of subservience, alcoholism, and prostitution. "We are making," he argued in reference to the majority of the Cherokee population, "a rapid tendency to a general immorality and debasement. What more evidence do we need, to prove this general tendency, than the slow but sure insinuation of the lower vices into our female population?"[56]

Boudinot criticized Ross for primarily thinking like a businessperson rather than someone interested in preserving the Cherokee Nation. His fight against the treaty, Boudinot argued, was concerned with how "to get more money, a full compensation for . . . gold mines . . . marble quarries . . . forests . . . watercourses. . . ." Forget about the money, Boudinot declared, and "fly for your lives. . . . I would say to my countrymen, you among the rest fly from the moral pestilence that will finally destroy our nation."[57]

On December 29, 1935, a group of 20 men gathered in the parlor of Boudinot's house at the Cherokee capital of New Echota. The men signed the Treaty of New Echota, which provided for the exchange of Cherokee lands in the East for lands in Indian Territory. According to a Cherokee law designed to protect Cherokee lands from fraudulent treaties, anyone convicted of signing a treaty without the full authorization of tribal government was to be sentenced to death. When The Ridge placed his mark on the treaty, he reportedly said, "I expect to die for it."[58]

REMOVAL AND DEATH

When John Ross heard about the treaty signing, he immediately gathered signatures on a petition protesting the treaty. The Cherokee nation was up in arms. The majority of Cherokees believed that they were literally sold down the river by the Treaty of New Echota. Reflecting the interests of the U.S. government, U.S. officials accepted the treaty as legitimate. Concluding that he could not get the treaty reversed, Ross fought for a larger compensation for Cherokee lands. But now removal was inevitable.

Similar to the Choctaws, the Cherokees faced the hardships of travel, exposure to the elements, sickness, and problems with supplies. But they experienced a worse horror in the actual physical roundup of people by the U.S. Army. Unlike the Treaty of Dancing Rabbit Creek, the Treaty of New Echota contained no provisions for Cherokees to remain in the East. By 1838, only 2,000 of the 17,000 Cherokee population had made the trip west. The remaining 15,000 did not seem to believe that they would be driven out of their country.[59]

In 1838, General Scott, with a combined military force of 7,000, was placed in charge of the removal process. Establishing his headquarters at New Echota, General Scott issued a proclamation that within a month, every Cherokee man, woman, and child should be headed west. Scott's troops moved through the countryside surrounding houses, removing the occupants, looting and burning the houses, and forcing the families into stockades. Men and women were run down in the fields and forests as the troops viciously pursued their prey. Sometimes the troops found children at play by the side of the road and simply herded them into stockades without the knowledge of their parents. Besides stealing directly from the Cherokees, the troops and White outlaws drove off cattle and other livestock. The Cherokees placed in stockades were left destitute. A volunteer from Georgia, who later served as a colonel in the Confederate Army, said, "I fought through the civil war and have seen men shot to pieces and slaughtered by thousands, but the Cherokee removal was the cruelest work I ever knew."[60]

Similar to the Choctaws, some Cherokees arrived in Indian Territory with considerable wealth but most arrived destitute. The three wealthiest to arrive in Indian Territory were The Ridge, Joe Vann, and Lewis Ross. Principal Chief John Ross and his family were forced on the Trail in 1839, resulting in his wife's death and burial in Little Rock, Arkansas. Elias Boudinot arrived in Indian Territory without any money but received support from Reverend Samuel Worcester to translate the Bible into Cherokee. John Ridge and The Ridge decided to devote themselves to agriculture.

Then, in 1839, in the Cherokee Nation, Indian Territory, a secret meeting was held by members of the antitreaty faction who voted that the signers of the Treaty of New Echota violated Cherokee law and must be executed. On June 22, 1839, executioners went to John Ridge's house, dragged him from his bed, and in front of his screaming wife and children stabbed him 26 times. Executioners stopped Elias Boudinot as he left Reverend Worcester's house, stabbed him in the back, and split his skull open with a tomahawk. Executioners hunted down The Ridge, Jefferson's noble yeoman, and shot him from his horse with five bullets.

THE TRIBES TAKE CHARGE OF THEIR OWN CULTURAL TRANSFORMATION

Removal to Indian Territory provided the opportunity for the elite members of tribes to control their own cultural transformation through the power of tribal governments and school systems. The entire removal process included what were to be known as the "Five Civilized Tribes." Besides the largest of the "civilized" tribes, the Choctaws and Cherokees, the Creeks, Chickasaws, and Seminoles experienced the terror and sadness of the Trail of Tears. These were the southern Indians that concerned President Washington when he entered the White House. The removal of the majority of these tribes provided land for White settlers in Tennessee, North Carolina, Georgia, Florida, Alabama, and Mississippi. It made possible the final expansion of the cotton culture and the use of enslaved Africans. The growth of cotton contributed to the growth of the U.S. economy during the antebellum period. Therefore, in part, the U.S. economy grew as a result of the removal of Native Americans and enslavement of Africans.

How "civilized" were the five civilized tribes when they entered Indian Territory? Using the Choctaws and Cherokees as examples, the "civilized" part of the tribes were a small, educated, and wealthy elite primarily composed of mixed-bloods. Being civilized in this context meant being Christian, literate in English, and living in a patrilineal nuclear family. Civilized also meant believing in the Protestant ethic, which valued hard work, accumulation of wealth, and the curbing of desires.

Most of the full-bloods were not "civilized" in the foregoing meaning of the term. Prior to removal, full-bloods were influenced by tribal laws passed by the mixed-bloods, ending such practices as polygamy. They were influenced through contact with White traders. But most full-bloods were illiterate, did not speak English, and did not live according to the values of the Protestant ethic.

Indian Territory, as Andrew Jackson promised in his First Annual Address to Congress, provided the opportunity for tribes to create their own unique governments. Reacting to this opportunity, the elite mixed-bloods created governments that guaranteed their continued power. Through the laws of these governments and the school systems that were created, the elite mixed-bloods tried to control the cultural transformation of the tribe.

As an example of what happened when the tribes took charge of their own cultural transformation, I focus on the cultural evolution of the Choctaws in Indian Territory. The cultural changes between the time of removal and the early 20th century resulted in only partial extinction of Indian traditions. There exists a photograph taken in 1899 showing Samuel Bailey Spring, acting as clerk of the Choctaw Tribal Court, standing behind the seated figures of the judge, Reverend Solomon Hotema, and the tribal sheriff, James Usarey. This tribal court was responsible for the sentencing of three witches for execution. Choctaws believed witches inflicted illnesses on other people. According to Choctaw practice, those people sentenced to death were allowed to go free on the promise that they would return for their own execution. As the tribal court's decision indicates, Choctaw traditions were not completely eradicated after more than a century of attempts by the U.S. government and civilization policies in Indian Territory.[61]

NOTES

[1]For a discussion of the Spring family see "Joel Spring, Pioneer Hugo Citizen, Played Important Part In History," *The Hugo Daily News* Cavalcade Edition, August 28–29, 1941, pp. 1–2, and Lee William Self, "Samuel Bailey Spring," in *Reflections of Goodland* edited by David L. Dearinger (Mt. Vernon, TX: Northeast Texas Publishing Co., 1993).

[2]Quoted in Angie Debo, *The Rise and Fall of the Choctaw Republic* (Norman: University of Oklahoma Press, 1961), p. 56. For the best account of the Trail of Tears, see Grant Foreman, *Indian Removal* (Norman: University of Oklahoma Press, 1972).

[3]Cushman, p. 114.

[4]William H. Goode, *Outposts of Zipon: With Limnings of Mission Life* (Cinncinnati: Poe & Hitchcock, 1864), p. 51.

[5]Ibid.

[6]Ibid., p. 115.

[7]Foreman, pp. 19–31.

[8]R. Halliburton, Jr., "Chief Greenwood Leflore and His Malmaison Plantation," in *After Removal: The Choctaw in Mississippi*, edited by Samuel J. Wells and Roseanna Tubby (Jackson: University of Mississippi Press, 1986), p. 58.

[9]Self, "Samuel Baily Spring...," pp. 45–47, and "Joel Spring...," p. 2.

[10]John Hebron Moore, *The Emergence of the Cotton Kingdom in the Old Southwest: Mississippi, 1770–1860* (Baton Rouge: Louisiana State University Press, 1988), pp. 1–17.

[11]For a discussion of the political pressures on Andrew Jackson see Ronald Satz, *American Indian Policy in the Jacksonian Era* (Lincoln: University of Nebraska Press, 1975), pp. 1–39. See chapter 2 for a discussion of the evolution of the civilization policies.

[12]For the political debate over removal, see Satz, pp. 39–64.

[13]"President Jackson on Indian Removal December 8, 1829" in *Documents of United States Indian Policy, Second Edition,* edited by Francis Paul Prucha (Lincoln: University of Nebraska Press, 1990), pp. 47–48.

[14]Ibid., p. 48.

[15]"Senator Frelinghuysen on Indian Removal April 9, 1830," in Prucha, p. 49.

[16]Prucha, p. 48.

[17]Moore, p. 16.

[18]Debo, p. 110.

[19]Ibid.

[20]"Treaty with the Choctaw Indians, September 27, 1830" in Prucha, pp. 53–58. See Foreman for discussion of preamble, p. 28.

[21]Goode, p. 51.

[22]Foreman, pp. 22–23.

[23]Ibid., pp. 25–26.

[24]See Halliburton, Jr.; Allene De Shazo, *Greenwood Leflore & The Choctaw Indians of the Mississippi Valley* (Memphis: C.A. Davis Printing Company, Inc., 1951); and N.D. Dupree, "Greenwood Le Flore," *Publications of the Mississippi Historical Society* (Oxford, MS: The Society, 1898–1914), Vol. 7, 1907).

[25]Ibid.

[26]Prucha, pp. 53–58.

[27]Foreman, p. 28.

[28]Prucha, p. 57.

[29]Ibid., p. 55.

[30]Ronald N. Satz, "The Mississippi Choctaw: From the Removal Treaty to the Federal Agency," in Wells and Tubby (Eds.), p. 8.

[31]Ibid., pp. 22–23.

[32]Samuel J. Wells, "The Role of Mixed-Bloods in Mississippi Choctaw History," in Wells and Tubby (Eds.), pp. 42–55.

[33]See Halliburton, Jr., DeShazo, and Dupree, p. 47.

[34]Prucha, p. 47.

[35]The speech is reprinted in Thurman Wilkins, *Cherokee Tragedy: The Ridge Family and the Decimation of a People, Second Edition Revised* (Norman: University of Oklahoma, 1986), p. 207.

[36]Ibid.

[37]Ibid.

[38]Ibid., p. 59.

[39]"Cherokee Nation v. Georgia 1831," in Prucha, p. 58.

[40]Ibid., p. 59.

[41]As quoted in McLoughlin, *Cherokees and Missionaries 1789–1839* (New Haven: Yale University Press, 1984), p. 260.

[42]Ibid., p. 265.

[43]"Worcester v. Georgia 1832" in Prucha, pp. 60–63.

[44]Ibid., p. 60.

[45]Wilkins, p. 207.

[46]Foreman, p. 235.

[47]Wilkins, p. 247.

[48]Quoted in Ibid., pp. 286–287.

[49]Gary E. Moulton, *John Ross Cherokee Chief* (Athens: The University of Georgia Press, 1978), pp. 7–10.

[50]Ibid., p. 32.

[51]Paula Gunn Allen, *The Sacred Hoop: Recovering the Feminine in American Indian Traditions* (Boston: Beacon Press, 1992), p. 37.

[52]Quoted in Moulton, p. 55.

[53]See Moulton, pp. 54–71, and Wilkins, pp. 242–263.

[54]Elias Boudinot's pamphlet is reprinted in Ralph Henry Gabriel, *Elias Boudinot Cherokee & His America* (Norman: University of Oklahoma Press, 1941), p. 161.

[55]Ibid., p. 162.

[56]Ibid., p. 163.

[57]Ibid., pp. 163–164.

[58]Wilkins, p. 289.

[59]See Foreman, pp. 251–315 for an account of the removal process.

[60]Quoted in Foreman, p. 287.

[61]Frances Imon, *Smoke Signals from Indian Territory* (Wolf City, TX: Henington Publishing Company, 1976), p. 48.

FIG. 5.1. Nanih Waiya Mound in Mississippi erected over 1,000 years ago is likely the "Mother Mound" referred to in Choctaw legends. Archaeologists estimated that the site was occupied since the time of Christ. In 1828, Chief Greenwood Leflore called a national assembly at this site to make laws to "civilize" Choctaws.

FIG. 5.2. Historical mural painted on the back of the Palace Drug Store, Hugo, Oklahoma. The building depicted on the top left of the mural is the Rose Hill plantation. The head of my grandfather, Joel Samuel Spring, is at the top of the mural next to the plantation building. The face below my grandfather is that of Robert M. Jones, the wealthiest man in the Choctaw Nation and owner of the Rose Hill Plantation.The female portrait represents women teachers from the east who brought "civilization" to the Choctaw Nation.

FIG. 5.3. Detail of Palace Drug Store's mural depicting the Rose Hill Plantation and the two enslaved Africans, Uncle Wallace and Aunt Minerva. While "on loan" to the Spencer Academy, Uncle Wallace and Aunt Minerva composed "Swing Low, Sweet Chariot," "Steal Away to Jesus," and "I'm A-Rollin'." Their songs were sung by the Fisk University's Jubilee Singers to Queen Victoria of Great Britain.

FIG. 5.4. Author standing in front of Old Chief's House designed by Greenwood Leflore and built according the terms of the Treaty of Dancing Rabbit Creek. First occupied by Chief Thomas Leflore, it is the oldest house in Oklahoma still standing on its original site.

FIG. 5.5. Road sign indicating direction to Fort Towson, one of the centers of early Choctaw life in the Choctaw Nation. Note that the sign indicates that the Army was there to "protect" the Choctaws.

FIG. 5.6. My great grandfather George C. Gooding's restored "sutlers'" store at Fort Towson. My great grandfather's tombstone is located only a short walking distance from the store.

FIG. 5.7. Author holding original timber from the Goodland Presbyterian Church built in 1852 at Goodland, Choctaw Nation. This is the oldest continuously used church in Oklahoma. Many of the author's direct ancestors attended this church.

FIG. 5.8. The author sitting on the porch of a cabin constructed from timbers from his great grandfather Basil Leflore's house at Goodland, Oklahoma.

FIG. 5.9. The author's great-grandfather's tombstone at Goodland, Oklahoma. Above the inscriptions is a Masonic symbol. The inscription "In Memory of Ex. Gov. B. L. Leflore Died at Goodland, C.N. [Choctaw Nation] Oct. 15 1886 Aged 76 years."

FIG. 5.10. Recent photograph of the main building of the Wheelock Academy, which provided a college preparatory education for Choctaw women.

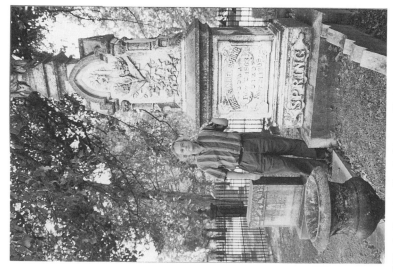

FIG. 5.11.   Author standing by his grandfather Joel Spring's tombstone in the Spring Chapel Cemetery, Hugo, Oklahoma.

FIG. 5.12.   The Hugo National Bank Building, Hugo, Oklahoma, built by my grandfather in 1905 during the boom period following the platting of townsites according to the recommendations of the Dawes Commission.

PART II

A CHOCTAW FAMILY AND ITS TRIBE AFTER REMOVAL

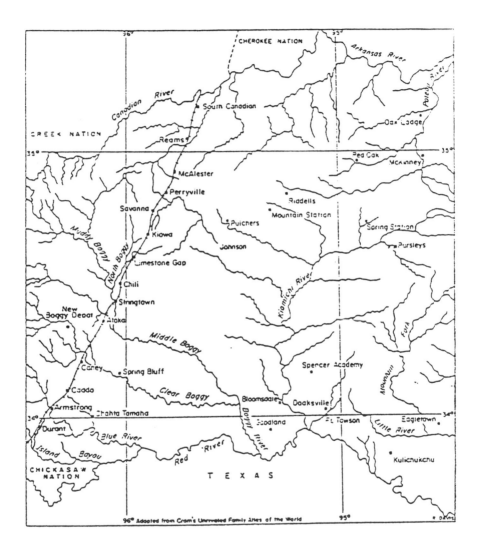

FIG. 6.1. Towns of the Choctaw Nation about 1872. Reprinted from Angie Debo, *The Rise and Fall of the Choctaw Republic* (Norman: University of Oklahoma Press, 1934), p. 119.

6

The Choctaw Republic and Its People

Approaching the Oklahoma border from Paris, Texas, travelers are often startled by the abrupt change between the dry, brush-covered plains of northern Texas and the green wall of trees that suddenly rises on the Oklahoma side of the Red River. Serving as the present boundary between Oklahoma and Texas, the Red River was the southern border of the Choctaw Nation, and it was used by Choctaw planters to ship cotton down to New Orleans. To the North, the Canadian River divided the Nation from the Cherokees, and the eastern and western borders separated the Choctaws from Arkansas and the Chickasaw District.

Although the area exchanged for Mississippi lands contained forests of hardwood trees filled with deer, wolves, bear, and other game animals, the earth was not as rich for growing cotton. Traveling through the Choctaw Nation in 1842 investigating charges of corruption against contractors who had provided inadequate and spoiled supplies on the Trail of Tears, General Ethan Allen Hitchcock recorded in his journal:

> Face of the country, wood lost in prairies, rolling, rich . . . mostly oak, post oak, red oak, Spanish oak, water oak . . . hickory, black jack in the up-country. . . . All streams big and little lined with timber . . . and the small creeks adjacent to the larger streams are all marked in the distance by timber presenting one of the most beautiful features of the country . . . and around springs are spots of wood adding to the beauty.[1]

Doaksville was the largest of the earliest towns in Indian Territory. Here the U.S. government established the first post office in the Choctaw Nation. In 1831, the town began as a camp for civilian workers rebuilding the nearby Fort Towson in anticipation of the Choctaw removal. The town was named after Josiah Doakes, who opened a small store at the camp. By 1842, the town had five stores, three of them owned by mixed-blood Choctaws and the other two by U.S. citizens licensed as traders. In the 1850s, the bilingual newspaper, the *Choctaw Intelli-*

113

gencer, was published in Doaksville. Indian Agent William Armstrong wrote in 1842:

> ....Doaksville is one of the most orderly and quiet towns that you will find in the west . . . There is a resident physician, a good tavern, blacksmith shop, wagonmaker and wheelwright. A church has been erected . . . a temperance society is organized which numbers a large portion of the most respectable Choctaws. . . .[2]

A photograph, taken sometime in the second half of the 19th century, shows a wide dirt street separating the businesses in Doaksville. The street is dusty and full of ruts. Several men dressed in cowboy hats, thigh-length coats, and vests are standing on the street and others are resting on the covered porch of a weatherbeaten frame building. Several horses attached to wooden wagons with high wheels are standing next to the building. The only words discernable on a sign on the building are, "Your money back."[3]

Once a year, Doaksville's population would be transformed into a wild scene of mixed-bloods and full-bloods gathering for their annual receipt of annuities owed by the U.S. government from the many treaties signed over the years. Reverend Goode wrote the following description of an annuity gathering in 1844:

> Some thousands of Indians are scattered over a tract of nearly if not quite a mile square around the payhouse. . . white, red, black, and mixed in every imaginable shade and proportion and dressed in every conceivable style from the tasty American fop to the wild costume of the savage; buying, selling swapping, betting, shooting, strutting . . . fiddling, eating, drinking, smoking . . . all huddled together in one promiscuous and undistinguishable mass.[4]

Near the former site of Doaksville, the Old Chief's house still stands as the oldest house in Oklahoma on its original site. It is a landmark from the early days of the Choctaw Republic. The federal government built the house according to the provisions of the Treaty of Dancing Rabbit. Why Greenwood Leflore, who had already made a decision not to travel the Trail of Tears, designed the house in 1832 is not altogether clear. But in 1837, using Greenwood Leflore's plans, a 52- by 20-foot house was built of rough-hewn logs. Modest, in comparison to Greenwood's plantation house of the 1850s, the first floor of the house has two 20-foot square rooms connected by an open passageway and an upstairs of two rooms connected by an indoor passageway over the open passageway of the first floor. Two covered porches 10-feet wide extend the length of each side of the building.[5]

The lifelong resident of the house was Greenwood's cousin, Chief Thomas Leflore. Even when his term expired as chief, Thomas remained in the house and, using enslaved Africans, cleared 1,000 acres of surrounding land for a plantation. Today, a display case at one end of the building contains articles found in Thomas' trunk. Looking down on the display case is a painting of Greenwood Leflore, with a note reminding the visitor of the removal treaty and Greenwood's design of the house.

What are the tokens from Thomas' life? There are two copies, one in English and one in Choctaw, of the Choctaw constitution first written in 1832 and revised in 1838, 1843, and 1860. There is a *Scripture Question Book* with a hand-scribbled sign, "Elementary." There is also a *Choctaw Alphabet Book* and *Choctaw Scriptures*. Placed around the display case are various denominations of Confederate currency.

Did Thomas Leflore read Choctaw? The display indicates that he might have been literate in Choctaw. I do know that he was illiterate in English in the 1840s, when he put his mark to a letter written for him by his clerk and cousin, my great-great grandfather, Basil Leflore. As Chief, he was active in the government. Could he read the Choctaw version of the constitution? The Confederate money indicates his allegiance and that of the tribe to the Confederate cause during the Civil War.

The exact date that Basil Leflore began working with Thomas is not known. After his education at the Presbyterian missionary school at French Camp and the Choctaw Academy in Kentucky, his father sent him to Tennessee to study law. He and his brother Forbis were the only children of Louis Leflore to travel the Trail of Tears. The other nine siblings remained in Mississippi as Basil made the trip with my great-great grandmother, Narcissi Fischer. Being literate and having studied law, he was fully prepared to participate in the new Choctaw Republic.[6]

I could find several personal descriptions of Basil, but none of Narcissi. Apparently, he and I have similar blue eyes. After his death, his niece wrote, "Basil Leflore was built like an Englishman with ruddy skin, blue eyes and fair hair, showing his English great grandfather, Major Cravat."[7] Horatio Cushman, whose father was a missionary to the Choctaws and who grew up near the Leflores in Mississippi, described Basil in glowing terms, which, from my point of view, indicate a prudish character. "Basil Leflore," Cushman wrote after Basil's death, "was a man than whom a purer one is seldom found in this age of the world. He filled the highest public offices of his Nation. . . . Kind words and pleasant smiles spread sunshine throughout his whole actions; his home was a model home, where all the virtues known to man seem to congregate and delight to dwell."[8]

Narcissi and Basil selected a farm near Chief Thomas Leflore's home and Doaksville. Narcissi died in March, 1852 as a result of complications from giving birth to her son, Moore. The friendship of the Leflores with

missionary educator Kingsbury continued in Indian Territory as indicated by an entry in Kingsbury's diary, dated Wednesday, March 16,
1852: "Mr. Basil Leflore's son More [sic] is very sick, we fear he will not
live."[9] Moore died the same month as his mother. Basil Leflore would
find his next wife down the road at Fort Towson.

In the early days in Indian Territory, Fort Towson became a center of
social life. The Fort is located about mile from the original site of
Doaksville, and about the same distance from the site of Basil Leflore's
farm and the Old Chief's house. The army troops posted at the fort were
to fulfill Andrew Jackson's promise in his First Annual Address to
Congress to provide protection against Whites and bandits. Today, on
the main road, a sign with an arrow indicating the location of Fort
Towson inaccurately states, "Built in 1824 To Protect the Choctaw
Indians." Fort Towson was originally built in 1824 by General Scott, the
same general who brutally rounded up the Cherokees, to regulate trade
between frontier settlers and Indians. Rebuilt in 1831, Fort Towson
probably existed to assure the containment of the Choctaws, as well as
to protect them. It was expanded in the 1840s in preparation for the
Mexican-American War and the protection of the Republic of Texas.
Basil Leflore would eventually buy the remains of Fort Towson after it
was abandoned following the Civil War.[10]

Basil Leflore must have frequently visited the Sutlers' store at Fort
Towson, because he eventually took the Sutler's daughter, Carrie Gooding, as his second wife. In the 19th century, a Sutler was the person who
operated the trading post at military forts. Today, the only building
restored at Fort Towson is the sutler's store with baskets, brooms, and
farm supplies on display. Against one wall are supply boxes stamped
"CN [Choctaw Nation]" and with Carrie's father's name, George C.
Gooding. Down the hill from the sutler's store are gravestones, including
those of Carrie's parents. George Gooding never witnessed the wedding
of his daughter to Basil Leflore, as his tombstone indicates that he died
on October 8, 1851 at the age of 49. Carrie's mother, Esther Sprague
Gooding, lived to see the Choctaw Nation join the Confederacy. She died
January 22, 1863, at the age of 63.[11]

Although there did not seem to be any social repercussions from
mixed-breed Basil Leflore marrying Gooding's White daughter, there is
evidence of some ambivalence by other Whites about this type of marriage. Because Basil was described as blue-eyed and of ruddy complexion
with fair hair, and because he was relatively well educated for the
western frontier, he probably looked simiilar to and acted much the same
as other White European Americans. On the other hand, according to
the racial rules of some Whites, it was acceptable for White men to have
a relationship with mixed-blood women, but it was not acceptable for
White women to have a relationship with mixed-blood men. As he
traveled through Indian Territory, General Hitchcock jotted in his jour-

nal, "I confess I do not like to see White women marrying Indians or half-breeds, though I have not the least objection to White men marrying half-breeds."[12]

THE SOCIAL WORLD OF
THE EARLY CHOCTAW REPUBLIC

In the late 1980s, Smith Luton, the 70-year-old son of the operator of the Hugo Indian Territory Trading Post, hired a muralist to paint scenes from the early history of the area on the rear outside wall of the Palace Drug Store in Hugo, Oklahoma. About a quarter of the mural is devoted to the Rose Hill Plantation and two of its enslaved Africans picking cotton. Similar to other mixed-bloods who wanted to recreate the plantation life of Mississippi, Robert M. Jones cleared land to raise cotton and build a plantation house near the Red River and close to the military road that ran to Paris, Texas. He also owned a store in Doaksville, operated river boats, and, eventually, owned 500 slaves.[13]

Reputedly the wealthiest man in the Choctaw Nation, Jones represents one end of the social spectrum. At the other end of the social spectrum were the full-bloods living in cabins scattered through the hills of the Nation. Dressing in traditional clothing, these Choctaws gathered most of their food from hunting, fishing, and small garden plots. In 1855, another traveler to the Choctaw Nation in Indian Territory, Bishop George F. Pierce of the Episcopal Church, noted the differences in social class. Bishop Pierce wrote, reflecting both economic and cultural differences, "There was the Christian Indian dressed like the white man; there was the half-civilized, an odd combination of the apparel of the two races, and here was the genuine man of the woods, strutting in the costume of his ancestors. . ."[14]

As representative of the wealthy Christian Indian, Jones, as I discuss in chapters 7 and 8, played an active role in education and in the political life of the Republic. Completed in 1843, the Rose Hill Plantation stood on several acres of land with a large rose garden, for which it was named, and a fenced-in deer park. Similar to other two-story plantation houses of the antebellum period, the large front porch was supported by four columns, and marble steps ran from the porch to the military road. In back were separate buildings for the kitchen and slave quarters. The only element still remaining of this historic plantation is the family's Rose Hill cemetery.[15]

Exemplifying the social differences in the tribe, the "upper crust" of Choctaw society would dress in their finest clothes to gather at the Rose Hill Plantation for an occasional ball, whereas partially clothed full-bloods gathered for a traditional game of Choctaw ball. Traveling in Indian Territory in the 1830s, American artist George Catlin painted many scenes of traditional Choctaw games and dances. Choctaw ball was the most famous of the games. Players used sticks with woven leather baskets at one end and a leather ball. At each end of a playing field of 200 to 300 yards were goals. The object was for a team member to scoop up the ball in the basket and toss it against the goal. Players would leap, run, and attempt to foil their opponents. Serious injuries and death frequently resulted from these contests.

One of Catlin's paintings completed in 1834 depicts the Choctaw Ball Play Dance that traditionally occurred the night before the game. In the painting, male participants dressed in breechcloths are dancing around a goal while others beat drums. Long lines of women facing each other are shown dancing near the goal. In the same year, Catlin did a painting of "Tullock-Chisk-Ko Champion Choctaw Ball Player" who is dressed in an ornate breechcloth with a bent tail of mane sticking out from his lower back. His head is partially shaven so that his hairstyle looks similar to a Mohawk haircut of the 1990s. One painting shows an actual ballgame scene, with players wrestling on the ground and running in a frenzy with their tails of mane bouncing behind them. In Catlin's "Choctaw Eagle Dance," completed in the same year as his series of ballgame paintings, dancers in breechcloths with heavily painted faces dance with eagle feathers held in their hands and stuck in their hair.[16]

In 1842, General Hitchcock encountered a full-blood Choctaw, Colonel McKinney, who claimed that many in the Nation still followed ancient traditions. In the course of telling Hitchcock about the custom of putting dead people on scaffolds until their bones were almost clean of all flesh, McKinney revealed some of the changes that had taken place in these ancient customs. Hitchcock recorded McKinney's description: "The dead are buried, now, throughout the nation. Some few bury at their houses, under the porch. Nearly all their old dances are done with."[17]

Somewhere in between the social world of frolicking ball games and life at the Rose Hill Plantation were the stiff and prudish mixed-blood church members, who filled the meetings of the temperance groups at Doaksville and Fort Towson. Often leading these groups were the Presbyterian missionaries who traveled with the Choctaws on the Trail of Tears. The most famous was Kingsbury, the first missionary sponsored under the Civilization Fund Act to the Choctaw Nation. He crossed on the Trail in 1836 and built a home and mission near Fort Towson and Doaksville. In the 1840s, he led church services at Doakesville and Fort Towson. Apparently a frequent attender of church services, General Hitchcock noted in his journal: "Attended the preaching of the Rev. Kingsbury, morning in Doaksville and afternoon in the Garrison of Fort Towson."[18]

In conversation with General Hitchcock, Kingsbury restated his complaint that the major problem with Indians was their laziness. This laziness, Kingsbury told Hitchcock, was originally caused by living in a land of plenty, and now it was reinforced by government annuities. Hitchcock transcribed the following expression of these sentiments by Kingsbury:

> Where the bounties of nature have relieved a population from the necessity of labor have they not lived for ages in sloth, with all its evils, and is not the reliance upon annuities calculated to produce the same effect? Is not weal a dangerous inheritance among ourselves and infinitely less valuable than habits of industry?[19]

So even in Indian Territory, after the Choctaws were forced to give up their lands, Kingsbury continued to rail against their laziness and lack of a work ethic. By the 1840s, Kingsbury was in his middle 50s. Methodist minister Goode provided the following description of Kingsbury after he met him at Doaksville and Fort Towson: "This veteran missionary was of small stature, unimposing in outward appearance, and with a deformed foot, which caused quite a halt in his gait." Kingsbury's character was captured by Goode in an incident at Fort Towson. Goode recorded that a visiting church leader was engaged in "a social game . . ." with an army officer when Kingsbury was spotted limping toward the door of the building. "Have these away," the officer hastily said, "Parson Kingsbury is coming." The two hurriedly hid the game. "So it was," Goode commented, "this 'Right Reverend' dignitary of 'the Church' was compelled to cower before the simple, unaffected piety of a little, old, club-footed, Presbyterian missionary. Such is true, consistent piety; such is Christian, ministerial dignity everywhere; and the effects will follow."[20]

Within this small social world of Doaksville and Fort Towson, the Spring, Leflore, and Gooding families began to mingle. The historical trail of their relationships runs through services and social events at Kingsbury's church, to merchant establishments in Doaksville, to temperance society meetings, and through the social gatherings at Fort Towson and in family homes. Kingsbury probably officiated at Basil Leflore's marriage to Caroline Gooding in the 1850s. Certainly, most members of all three families were gathered at Fort Towson on June 3, 1863, when Reverend Kingsbury married Basil's daughter from his first marriage, Roseanne Leflore, to Basil's second wife's brother, Henry Gooding. One of the Spring clan who probably missed the ceremony was my great grandfather, Samuel Spring, who died that year while serving in the Choctaw regiment of the Confederate Army. But his wife, the former Elizabeth Leflore, was probably there, holding my grandfather who was 4 months old at the time of the wedding.[21]

AFRICANS AND CHOCTAWS

Enslaved Africans in the Choctaw Nation filled a variety of roles, from simply working independently for full-blood Choctaws, to working in field gangs, planting and harvesting cotton for mixed-blood plantation owners such as Thomas Leflore and Robert M. Jones. It was customary for enslaved Africans owned by full-bloods to live and work on their own small farms and pay a tithe once or twice a year to their owner. One thing that made this arrangement possible was the common ownership of land in the Choctaw Nation. A slave could simply find an unused plot of land, clear it, and start farming. General Hitchcock captured in his journal the differences in treatment of enslaved Africans: "The full-blood Indian rarely . . . make[s] their slaves work. A slave among wild Indians is almost as free as his owner, who scarcely exercises the authority of a master beyond requiring something like a tax paid in corn or other product of labor . . . more service is required from the slave . . . among the half-breeds and the Whites who have married natives. . . ."[22]

Enslaved Africans sometimes became regular members of full-blood families. Methodist minister Benson, who worked at the Fort Coffee Academy in the Choctaw Nation, described in his journal a full-blood family, the Joneses, who sent their son to Fort Coffee as a day student. The family consisted of a father, mother, grown-up daughter, four young children, and one slave. The slave, Hannah, claimed to be over 100 years old, because these events were recorded in the 1840s, placed her birth date in the 1740s. After being the property of several masters, she was bought by Jones before the migration to Indian Territory. As a slave, she provided little work for the Joneses, because, according to Benson, her age had rendered her as helpless "as an infant child." Benson describes the family as poor, with their means of support coming from a small farm and herd of cattle. They knew only a little English and kept track of dates by referring to the number of "sleeps."[23]

In contrast to the lifestyle of the Joneses was that of the Rings. Mr. Ring was White and his wife was Choctaw. Unlike the Joneses, the Rings had several slaves who actually worked to maintain a prosperous farm. Mrs. Ring, according to Benson, was well educated. "Having slaves to do her work," Benson recorded, "she devoted a considerable portion of her time to reading, was fond of novels, knew something of Dickens, and would, with confidence, criticize the magazine literature of the day."[24]

There was also a more ambiguous status for some slaves in Indian Territory. Benson recounts the situation of "Uncle Phil," who acted as a ferryman near the Fort Coffee Academy. Uncle Phil's master and mistress died, leaving him on their farm with their four small children. No guardian was ever assigned to the children, so Uncle Phil took over the farm and the raising of the children. Benson noted that because the Choctaw Nation had no fugitive slave law to bring him back at national expense, Uncle Phil could have appropriated all the property and absconded. Instead, he operated the farm and the ferry, and raised the family on his own. Benson wrote, "a neighbor facetiously remarked that Phil owned the farm, the ferry, and four Indian children. He was regarded by his neighbors as a man of unflinching integrity, honesty, and truthfulness."[25]

There were also freed slaves in Indian Territory, but they remained in a social status below that of the Native Americans. The superintendent of the Fort Coffee Academy, William Goode, after he was criticized for not hiring slaves because it gave the impression that he was an abolitionist, employed a freed slave and his family to cook, do the laundry, and maintain the dormitories at Fort Coffee. The freed slave purchased his freedom and was able to hire his wife and children from their master for a contracted price.[26]

Some slaves experienced a cultural transition from African to Choctaw society instead of from African to European-American society. For instance, Aunt Hetty, who worked at the New Hope Academy, lived from infancy among the Choctaws and, consequently, shared many of their cultural characteristics. The teacher at the New Hope Academy, William Graham, wrote that she was a vital part of the school because she spoke Choctaw and she was "well acquainted with their peculiarities, tricks, and turns, but she also partook of them largely herself. . . ."[27] Aunt Hetty was also bilingual, and she was a translator for the missionaries. Bilingual slaves such as Aunt Hetty could occupy important positions in an informal power structure because most missionaries did not speak Choctaw. At New Hope, Graham wrote "we had to depend on her even for interpreter, in which position she appeared to a surprisingly good advantage."[28] Students used her as a mediator with the missionaries.

One of the famous stories associated with Spencer Academy was the musical talents of two enslaved Africans, Uncle Wallace and Aunt Minerva. According to Smith Luton, these were the two slaves portrayed picking cotton at the Rose Hill Plantation on the mural at the Palace Drug Store. Robert M. Jones loaned the two enslaved Africans to the Spencer Academy. Uncle Wallace and Aunt Minerva composed songs that were written down by a missionary teacher at the school, who later taught them to the Jubilee Singers in Newark, New Jersey. The Jubilee Singers made famous the songs "Swing Low Sweet Chariot," "I'm a Rollin'," "The Angels are Comin'," and "Steal Away to Jesus."[29]

Although enslaved Africans worked under varying conditions, there did develop an extreme racism among Choctaws toward Africans. This racism lasted well into the 20th century. In the racial hierarchy of the Choctaw Nation, Whites and mixed-breeds were at the top, followed by full-bloods, with African Americans at the bottom.

An example of the extreme racism developing in the Choctaw Nation prior to the Civil War is a story titled "A Suicide" recorded by Henry

Benson. The story is about a 14-year-old day student at the Fort Coffee Academy named Issac M'Kee. The students at the Academy taunted Issac by calling him "nigger." While angry, Benson wrote, "when he had time to reflect coolly upon the subject, he was forced to admit that his complexion was peculiar and his hair curled. . . ." Issac went to the U.S. Interpreter William Riddle and questioned him about his ancestry. Riddle told him, "Your father lived on Red River, and was once a chief; he was an honorable man, and died when you were an infant. Your mother was a servant—a mulatto, a beautiful woman, of excellent character."[30]

Within an hour of the conversation, Riddle heard a gunshot and eventually found Issac M'Kee dead by his own hand. Certainly, this must have been one of the most extreme forms of racism, causing the boy to take his own life because of his attitude toward his racial ancestry. In Benson's words, "He had regarded a life of degradation as more intolerable than death itself; he could not endure the odium which he believed attached to the word *negro*."[31]

SCHOOLMARMS

An important addition to the social world of Indian Territory were the single female teachers sent from the east by the Board of Foreign Missions of the Presbyterian Church in the United States of America. Indeed, these teachers played an important role in the cultural transformation of the Choctaws. The Board of Foreign Missions was created in 1838 as a result of a schism in the Presbyterian Church. Wanting to exercise control over their own religious programs, one faction in the schism broke away from the interdenominational American Board of Commissioners for Foreign Missions. The newly created Board of Foreign Missions served as a major source of missionaries and teachers sent to Indian Territory.[32]

Why did young women decide to become missionary teachers? One factor was the development of common schools during the 1830s and 1840s, which resulted in women being encouraged to make a career of teaching. In fact, this was the only major career open to women during this period. Women were openly recruited into teaching because they could be paid less than men and because they were considered to be of higher moral character than men. Because women at this time could not enter the ministry, those with missionary zeal had to choose teaching to fulfill their religious goals.[33]

In her study of women teachers on the frontier, Polly Welts Kaufman found that many female teachers went west because of economic necessity. From the 1830s through most of the 19th century, there was a rush of single women into the teaching profession in New York and New

England. Consequently, job opportunities began to shrink in the northeast. Kaufman, based on her study of the teachers sent to the frontier by the Board of National Popular Education founded in 1846, concluded that two thirds of the female teachers were self-supporting by necessity. One half of the teachers mentioned that they had to become self-supporting because of the death of one or both parents. Catherine Beecher founded the National Popular Education Board for the specific purpose of sending west the surplus of single eastern women trained as teachers.[34]

Prior to the establishment of the National Popular Education Board, Emma Willard's educational network at the Troy Female Seminary in New York was busily engaged in finding teaching positions for single women in the South and the West. In the 1830s, Zilpah Grant's Female Seminary in Ipswich, Massachusetts also began to place single female teachers in jobs in the South and the West. A year before the establishment of the National Popular Education Board, the Ladies' Society for the Promotion of Education in the west began sending single women out to remote areas.[35]

Female teachers sent to Indian Territory by the Board of Foreign Missions probably went West for reasons similar to those of other single women. Although the main reason for female teachers' leaving the East was a shortage of teaching positions, there was also an evangelical impulse to save the world. Most female teachers traveling west experienced an evangelical conversion, which, according to Kaufman, allowed them to break with their families and communities and to develop an independent identity. Rather than depending on men, they now depended on God. Kaufman wrote,

> If God willed that they were to serve Him by teaching in the West, the women believed it was their duty to go. By transferring authority to God, each woman began the process of separating herself from dependence on her family to reliance upon her own conscience and her own self.[36]

The other reason for traveling West, Kaufman found, was the romantic vision of frontier life.[37] For those living in the more developed areas of the United States, the West promised an adventure in frontier living that had once been experienced by Whites in the New England Colonies. For teachers sent to Indian Territory by the Board of Foreign Missions, there was the added romance of living among Native Americans. One of these teachers, Sue McBeth, sent to teach among the Choctaws in 1860 and 1861, expressed in her journal this combination of evangelical religious zeal and romantic feelings about Native Americans:

> Standing on my rude porch, looking down into the deep forest that skirts my home, I ask myself, Is this a reality or am I dreaming . . . as when long ago I sat upon rocks . . . of the Ohio at low water . . . covered with hieroglyphics [sic] traces by Indians . . . [and] felt such sorrow for the

vanished race and thought that if God spared me to be a woman I would
go to the handful that remained and tell them of Jesus and show them the
ways to a home from which they could never be driven out.[38]

Motivated by a combination of economic necessity, religious mission,
and romantic visions of Indian life, missionary teachers to Indian
Territory faced hardships as soon as they started on the trail. In 1820,
prior to the Choctaw removal and the founding of the Board of Foreign
Missions, the American Board of Commissioners for Foreign Missions
sent a group of teachers to the Osages in what would later be Indian
Territory. "Muddy river water had to be used for drinking water," wrote
Ethel Brewer McMillan, "and mosquitoes infested the adjacent swamps,
so that a virulent form of malaria soon wrought havoc. After seventeen
days of suffering Dolly E. Hoyt's [age 23] life was over. . . . [five] days
later . . . Susan Lines died."[39]

Grant Foreman provided an even gloomier picture of the problems
facing these early teachers to Indian Territory. Foreman wrote, "Among
the Choctaw they [teachers sent by the Missionary Board] labored for a
stipend of twelve to fifteen dollars monthly. Invariably they succumbed
to the unhealthful climate in which they labored, and suffered through
long sieges of enervating illness, and often their emaciated bodies were
interred in the malarial soil of the far-off wilderness."[40]

Whereas many of these missionary teachers died shortly after arrival
or returned east to escape the hardships of frontier life, many remained
to teach for many years. Some married Choctaw citizens. For instance,
Robert M. Jones' third marriage was to a Presbyterian missionary
teacher. Across the state of Oklahoma are old graveyards filled with the
tombs of pioneer women teachers.[41]

Ethel Brewer McMillan was chairperson in the 1940s of the Committee on Pioneer Women of the Delta Kappa Gamma Society of Oklahoma,
which worked to preserve the records of pioneer women teachers in
Oklahoma. After sifting through their journals, McMillan concluded
that isolation created major psychological problems for these young
teachers. One young missionary teacher, Eliza Cleaver, "was found
wandering over the prairies with mind so disordered as to make her
return home imperative."[42]

Among the Choctaws, Sue McBeth expressed feelings of longing in
her 1860 journal, "I have been so depressed in spirit for several days, I
scarcely know why, a sence [sic] of impending danger, I scarcely know of
what kind, seems to hang over me. I could scarcely wait for my letters
(our post office was ten miles distant)."[43] In McBeth's case, the problem
was not only isolation but the real danger of an impending Civil War.
Most of the male and female missionary workers were abolitionists, and
they feared attacks from Texans who were roaming across the border
into Indian Territory to attack missionary stations.

Many of the young female teachers were recruited from New England and areas that had been for many years relatively free of natural dangers, such as those from animals and reptiles. Even McBeth, who was raised in Stuebenville, Ohio, expressed fear of the natural dangers in Oklahoma. Working at her school, she worried about the scorpions she killed in her room and the poisonous lizards that swarmed over the porch. She recorded, "I killed one the other morning as it was mounting the steps of the porch. The girls killed a ferocious looking reptile, as little distance from my door one day. They called it a 'red head scorpion', but its body looked much more like that of a lizard."[44]

The fear of isolation and natural dangers took a toll on McBeth's health. She found it difficult to sleep alone in her cabin. "All these things were new to my experience," she wrote in her journal. "I had never even lived in the country or alone before, and at first I suffered with fear. I was ashamed to acknowledge myself such a coward . . . I was very brave in the day time, but when the shadows began to creep among the thick trees around my lonely little house, I could not keep them from stealing in to my heart too." McBeth solved part of the problem by inviting students to stay overnight with her.[45]

The large number of female teachers who traveled from New England to Indian Territory had a major effect, as I discuss in chapter 7, on the cultural transformation of their students. They were the ones given the responsibility for teaching Indian students. McMillan provides an extensive list of these teachers and their contributions to mission life. In reading through the pages of this list, I found that the majority of young female teachers making the trip to Indian Territory were from Massachusetts, New Hampshire, New York, and Vermont. Most came from middle-class backgrounds, and a large number had fathers who were ministers. They brought with them a missionary zeal to turn Indians into Christians, and a sense of adventure and independence that allowed them to leave their homes. McMillan argues that the development of Indian Territory "cannot be accounted for until...we see in part the role played by its women teachers."[46]

ORGANIZING A CHOCTAW GOVERNMENT

One of the significant cultural transformations of the Choctaws was organizing a formal government with written laws, formal courts, and police. Obviously, this form of government required a degree of literacy and tended to favor educated mixed-bloods. Traditionally, crimes were punished by the clan. For instance, if a member of a clan was murdered or physically harmed by a member of another clan, then members of the aggrieved clan would kill or harm a member of the guilty clan. Because sharing rather than accumulation of wealth was a traditional practice, there had been little concern about stealing. But all this changed with the accumulation of property and with the attempts to eradicate traditional practices of polygamy and infanticide. Also, European values stressed the punishment of the criminal rather than revenge on any member of the clan or family.[47]

Shortly after removal, the Choctaw constitution of 1834 was written, which gave legislative power to a General Council with 27 elected members paid out of tribal annuities. In addition, there were three District Chiefs, two of whom had veto power over legislation. In the constitutional changes that began in 1857 and concluded in 1860, the power of the District Chiefs was replaced by the office of Principal Chief. The Principal Chief was often called Governor. For instance, Basil Leflore was elected as Governor or Principal Chief.

Under these constitutions, the Choctaws developed a code of laws that Debo referred to as "a curious mixture of English law and savage customs."[48] In Mississippi, the tribe began its transition from a system based on revenge to a system based on formal punishment with the creation of a police force called the lighthorse. The lighthorse acted as police and judge and provided whatever punishment decided on. If the lighthorse captured a criminal, they would hold an informal trial and provide summary punishment. Under the constitutions in Indian Territory, the Choctaws established a system of county, district, and national courts.

The marriage law of 1875 was important for regulating marriage between Choctaw citizens and noncitizens. A problem plaguing the Choctaw nation throughout its existence was White noncitizens' marrying Choctaw citizens as a means of gaining Choctaw citizenship. When McBeth entered the Choctaw Nation in 1860, she noted in her journal that some of the "half-breeds I had seen were as fair as Europeans." While taking supper at a home in Skullyville, Choctaw Nation, she commented on the number of half-breeds. A White mechanic replied, "If a white-man marries an Indian woman he becomes a citizen of the Nation and can have a share of land. As soon as he is able he gets a slave or two and takes in more and more land. Some of the whites and half-breeds have large plantations and are rich." After complaining about "the evil-looking white men" she saw in town, she was told, "Wicked men who have broken away from the restraints of the States, I suppose the most of them were, he said. These depraved whites are a curse to the Indians, and always have been."[49]

The marriage law of 1875 was designed to correct the problem of "depraved whites" marrying into the tribe. The law required a White man marrying into the tribe to obtain a license from a county official, and a certificate of good moral character. This certificate had to be signed by 10 "respectable Choctaw citizens" who had known the man for over 12 months. The man was then required to take the following oath:

I do solemnly swear that I will honor, defend, and submit to the constitution and laws of the Choctaw Nation, and will neither claim nor seek from the United States government or from the Judicial tribunals, thereof any protection privilege or redress incompatible with the same, as guaranteed to the Choctaw nation by the treaty stipulations entered into between them so help me God.[50]

EDUCATION AND POLITICAL POWER

In the 1930s, Peter James Hudson (1861–1938), a noted Choctaw educator and graduate of the Spencer Academy, compiled a series of sketches of the governors, or Principal Chiefs, of the Choctaw Nation. He personally knew many of these Choctaw political leaders. One of the striking features of these sketches was how many of the governors attended either the Choctaw or Spencer Academies. Although the sketches indicate that most governors were literate, there is one exception. This exception was Wilson N. Jones, who served as governor of the Choctaw Nation between 1890 and 1894. According to Hudson, "He was uneducated but was a good businessman. He got rich in spite of the fact that he could hardly write his name. He talked broken English."[51] Despite his illiteracy, Jones opened two new boarding schools while he was in office. The boys' school was called the Jones Academy and the girls' school was called the Tuskahoma Female Institute. Hudson, the author of these sketches, was superintendent of the Tuskahoma Female Institute.

The following list of educational backgrounds of Choctaw governors is based on Hudson's sketches and a list of notable Spencer Academy graduates by W. David Baird.[52] It provides an important history of the relationship between education and political power.

Governor	Education
Alfred Wade (1857)	Choctaw Academy
Basil Leflore (1859)	Choctaw Academy
George Hudson (1860)	Mayhew Missionary School, Mississippi
Sam Garland (1862)	Choctaw Academy
Peter Pitchlynn (1864)	Choctaw Academy
Allen Wright (1866)	Union College, Schenectedy, New York
William J. Bryant (1870)	Choctaw Academy
Coleman Cole (1874)	Elliot Missionary School, Mississippi
Issac Garvin (1878)	No school listed, but apparently literate

All of the Following governors were Raised in Indian Territory

Jack McCurtain (1880)	Spencer Academy

Edmond McCurtain (1884)	No school mentioned—but he was apparently literate because he served as superintendent of schools for the Nation
Thompson McKinney (1886)	Full-blood Hudson states: "I do not know where he received his education."
Ben Smallwood (1888)	Spencer Academy
Wilson N. Jones (1890)	Illiterate
Jefferson Gardner (1894)	Spencer Academy-father attended Choctaw Academy
Green McCurtain (1896)	No school listed
Gilbert Dukes (1900)	Spencer Academy

According to this list, the overwhelming majority of governors until the election of Issac Garvin in 1878 were graduates of the Choctaw Academy. They represent the early educated elite that attended the Choctaw Academy prior to, and just after, removal. Little is known about Gardner except that he was born in Mississippi and traveled the Trail of Tears. On the other hand, Jack McCurtain, elected in 1880, moved to Indian Territory at the age of 3 in 1833 and was educated at the Spencer Academy. He represents the new generation of political leaders educated in the Choctaw Nation in Indian Territory. With the exception of Wilson N. Jones, all those elected after 1879 were literate, with 50% having attended the Spencer Academy.

Therefore, more than a majority of the Principal Chiefs of the Choctaw Nation attended either the Choctaw or Spencer Academy. These two institutions served the function of establishing and maintaining a political elite in the Choctaw Republic.

EDUCATIONAL LAWS AND SCHOOL FINANCE IN THE CHOCTAW REPUBLIC

Most of the Presbyterian missionaries in Mississippi followed the tribe to Indian Territory, where they quickly built missions and schools. They were aided by the willingness of the U.S. government in 1833 to allow the tribe to spend $6,000 of their annuities on the building of 12 log-cabin schools, the purchase of schoolbooks, and the hiring of teachers. With this money, the Choctaw Nation was able to pay for the salaries and expenses of teachers sent to Indian Territory by the ABCFM (later Board of Foreign Missions). Even before the receipt of the treaty money, the small community of Eagletown built their own school and hired Eunice Clough as teacher.[53]

The teachers hired by the annuity money were called "treaty teachers" or "United States school teachers." By 1836, all 12 of the schools were completed with the use of annuity money and were staffed by a combination of Presbyterian missionaries and treaty teachers.[54]

In 1842, the Choctaw Nation passed legislation for a comprehensive school system. One of the reasons for the legislation, as I discuss in chapter 3, was the large number of complaints by mixed-bloods about the treatment of students and the introduction of a manual training program at the Choctaw Academy in Kentucky. By 1840, the tribe announced it would no longer send students to the Choctaw Academy. Peter Pitchlynn, who had been a critic of the Choctaw Academy for many years, wanted the tribe to establish a national school in Indian Territory. In addition to the issue of the Choctaw Academy, there was concern about the education of the children of the full-bloods.

Working within the National Council, Pitchlynn played a major role in the passage of the 1842 School Act, which provided for two male and four female academies. The legislation placed one male academy, Fort Coffee Academy, and one female academy, the New Hope Academy, under the management of the Methodist Missionary Society and assigned the third school, the Wheelock Academy, to the Board of Foreign Missions.[55]

The fourth school was the Spencer Academy, which was kept under tribal control. In Pitchlynn's mind, the Spencer Academy would be the national school of the Choctaws. The tribe kept the Spencer Academy under its control and created a board of trustees to administer the educational system with Pitchlynn as its president. When tribal management of Spencer proved difficult in 1845, 1 year after the actual opening of the school, management of the school was turned over the Presbyterian Board of Foreign Missions.[56]

The Spencer Academy and Wheelock Academies were preparatory schools for colleges in the "states." The Treaty of Dancing Rabbit Creek provided a 20-year annuity for the education of 40 Choctaw men. In 1842, the National Council discussed sending students away to college, but Pitchlynn argued that they should wait until students received training in tribal schools. In 1848, tribal money was used to send seven Spencer-educated boys, including Pitchlynn's son and two nephews, to Delaware College in Newark, New Jersey. Pitchlynn chose the small conservative Delaware College because he believed that Princeton, Harvard, and Yale were "Dissipated and full of wild fellows." In addition, female students from the Wheelock Academy, including Basil Leflore's future second wife, Carrie Gooding, were sent to college. The numbers going to college increased dramatically after the Civil War.[57]

Tribal accounts indicate that larger amounts of money went to support the Spencer Academy than the other academies. This inequality of school finance was linked to social class. The situation was noted at the time by the superintendent of the Fort Coffee and New Hope Academies,

William Goode. In comparing the Spencer Academy to his school, Goode wrote, "Our endowment was inferior . . . and as a result, the apparent advantages of Spencer Academy led the prominent families of the Nation, principally half-breeds, to seek admission for their students, while ours was filled up mainly with full-bloods from families of smaller influence and wealth."[58]

Neighborhood day schools were first started by missionaries and spread across the Nation. By 1860, the Choctaw government reported 500 children enrolled in neighborhood schools. Legislation bringing the neighborhood schools under government control was passed by the National Council in 1866. When the neighborhood schools opened in January 1867, they were placed under the control of superintendent Forbis LeFlore, Basil's brother. In 1869, LeFlore reported 69 schools in operation with 1,847 children. In 1876, there were 54 day schools and 1,118 students.[59]

One event that helped finance the school system and increase the wealth of the Nation was the coming of the railroad in 1872. Almost overnight, the coal reserves on Choctaw land became extremely valuable. By 1885, revenues were $54,611.52. The revenues increased to $91,794.22 in 1890 and to $181,756.47 in 1897. By 1883, the Choctaw Nation was able to appropriate $5,000 for each district neighborhood school. In addition, a day school was provided, where 10 or more students could gather. By 1887, there were 168 neighborhood schools with 3,512 students in attendance.[60]

In addition to the growth and prosperity of the school system, it became compulsory and professionalized. In 1884, the Nation passed a compulsory attendance law for all children between the ages of 7 and 18. Parents of children who did not attend school were fined 10 cents a day.[61] The School Act of 1890 created standards for certification of teachers and supported the publication of the *Choctaw School Journal*. Applicants for teaching certificates were examined in reading, writing, spelling, English grammar, geography, history, and the Constitutions of the United States and the Choctaw Nation. The 1890 School Act also refined the procedure for admission to the Spencer Academy by requiring selection by county judges on the basis of ability to learn, school attendance record, and proficiency in reading.[62]

CONCLUSION: IDEOLOGICAL MANAGEMENT IN THE CHOCTAW NATION

Unlike the attempt by the U.S. government to "civilize" the Choctaws in Mississippi, the Choctaw government in Indian Territory consciously assumed the role of ideological manager. The Christian mixed-breeds educated at the Choctaw Academy assumed leadership in the new government and were responsible for the passage of the School Law of 1842, which, as I discuss in more detail in chapter 7, created academies that paralleled social classes and religious affiliations. The Methodists, the Christian denomination most often associated with the full-bloods, were given control of the Fort Coffee and New Hope Academies for the purpose of turning full-blood boys and girls into good Christian farmers and domestic workers. The Presbyterians, who were the religious mentors of the mixed-bloods, were given control of the Spencer and Wheelock Academies to educate students for college.

The missionaries that made the trek over the Trail of Tears brought with them the desire to culturally transform Native Americans by destroying Indian traditions, instilling a Protestant work ethic, curbing desires, creating patrilineal families, and winning hearts to Christ. Joining the missionaries in this endeavor were single female teachers from the East. In part out of economic necessity, these New England schoolmarms headed West to save Indian souls. Full of romantic visions about the frontier and Native Americans, they did much of the real work of education.

The full-bloods were the primary target of cultural control by the mixed-breeds, the missionaries, and the schoolmarms. From accounts of the period, many full-bloods continued to resist the conversion to "civilization." After the Civil War, the African Choctaws would be included in these educational efforts. And, of course, influencing cultural change and adding to the cultural mix of Indian Territory were Whites in search of Choctaw citizenship, members of the U.S. Army, and cowboys who drove cattle up from Texas, and frontier drifters. All of these factors contributed to the culture of the Choctaw Nation.

NOTES

[1]*A Traveler in Indian Territory: The Journal of Ethan Allen Hitchcock, late Major-General in the United States Army*, edited and annotated by Grant Foreman (Cedar Rapids Press, IA: The Torch Press, 1930), pp. 181–182.

[2]Quoted in Frances Imon, *Smoke Signals from Indian Territory* (Wolf City, TX: Henington Publishing Company, 1976), pp. 26–27.

[3]Ibid., p. 38.

[4]William H. Goode, *Outposts of Zion, With Limnings of Mission Life* (Cincinnati: Poe & Hitchcock, 1864), p. 194.

[5]This description is based on a visit to the site and photographs taken by my wife, Naomi Silverman.

[6]H. B. Cushman, *History of the Choctaw, Chickasaw and Natchez Indians*, edited with a foreword by Angie Debo (New York: Russell and

Russell, 1972), p. 347. The book was first published in 1899 (Greenville, TX: Head Light Printing, 1899).

[7]Goode, pp. 81–82.

[8]Cushman, p. 348.

[9]Ralph Folsom McBride and Alberta Patrick McBride, *A Family Makes Its Mark: The Leflores of Mississippi* (Jacksonville, FL: The Louis LeFlore Association, 1976), p. 80.

[10]The Oklahoma Historical Society, *Fort Towson*, a pamphlet published by the Society (Oklahoma City: Oklahoma Historical Society, 1981); "Mrs. Griffith Relates Tales Told Her By Her Grandfather of Pioneer Life Here," *The Hugo Daily News*, Cavalcade Edition, Section 3, p. 4. Mrs. Harold (Spring) Griffith is my aunt.

[11]This description is based on a visit to the site and photographs taken by my wife, Naomi Silverman. Also see Imon, p. 28.

[12]Hitchcock, p. 224.

[13]Imon, pp. 32–34.

[14]As quoted from George Smith's *The Life and Times of George Foster Pierce, D.D. LL.D.* (Nashville, TN, 1888) by Carolyne Thomas Foreman in "New Hope Seminary 1844–1897," *Chronicles of Oklahoma* 22(1944): 282.

[15]Imon, pp. 32–34.

[16]Copies of these paintings can be found in Angie Debo, *The Rise and Fall of the Choctaw Republic* (Norman: University of Oklahoma Press, 1961).

[17]Hitchcock, pp. 217–218.

[18]Ibid., p. 190. See "Diary of Rev. Cyrus Kingsbury," *Chronicles of Oklahoma* (June 1925), pp. 150–157.

[19]Ibid.

[20]Goode, pp. 199–200.

[21]"Mrs. Griffith Relates Tales...," p. 4.

[22]Ibid., p. 187.

[23]Benson, pp. 95–99.

[24]Ibid., pp. 99, 135–136.

[25]Ibid., p. 136.

[26]Goode, p. 150.

[27]Quoted by Foreman, p. 274.

[28]Ibid., p. 274.

[29]Spear, p. 77.

[30]Benson, p. 217.

[31]Ibid., p. 19.

[32]Michael C. Coleman, *Presbyterian Missionary Attitudes toward American Indians, 1837–1893* (Jackson: University of Mississippi Press, 1985), pp. 9–33.

[33]See Joel Spring, *The American School 1642–1993, Third Edition* (New York: McGraw-Hill, 1994), pp. 97–127.

[34]Polly Welts Kaufman, *Women Teachers on the Frontier* (New Haven: Yale University Press, 1984), pp. 1–51.

[35]Ibid., pp. 6–8.

[36]Ibid., p. xxii.

[37]Ibid., pp. 18–19.

[38]"Notes and Documents: The Diary of Sue McBeth A Missionary to the Choctaws, 1860–1861," edited by Anna Lewis, *Chronicles of Oklahoma* (Spring 1949), p. 186.

[39]Ethel McMillan, "Women Teachers in Oklahoma, 1820–1860," *Chronicles of Oklahoma* (Spring 1949), p. 4.

[40]Grant Foreman, *The Five Civilized Tribes* (Norman: University of Oklahoma Press, 1934), p. 42.

[41]Ibid., pp. 2–32.

[42]Ibid., p. 7.

[43]Lewis, p. 193.

[44]"Diary of a Missionary to the Choctaws," edited by Anna Lewis *Chronicles of Oklahoma* (December 1939), p. 430.

[45]Ibid., p. 430.

[46]McMillan, p. 16.

[47]This section on the development of the Choctaw Republic is primarily taken from Debo's *The Rise and Fall of the Choctaw Republic*.

[48]Ibid., p. 76.

[49]Lewis, p. 188.

[50]Quoted in Debo, pp. 180–181.

[51]Peter James Hudson, "A Story of Choctaw Chiefs," *Chronicles of Oklahoma* (June, 1939), p. 206.

[52]W. David Baird, "Spencer Academy, Choctaw Nation, 1842–1900," *Chronicles of Oklahoma* (1967), pp. 42–43.

[53]Foreman, p. 36, 42.

[54]For a list of these schools see Foreman, pp. 45–46.

[55]Baird, p. 64.

[56]Ibid., pp. 65–66.

[57]Ibid., pp. 66–67. Eloise G. Spear, *Choctaw Indian Education with Special Reference to Choctaw County, Oklahoma: An Historical Approach*, Dissertation, University of Oklahoma, Norman, 1977 (Ann Arbor, MI: University Microfilms International, 1977), pp. 167–168.

[58]Goode, p. 184.

[59]Ibid., pp. 150–154.

[60]Debo, pp. 125–130; Spear, pp. 156–158.

[61]Spear, p. 157.

[62]Ibid., p. 159.

7

Academies and Anglo-Saxon Culture

"The principal lever by which the Indians are to be lifted out of the mire of folly and vice in which they are sunk," wrote T. Hartley Crawford, Commissioner of Indian Affairs, in his 1838 annual report, "is education."[1] Sharing similar beliefs, Pitchlynn, who had complained of dirty slaves at the Choctaw Academy and who believed that the model of his Christian marriage would end polygamy among the Choctaws, was primarily responsible for the enactment of the Choctaw government's School Act of 1842. For Pitchlynn and other mixed-breeds, the Fort Coffee, New Hope, Spencer, and Wheelock Academies provided the means of bringing civilization to full-bloods and of improving the cultural level of the planter and trader class. Similar to missionaries, Pitchlynn believed in the superiority of European and Christian values over traditional tribal practices. Filling the temperance meetings and religious services at Doakesville and Fort Towson, these self-righteous mixed-bloods, such as Pitchlynn and Basil and Forbis Leflore, wanted to bring about the final eradication of Indian values and traditions, and their replacement with the culture of the most pious of Protestant European Americans.

The educational policies of the U.S. government complemented the policies contained in the School Act of 1842. In 1835, President Jackson argued before Congress that Indian removal was a humanitarian act. "All preceding experiments for the improvement of the Indians have failed," he told Congress. "It seems now to be an established fact that they can not live in contact with a civilized community and prosper." Referring to the "moral duty of the Government . . . to preserve and perpetuate the scattered remnants of this race," Jackson assured Congress that, "Ample arrangements have also been made for the support of schools. . . ."[2]

The first, at least to my knowledge, affirmative action hiring procedure was made part of Jackson's civilization plan. For Jackson, affirmative action hiring would act "as a stimulus for exertion" on Native

134

Americans. The law provided that "in all cases of the appointment of interpreters or other persons employed for the benefit of the Indians a preference shall be given to persons of Indian descent. . . ."[3]

T. Hartley Crawford, appointed Commissioner of Indian Affairs in 1838 and serving in that position for 7 years, advocated a manual training program that was similar to the one used at Fort Coffee and New Hope Academies. Crawford believed that Native Americans were not advanced enough in moral and social values to benefit from a liberal education. In Crawford's words, "To teach a savage man to read, while he continues a savage in all else, is to throw seed on a rock. In this particular there has been a general error."[4]

Obviously, Crawford's view of education was in sharp contrast to the Cherokee ghost dance visions, in which learning to read was a means of protecting "savage" culture. For Crawford, literacy should be accompanied by the destruction of traditional values and their replacement with European-American values. Similar to most Whites, Crawford believed the central moral failure of Indians was the lack of a work ethic. "If you would win an Indian from the waywardness and idleness and vice of his life, you must improve his morals, as well as his mind. . . ."[5]

Commissioner Crawford championed the manual training school plan advocated by the Missionary Society of the Methodist Episcopal Church. Manual training, Crawford believed, was the key to ending the idleness of Native Americans. Once trained in farming, mechanical arts, and "how to labor profitably," he wrote, "he will fall into those habits which are in keeping with the useful application of such education as may be given him."[6] In other words, literacy needed to be controlled so that it did *not* lead to a maintenance of Native American values but rather to their erosion.

Originally, members of the Missionary Society of the Methodist Episcopal Church proposed to Commissioner Crawford the establishment of a central school to be attended by students from all Native American tribes living in the West. The Missionary Society believed separate schools for each tribe would not be as beneficial as a single school for all tribes. A single school would provide an opportunity to break down cultural barriers between tribes. The major problem with the plan, Commissioner Crawford argued, was that each individual tribe controlled its own money and the federal government could not take away that money to fund a central school. On the other hand, he felt, if such a school could be created, it would train teachers for tribal schools.[7]

MISSIONARY SOCIETY OF THE METHODIST EPISCOPAL CHURCH

Under the 1842 School Act, the Choctaws were the first tribe to adopt the Missionary Society's plan for a manual training school. With the failure to establish a central school, Methodists focused their efforts on tribal schools. Meeting in May of 1840, the Missionary Society appointed Reverend E.R. Ames to travel through the West in search of possible areas for building missions. During the summer, Ames traveled through the upper tributaries of the Mississippi in search of Native Americans who had not been touched by "civilization." He did not want to build his mission "upon another man's foundation." When reaching what he thought was a remote area, Ames was surprised to find an Indian sitting on the root of a tree and singing a Gospel song. Discouraged at his inability to find an untouched pagan Indian, Ames traveled south until he came upon the Choctaws, who provided him with the best accommodations he had encountered on the trip. Impressed by the Choctaws and the availability of money for schools, Ames approached the National Council with the Missionary Society's plan for manual training schools. He spent a great deal of time convincing the educated mixed-breeds of the value of manual training schools for full-bloods. His ideas resulted in the Missionary Society being given management of the Fort Coffee and New Hope Academies in the School Act of 1842.[8]

The leaders of the Missionary Society shared the same sentiments with Andrew Jackson that, "Heathenism and Christian civilization can never flourish on the same soil. The life of one is the death of the other." But, they believed, the death of heathenism did not necessarily mean the death of its practitioners. They could be saved by conversion to Christian civilization. After all, they reasoned, wasn't Jesus supposed to save lives? Therefore, they believed, "whatever can be done to save the Indians from their delusion and wretchedness, should be accomplished."[9]

Indeed, leaders of the Missionary Society felt that Christian Americans had a special obligation to convert Indians because, "We owe them this kind office for depriving them of their country." In other words, "civilizing" Native Americans was a form of repayment for their lands, in contrast to Jefferson's argument that "civilizing" Indians was a means of obtaining Native American land. They supported government policies for Native Americans as a magnanimous gesture of the strong to the weak. But, similar to McKenney, they felt government efforts failed because depraved Whites supplied alcohol and seduced Indian women.[10]

METHODIST MISSIONARIES: "SCARCELY EVER SHAKEN THE HAND OF A RED MAN"

Apparently, the Methodists and the Choctaw government officials did not think it was strange to appoint as superintendent of the two manual training academies a man who had never met an Indian, experienced frontier living, or worked in a manual training school. When William H. Goode received the call to Indian Territory, he was in the midst of a glorious season of revival in Indiana. Writing about the winter of 1842–43, Goode jubilantly described, "The flame of revival was kindled far and near. Zion had put on her 'beautiful garments'; the ministers of Christ had received a fresh anointing; the hosts of the Lord were girded anew for the conflict; sinners were pressing to the cross by scores and hundreds. . . ."[11]

On February 4, 1843, Reverend Goode received a letter from the Missionary Society asking, "Will anything induce you to consent to go to the Indian country in the South-West? The Choctaw Indians, at their late General Council, appropriated six thousand dollars *per annum* . . . to support the Fort Coffee Academy. This institution they have placed under the care of our Missionary Society."[12] The letter informed Goode that, as superintendent of the school, he would hire and supervise teachers, mechanics, and laborers and that he would be assisted by a principal for the female department. The female department would become the New Hope Academy. Feeling hopeful from the conversion of many sinners, Goode left his revival meetings to lead the Choctaws to salvation.

Goode received his final letter of appointment while preaching in South Bend, Indiana. While moving his family to Indianapolis before he started his journey west, he was greeted by the spirit of revival meetings throughout Indiana. Everywhere he turned, he felt the evangelical spirit of Christ. He traveled from Indianapolis to Cincinnati to embark on his journey by steamboat on the Ohio River and, eventually, by a small boat that unloaded him in the late afternoon of April 27, 1843 on the beach in front of the abandoned and ruined buildings of what had been the military post of Fort Coffee.

Goode embodied the romantic and religious quest to save the souls of Indians. Similar to other missionaries and teachers, Goode knew very little about Indians and never had much personal contact with them. To him, they were savages who in a previous era had slaughtered White settlers in the Ohio River Valley. Standing that first evening on the beach at Fort Coffee, which was located near the dividing line between the Choctaw and Cherokee nations, Goode wrote, "We were now fairly beyond the bounds of civilization, surrounded by two powerful Indian tribes." He admitted that night he had "scarcely ever shaken the hand of a red man, and was, to a great extent, unacquainted with their habits and customs."[13]

Also, Goode had little experience with outdoor life. The first night on the Fort Coffee beach was the first time in his life that he had ever slept outdoors. Goode compensated with intelligence and religious zeal for what he lacked in knowledge about Indians and frontier living.

The money set aside for the Fort Coffee and New Hope Academies, Goode quickly discerned, represented a major policy decision by the Choctaw government. The General Council of the Choctaw Nation passed a law that changed the distribution of interest on annuity payments from a per capita basis to a fund for education. This was essentially an indirect tax on Choctaw citizens who would otherwise have received the interest money. Goode applauded the measure and, after realizing that Choctaws similar to Pitchlynn and Leflore were not savages, claimed, "Probably no nation on earth has ever applied so large a proportion of its public revenue to the cause of education."[14]

Goode adhered to the plan in the School Law of 1842. The Choctaw plan was that the General Council would select the students and that the students would be boarded and clothed at the expense of the institution. Boys were to be instructed in agriculture, mechanical arts, literature, and morals. Girls were to be trained in domestic arts, literature, and morals. In practice, this curriculum would also include instruction on grooming, manners, and religion.

Goode arrived at Fort Coffee less than 3 months after receiving the request to manage the Fort Coffee Academy. Between preparation for the trip and the actual trip itself, Goode found little time to prepare to interact with Native Americans or to run a manual training school. His first problem was repairing the buildings of Fort Coffee and making them suitable for admitting students by the fall. In addition, the farm lands attached to the Fort needed to be planted and cultivated. No arrangements had been made to hire laborers, provide construction material, or plant crops.

The distorted view of Choctaws and Cherokees as "savages" kept the German family, whom Goode brought from Cincinnati to cook and do domestic chores, living in a state of fear. Their little colony consisted of Goode, the German family, and a dog. Commenting on the fear of Indians, Goode wrote, "And so exceedingly timid were my Germans among 'the Indians,' that it was with difficulty I could leave them for an hour."[15]

Over time, Goode developed a sympathy for the plight of the Choctaws, but this sympathy was tempered by a belief that Indians were culturally inferior to Whites. Goode expressed this combination of sentiments when reflecting on a graveyard filled with the remains of Choctaws who died on the Trail of Tears. Goode wrote, "The spectacle gave melancholy proof of the effect of the 'removal policy,' while it presented affecting evidence of the working of the finer feelings of humanity, *even in the savage heart*, [italics added] in the little houses built over the graves. . . ."[16]

Prior to the fall opening of the Academies, the Missionary Society assigned Reverend Henry C. Benson as a teacher to work with superintendent Goode. Although Benson shared the sentiments of the Missionary Society and Goode regarding the necessity of converting Native Americans to Christian civilization, he was much more sensitive to Native American customs and traditions. The memoirs of his teaching experience contain details about cultural transitions occurring within the Choctaw Nation.

Similar to most Christian missionaries, Benson was concerned about the lack of a work ethic among Native Americans. He wrote, "Indians are known to cherish an invincible disgust for manual labor."[17] The ownership of slaves, he felt, was a result of this disgust with manual work. Surprising to him was the discovery that Choctaw women were *not* overburdened with work. One of the legends among Whites of the 18th and 19th centuries was that Indian women were simply slaves to men. As I discussed earlier, this concept seemed to be disproved by the number of White female captives who preferred to remain with their Indian captors as opposed to returning to the male-dominated households of White Americans. Expressing his astonishment, Benson wrote, "I *never* discovered that the burdens were heaped upon the females, *as we are assured is the custom in savage life* and with the wild tribes who roam over the forests, depending upon the chase for their subsistence [italics added]."[18]

The major problem, Benson believed, was the poor educational level of the Choctaws—the very group that he would be teaching. For instance, he observed that most traditional rites had been discarded except among "the least intelligent portion of the tribe."[19] Of course, Benson applauded the abandonment of traditional rituals as a necessary step in becoming civilized. He was also pleased with the abandonment of tattooing and painting of faces and bodies and the wearing of rings in noses and feathers in the hair.

Arriving with his wife during the summer months of 1843, Benson helped refurbish the buildings and prepare them for students. The opening of the Fort Coffee Academy was delayed until January 9, 1844 because of construction work and the delay in receiving school supplies. On opening day, Goode and Benson commenced their efforts to eradicate the last vestiges of traditional values and customs, and replace them with the values and customs of a Christian culture.

FORT COFFEE ACADEMY

Manual training at Fort Coffee and New Hope Academies taught gendered work roles. Imitating the domestic functions of a nuclear family, Goode and Benson had the boys at Fort Coffee supply the girls at New Hope with agricultural products. In turn, the girls supplied the boys at Fort Coffee with the products of their domestic labor, including pants, shirts, and bedding.

On February 9, 1844, Goode and Benson received their first group of male students. The students were from traditional Choctaw families and had been selected personally by chiefs and trustees in the three Choctaw districts. Thirty students ranging in age from 8 to 20 arrived with signed certificates of admission, which entitled them to clothing, food, and instruction.

The first step in deculturalization was changing the dress and grooming of the students. Most of the students arrived barefoot, with calico hunting shirts and pants. Several wore hats, but many wore turbans made of twisted cotton. Late 18th and 19th century paintings of Choctaws and Cherokees in traditional clothing show men wearing a similar type of turban. All the children had long hair, and some wore it in braids.

With missionary zeal and "stout shears," Benson wrote, "[we] soon reduced their hair to our notions of taste and comfort. They generally submitted to our requirements without a murmur, but occasionally one would reluctantly consent to be shorn of his locks." They were then bathed and given a new suit of clothing. With heads shorn of long hair and braids, the students donned a coat and pants of "Kentucky" jeans, white shirts, "stout" shoes, and sealskin hats. As they came out of the dressing room, Benson noted, their friends could not recognize them.[20]

Benson's story of introducing a student to European-American sleeping arrangements exemplifies the cultural changes experienced by the students. The first evening, after the arrival of the students, Benson found an 8-year old boy standing behind the dining room, crying. Using an interpreter, because neither Benson or Goode spoke Choctaw, Benson asked what was wrong. The boy replied, "[he] had good pants, good jacket, good shoes and cap, and was much glad, but [he] had no blanket to wrap himself in, and thought that lying upon the ground without a blanket he would be cold."[21]

Benson proceeded to take him into the dormitory and explain, through an interpreter, the method of sleeping on a raised bed with a mattress, pillows, sheets, and blankets. Benson wrote, "He had never before conceived the idea of any better sleeping arrangements than the earth and a blanket could afford." Unlike Pitchlynn, who complained of sleeping on a straw mattress at the Choctaw Academy, many of the boys attending Fort Coffee had to be shown how to use a mattress, sheets, and pillows. They were used to sleeping on the ground, wrapped in blankets.[22]

The next step in the deculturalization process involved names. Goode wrote, "Some of our boys had already received English names, while others had only their heathen or Indian names." It might seem ironic from the standpoint of the late 20th century that Goode decided to replace "heathen" names with names "of persons known as active and benevolent friends of the cause of missions in the States."[23]

With their new hairstyles, clothing, and names, the students were introduced to the plan devised by Goode and Benson to regulate their study, labor, and play. A large bell woke the students in the morning at roughly 5:00 a.m. and then called them to morning worship services.

After services they proceeded to the dining room, where they were required to eat their meals in silence. After breakfast, the bell summoned them to an hour and a half of labor through which they learned agricultural skills and husbandry. The next bell announced a period of recreation, which was followed by the bell indicating the beginning of a 3-hour study period until the noon bell. After lunch and recreation, another ring of the bell announced 3 hours of study. The bell was rung again around 4 p.m. to call the students to another hour of labor. Then the bell announced recreation, worship, and supper. The students went to bed after hearing the final bell of the day. This was certainly a schedule designed to avoid idleness and instill a work ethic.[24]

The two missionary teachers were also concerned about maintaining authority. They both expressed surprise at the lack of insubordination by the students. On the other hand, although the boys did not rush to participate in manual labor, with direction they used axes, hoes, and rakes, and drove teams of horses for plowing. Some of the students learned to use carpentry tools.

The major disciplinary problems, as one might suspect, occurred during recreation period. The missionaries found the boys very rough in their play, often inflicting wounds on each other. Consequently, they restricted the use of bows and arrows, and forbade throwing stones and sticks. Benson recorded one incident when a student, Robert Frazier, threw a rock and hit Sam Magee in the face, causing considerable swelling. Before the assembled students, Robert admitted throwing the rock. Benson asked him, "Now, what ought to be done? What shall I do with you for breaking our rules?" Robert replied, "I must be whipped." When Benson asked the other students, they also replied, "He must be whipped." Benson wrote, "The rod was accordingly applied with considerable energy, but it was patiently borne, and Robert loved and respected us none the less for the promptness with which *we maintained the authority of the school government* [italics added]." Benson also recorded a similar tale about a group of students who violated the rule about playing marbles and were promptly punished.[25]

It is important to consider these incidents against the background of traditional Native American childrearing practices and the belief by White schoolmasters of the value of the "authority of school government." The permissive childrearing practices of traditional Choctaws would not have involved rules for playing or punishment for violation of rules. Within the context of traditional practices, the missionaries were socializing these students into a system of laws and punishment. Indeed, among educators of the 19th century, it was believed that "the authority of the school government" prepared children for obedience to the law of the state.[26]

The major focus of classroom instruction was on teaching reading and writing in English. This presented a problem because many of the students did not speak English, only eight knew the alphabet, and three could spell in one or two syllables. To help with the language problem, Benson had the assistance of Reverend John Page, a bilingual Choctaw who was educated at the Choctaw Academy. The beginning lessons focused on the teaching of the alphabet, followed by reading and spelling exercises.

Goode complained, "Their pronunciation is usually defective, some sounds being never mastered." On the other hand, Goode praised the students for their quickness at learning to read, spell, and write. But, he felt their capacity to learn English was limited. "For grammar," Goode wrote, "and the higher branches of lingual study they have little capacity." Obviously, because Goode was not trained to teach what is currently referred to as English as a Second Language, he did not understand the differences in grammar and pronunciation between language groups. He simply dismissed the problems by branding the Choctaw children as having "little capacity."[27]

As their teacher, Benson made no effort to learn to speak or write in Choctaw. There was no attempt on his part to communicate in Choctaw or teach literacy in Choctaw. He simply taught them English by having them learn to pronounce two or three letters formed into syllables placed on a chalkboard. The syllables were then organized to form words.[28] Textbooks used at both Fort Coffee and New Hope included Goodrich readers, Ray's *Arithmetic*, Kirkham's prose or poetry lessons, Mitchell's *Geography*, and Noah Webster's *Dictionary*.[29]

THE NEW HOPE ACADEMY

In the fall of 1845, the New Hope Academy was ready to receive its first group of 30 female students. By 1848, the number of students increased to 95. The school was considered to be a branch of the Fort Coffee Academy. Goode stated that his plan was "to connect the interests and labors of the two as to render them mutually subservient to each other's support and advancement."[30] According to Benson, manual training at New Hope would focus on "plain and fancy sewing, the duties of the kitchen, the dairy, the laundry, and the mysteries of housekeeping in general."[31]

In the New Hope and Fort Coffee Academies, Goode and Benson created schools that were symbolically Protestant models of husband and wife. The buildings at New Hope were modeled on those of the boy's school, with two one-story frame buildings 100 feet long. Also, the organization of the day, punctuated by bell ringing, was the same at both schools, and the same studies were followed in the classroom. The main difference between the two schools was the manual training.

The language problem was more severely dealt with at New Hope. A student who entered the first year of operation of New Hope, Elizabeth

Jacobs Quinn, who was interviewed by Carolyn Foreman sometime in the 1930s, said that students at New Hope were not allowed to speak Choctaw, which made it difficult because most of them knew no English. Quinn stated, "If they talked Choctaw they gave them a teaspoonful of red pepper."[32]

Interestingly, the interpreter at the New Hope Academy was the enslaved African named Aunt Hetty. She had lived from infancy among the Choctaws and, consequently, shared many of their cultural characteristics. A teacher at the New Hope Academy, William Graham, wrote that she was a vital part of the school because she spoke Choctaw. Students used her as a mediator with the missionaries.[33]

The interview with Quinn provides a firsthand account of the early days at the New Hope Academy. At the time of the interview, she was 112 years old. Her account of life at New Hope, according to Foreman, was carefully recorded by a stenographer. Quinn reported, "We had to make pants and coats—had to make all the shirts for the boys at Fort Coffee."[34] These clothes were probably picked up when the boys made their weekly trip to deliver vegetables and corn.

Even at the age of 112, Quinn referred to the first superintendent of the New Hope Seminary, Reverend W. L. McAlister, as "Old Man McAlister." There were five teachers and four seamstresses to teach domestic arts. Quinn recalled, "They made us do it right. If it wasn't right they made us rip it out. . . . Same way with the sewing. . . . We made bed clothes, sheets and pillow cases."[35]

Quinn remembered the school examinations combining academic studies with manual training. Parents and other observers watched the girls present their lessons on an outdoor stage while seated in the yard on chairs or on the ground. Quinn remembered, "We wore green with our grammar lessons and for the next class we all put on another colored dress. There were rooms right up the stairs and we would step into another room and all come out on the stage again with a different colored dress on." In addition to wearing the dresses they had made, put on display was their other handiwork including shirts, "fancy work," and garments made for themselves and the boys at Fort Coffee.[36]

Quinn could recall many people of the era. Her comment about Pitchlynn, who was mainly responsible for the School Law of 1842, is interesting. She told Foreman, "Peter Pitchlynn was an educated man; pretty smart man, but wasn't many people fancied him much."[37]

Apparently, the girls were prone to religious outbursts in the middle of the night, which teachers tried to control through whipping. In the middle of the night, one girl would begin singing a hymn and other girls would mount chairs to exhort the glories of Christ. This would lead to a chorus of groans and shrieks very similar to a Methodist camp meeting. Sometimes a girl would begin an Indian chant which would lead to a chorus of war whoops. Although these activities might have been child-

hood pranks, they did represent the apparent thin line between traditional Indian activities and the shrieking and falling down at Christian
revival meetings.[38]

Fort Coffee was burned down during the Civil War by Indians supporting the Union side, and it was rebuilt after the conclusion of the war.
The Fort Coffee and New Hope Academies remained under Methodist
management until 1884, when the Choctaw Nation assumed direct
control. A new agreement was then reached with the Missionary Society,
and the Methodists continued managing the schools until 1892 when
Thomas D. Ainsworth became the first superintendent of Choctaw
ancestry. By this time, the Academies were receiving students with prior
educational experience in neighborhood schools. As compared to its first
years, the highest classes in the schools were studying algebra, physi-
ology, grammar, composition, and rhetoric. The Fort Coffee Academy
continued as a manual training school until the end of the Choctaw
Nation, although the New Hope Academy was destroyed by fire in
1896.[39]

Apparently, my great-great grandfather Basil Leflore approved of the
Methodists' efforts at the Fort Coffee and New Hope Academies to
deculturalize the children from traditional families and, through a
schedule regulated by constantly ringing bells, manual training, imposition of dress codes, religious revivals, and language instruction, instill
the values of pious Protestants. One must assume that this was Leflore's
vision of the cultural transformation of traditional Choctaws. As Principal Chief in 1859, Leflore approved an act, providing for the repayment
of the debts of the Academies. After the Civil War, Basil's brother,
Superintendent of Schools Forbis Leflore, signed an agreement with the
Southern Methodist Church to manage the two schools. Mixed-bloods
similar to Pitchlynn and Basil and Forbis Leflore condoned attempts to
destroy traditional Choctaw ways of living.[40]

PRESBYTERIAN MISSIONARIES: "THE PEOPLE
WHO SPEAK ENGLISH . . . HELD THE GREAT
POWER OF THE WORLD"

Longtime friends of the Choctaw leadership, the Presbyterians were the
obvious choices to manage the Spencer and Wheelock Academies. Operating on the philosophy that the first step in civilizing Indians was
converting tribal leadership, Presbyterian missionaries, such as
Kingsbury, accompanied the tribe on the Trail of Tears. Remaining close
to the leadership, Kingsbury opened a church at Doaksville where he
preached to mixed-breeds such as Basil and Forbis Leflore, and Peter
Pitchlynn.

With the organization of the Board of Foreign Missions in 1838, Presbyterian leadership began to articulate a concept of missionary work that included a belief in the manifest destiny of Anglo-Saxon culture to spread around the world. And, of course, the concept of manifest destiny applied to the United States meant it was God's will that the U.S. government extend its power across the continent and over all Native American tribes. The Board of Foreign Missions believed it was proper for the U.S. Commissioner of Indian Affairs to aid missionary efforts, because the spread of republican government over Indian nations required the spread of Protestantism and Anglo-Saxon culture.[41]

The first Presbyterian superintendent of the Spencer Academy, James Ramsey, was appointed by the Board of Foreign Missions in 1845. He was a native of New York and a graduate of Princeton. When the school opened under the management of the Board of Foreign Missions on June 1, 1846, Ramsey immediately lectured students and trustees about the importance of the cross and the flag marching across the country, and the superiority of Anglo-Saxon culture.

Ramsey described his initial lecture to students and trustees in the following words: "I showed them [on a map] that the people who speak the English language, and who occupied so small a part of the world, and possessed the greatest part of its wisdom and knowledge; that knowledge they could thus see for themselves was power; and that power was to be obtained by Christianity alone."[42] Then he told them that the key to their success would be to continue the practice of establishing religious schools. In this way, they could share in the glory of Anglo-Saxon culture and Christianity.

Being a male-oriented ministry, the Board of Foreign Missions believed the graduates of the Spencer Academy would spread Anglo-Saxon culture and religion through the nation. The *Annual Report* of the Academy in 1850 stated: "To the youth taught here . . . [the Choctaw Nation could] look for their future ministers, physicians, legislators, judges, lawyers, and teachers."[43] From these positions, Spencer graduates could assure that the Nation abided by the maxims of Anglo-Saxon Protestant culture. They would assume the leadership in planting the cross and flag in Indian Territory.

Although Presbyterians emphasized the superiority of Anglo-Saxon culture, they did believe that racial equality was possible. However, this equality depended on conversion to Christianity and the adoption of Anglo-Saxon culture. In other words, as long as Indians clung to traditional beliefs and practices, they were an inferior race. With conversion and education, the members of the Board of Foreign Missions believed, Indians could achieve equality with White people. It is important to emphasize that this concept of equality depended on the eradication of all tradition beliefs and practices among Native Americans.[44]

For these Presbyterians, conversion also eliminated the dilemma of the extinction of Indian tribes through contact with White culture. Once converted, the Indian would be able to distinguish between good and evil. With this religious power, Indians would be able to distinguish between the good and bad aspects of White frontier culture. In other words, the cross and the flag would make Indians equal to Whites and protect them from extinction.[45]

Similar to the Methodists, the Presbyterians believed in the importance of creating Christian families. Obviously, the sexual freedom of the Native Americans appalled the Presbyterians. In addition, missionaries and teachers complained about how easily Choctaws ended marital relations. Members of the Board of Foreign Missions also believed that Indian women did all the work, whereas Indian men were content with a lazy existence. One of the sources of this misconception was the belief held by many Whites that hunting and fishing was not work. For many years in England, hunting and fishing was a sport of the aristocracy. The common person was not given the opportunity to participate in this leisure-time activity. In farming and urban communities in the United States, hunting and fishing was considered a leisure-time activity for men. Even today, it is considered a leisure-time sport. So from the perspective of Protestant missionaries, men did not work; they only hunted and fished. Women did all of the real work.[46]

So, the Presbyterians wanted to create a Christian family similar to the ideal of Thomas Jefferson. They wanted to curb what they considered to be the sexual immorality of the Choctaws and to tighten the bonds of wedlock. For instance, Ramsey, the superintendent of the Spencer Academy, requested a married teacher "to give the boys a daily exemplification of a Christian, civilized society."[47] Of course, unmarried female teachers would be models of a chaste womanhood.

Consequently, the Spencer and Wheelock Academies were related in the same way as the Fort Coffee and New Hope Academies. They were both symbolic relationships of the ideal Christian family. The major difference was that of social class. The regulation and manual training of the Methodist-run Fort Coffee and New Hope Academies was to educate for an ideal Christian family of a lower middle-class farmer. The Presbyterian-run Spencer and Wheelock Academies were to educate for an ideal Christian family for the wealthy planter or professional class. One group would attend revival camp meetings whereas the other would take their place in the pews in front of Cyrus Kingsbury.

THE SPENCER ACADEMY

Historian Michael Coleman claimed, "Under the BFM [Board of Foreign Missions], Spencer Academy . . . soon became perhaps the most advanced Indian Academy by the standards of the time, advanced even compared to many white academies in rural areas."[48] Certainly, Choctaw leaders would have agreed with Coleman. After the passage of the School Act of 1842,tribal accounts indicate that more money went to support the Spencer Academy than the other three schools. This inequality of school finance was linked to social class. This situation was noted at the time by the superintendent of the Fort Coffee Academy, William Goode. In comparing the Spencer Academy to his school, Goode wrote,

> Our endowment was inferior . . . and as a result, the apparent advantages of Spencer Academy led the prominent families of the Nation, principally half-breeds, to seek admission for their students, while ours was filled up mainly with full-bloods from families of smaller influence and wealth.[49]

As Goode indicated, the National Council gave the greatest attention to the Spencer Academy. Located 10 miles north of Doakesville, in contrast to the remote location of the Fort Coffee and New Hope academies in the northern part of the Choctaw Nation, the Spencer Academy was easily accessible to the planters and traders in the Doakesville area. It was named for John Spencer, Secretary of War from 1841 to 1842, who donated to the school a bell weighing 250 pounds. When the academy opened in 1844, it consisted of three dormitories, a school building, and a superintendent's house. The two-story dormitories were 64 feet by 16 feet and divided into four equally sized rooms on each floor. One dormitory was named Pitchlynn Hall after the school's leading Choctaw advocate, Peter Pitchlynn. The second dormitory was named after the Choctaw Nation's wealthiest man and builder of the Rose Hill Plantation, Robert M. Jones. And the third dormitory was named after U.S. Indian Agent William Armstrong. By naming the Academy after the Secretary of War and a dormitory after U.S. Indian Agent, the Choctaw leadership indicated its loyalty to the U.S. government. At least until the Civil War, the Choctaw leadership indicated its support of the idea of combining the cross and the flag.[50]

The superintendent's house provided living space for the superintendent, principal, and female teachers and contained a kitchen and dining room. On the perimeter of the grounds were store houses and the slave quarters. Much to the displeasure of the Presbyterians, they had to lease slaves because the Choctaw students did not like to do menial labor. And, of course, two of these slaves from the Rose Hill Plantation, as I mentioned earlier in this book, Uncle Wallace and Aunt Minerva, sang for the students and missionaries their songs, "Swing Low, Sweet Chariot" and "Steal Away From Jesus." Eventually, the Fisk singers would perform these songs for Queen Victoria. It is a startling sidelight on history to think of songs created by enslaved Africans in a colonized Native American nation being sung to the greatest symbol of European colonial power of the 19th-century—Queen Victoria.[51]

Superintendent James Ramsey described the curriculum and social life at the Spencer Academy in a letter to the *Foreign Missionary Chronicle*. Dated July 16, 1846, the letter described the recent final examination of the students. Final examinations in the 19th century were sometimes major social events. The Spencer Academy's final examinations were attended by over 150 guests, many of whom brought an extra horse for their child to ride with the family. To feed the guests, Ramsey ordered the killing of a steer, two sheep, and three hogs, all of which, he stated, were eaten by the end of the evening.[52]

From the tone of his letter, Ramsey made the examination sound as if it were the major social event of the month for the upper crust of Choctaw society. And, out of all the 150 guests, Ramsey only mentioned the names of Pitchlynn and Jones. This might be some indication of their social status and importance to the community. Ramsey wrote, "There were a number of gentlemen and some ladies from Doaksville and Fort Towson present; among others Col. Pitchlynn's [Peter Pitchlynn's] two daughters and sister-in-law. Capt. Jones [Robert M. Jones] also, who you may be aware is one of our trustees, a very intelligent man, and of polished manners. . . . Ramsey went out of his way to note that the wealthiest man in the Choctaw Nation, Jones, "brought his family along in a very handsome coach—the only thing of the kind I have yet seen in the nation."[53]

The actual examinations took place in a small room of the schoolhouse where, according to Ramsey's estimates, 25 percent of the guests were represented in the constantly changing audience. When they weren't observing the examinations, the guests ate and visited in the yard of the school. Beginning at 7:30 in the morning, the examinations lasted until 3:00 in the afternoon, with a 1-hour break for lunch. The examinations were followed by speeches by Chief Thomas Leflore and other dignitaries. Reflecting his language problems, Ramsey wrote, "All these speeches were in Choctaw, and of course unintelligible to me."[54] From what he was told, the speeches emphasized the importance of education. By 4:00, the guests were on the road after consuming the butchered steer, hogs, and sheep. From Ramsey's perspective, it was a successful social event.

The examinations reflected several important things about the school's curriculum and pedagogy. First, Ramsey and most of the other superintendents and teachers at the Spencer Academy were educated at Princeton University to be ministers and teachers. This preparation was quite different from that of Goode and Benson, who were circuit riders at Methodist revivals. Second, Ramsey had noted in his speech to the students and trustees the importance of learning English and Anglo-Saxon traditions if the Choctaws were going to participate in what he considered to be the greatest and most powerful civilization in the world. Third, he believed that Latin and Greek classics were the basis of Anglo-Saxon culture. Consequently, Ramsey stocked the school library with Greek and Latin lexicons, Greek grammars, and Latin texts by Horace, Caesar, Virgil, and Cicero.[55]

The fourth important factor was that many of the students attending the Spencer Academy did not speak English, and, of course, Ramsey did not speak Choctaw. Even in the 1890s, 70% of the students entering the school did not know English. This situation created a problem in grouping students for lessons. At first, students were separated according to language ability, and later by age and years of schooling.[56]

The first examination of the day highlighted the problem of teaching English. Of course, Ramsey and other teachers were not trained for teaching English as a second language. Also, Ramsey complained that they did not have books suitable for teaching English. Because none of the missionaries spoke Choctaw, the instruction in English was turned over to a Choctaw named Jonathan E. Dwight, who attended Yale College in 1836. The examination in English, Ramsey wrote, which was a sample of the daily teaching, "was conducted simply by giving the names of various objects in Choctaw, and requiring from the scholars the English; repeating short sentences in Choctaw, and requiring a translation in English, and some conversation. . . ."[57]

The examination in English was followed by examinations in reading, writing, arithmetic, geography, natural philosophy, U.S. history, and algebra. In addition, Ramsey wrote, "I examined one boy in Horace, who had been reciting to me since I came."[58] Ramsey's successor in 1849, Alexander Reid, also a graduate of Princeton, dropped the idea of teaching Latin. The curriculum through the rest of the 19th century included English, geography, natural philosophy, United States history, algebra, Bible history, astronomy, and vocal music.[59]

The Spencer Academy closed during the Civil War when the dormitories served as a Confederate hospital. It did not reopen until 1871, under the direction of Reverend J.H. Colton of the Southern Presbyterians. Shortly after its reopening, my grandfather was enrolled in the school. By 1880, the deteriorating conditions of the buildings required that the Academy move to another location 20 miles west. The new location was closer to my family at Goodland and Spring Chapel. It was at this new location that my grandfather's children attended school. The Academy was restored in 1897, but the U.S. government took it over as part of its plan for dissolving the Choctaw Nation. That year, another fire consumed the buildings, and the Spencer Academy was permanently shut.[60]

The Spencer Academy of the 1840s and 1850s was somewhat of an historical oddity located in the vast area of Indian Territory, with its little library of Greek and Latin classics and its teachers exhorting the benefits of Anglo-Saxon culture to Indian youth whose lands had been taken away by the products of that culture. Equally odd was the

Wheelock Academy, with its pretensions of preparing young Indian women for the best of Anglo-Saxon society.

THE WHEELOCK ACADEMY

The Wheelock Academy began as a mission opened by Presbyterian missionary Alfred Wright shortly after he completed the Trail of Tears in 1832. By 1832, he had completed 12 years of missionary work among the Choctaws, and by the time of his death in 1853 at the Wheelock Academy, a major part of his life had been spent with the tribe. Similar to other Presbyterian missionaries, Wright was a well-educated man, having attended Williams College in Massachusetts and the Andover Theological College.[61]

Beginning his missionary work in 1820 at Mayhew, Mississippi, Wright became friendly with Pitchlynn and other mixed-bloods. During his time at Mayhew, he worked on developing a written Choctaw language with Cyrus Byington, Pitchlynn, and Loring S. Williams. By the time of the removal, Wright had translated many religious tracts and six books of the Bible into Choctaw. He was one of the few missionaries who was fluent in Choctaw.[62]

In 1833, when the Choctaw Nation was granted the right to use annuities for building schools, Wright received assistance to build a day school about 10 miles east of Doaksville. Because the area was sparsely populated, he found it difficult to attract students to a day school. In 1839, a dormitory was completed and the school became a boarding school. Using his friendship with Pitchlynn, he was able to persuade the Choctaw Nation to include his boarding school in the School Act of 1842 and, in 1843, the school opened officially as the Wheelock Academy with 48 girls and 4 small boys.

Wright remained superintendent until his death in 1853, when John Edwards took over the supervision of the school. Edwards remained superintendent until the outbreak of the Civil War, when he fled to California in 1861. The school fell into a state of disrepair until Edwards returned in 1882, rebuilt it, and remained as superintendent until 1896. Similar to Wright, Edwards was a scholar, having graduated second in his class from Princeton University. He learned Choctaw from Byington and translated part of the Old Testament into Choctaw, and revised Wright's translation of the New Testament.[63]

As the complement to the boy's Spencer Academy, the Wheelock Academy was to educate women as female companions for the ideal Christian marriage. As I have discussed previously, missionaries were very concerned about eliminating clans and replacing them with "Christian" families with the father exercising authority over the mother and children. Women, among these Protestant missionaries, were thought of as vessels of virtue as compared to men. One of the arguments for hiring female teachers as models of morality was the belief that evil and crime primarily emanated from men, and women served the role of tempering that immorality. The moral role of women was not as public preachers, but as mothers and teachers.[64]

During this time, it was believed by many men and women that educating women would enhance their ability to be companions for educated husbands, teachers and nurturers of their children, and teachers of other children. An educated woman, many men and women believed, should be modest and allow the public contacts of the family to be controlled by men. In the words of the secretary of the Board of Foreign Missions, John C. Lowery, "the ideal woman . . . [should be] consecrated and spiritual minded [and] adorned with the gifts of education and refined culture, but most all with the ornament of a meek and quiet spirit, which in the sight of God is of great price."[65]

As the head of the Wheelock Academy, Edwards espoused similar views of women and the education of women. Similar to other Whites, he did not consider hunting and fishing as work, and therefore believed Indian women were exploited. "The women did all the work at family," he wrote regarding Indians. "[T]he men, the lords of creation, did nothing there, but eat, sleep, talk and exercise themselves for games, or hunts, or war."[66] He believed that education would end the subservient and debased role of women in Native American society. Of course, one thing that made them debased in the eyes of White Christians was their sexual freedom and pleasure. An important aspect of Christian virtue was controlling desires for the glory of God.

Contrary to Edwards' statements about the subservience of Native American women, others commented on their independence. Even Sue McBeth, Presbyterian missionary teacher to the Choctaws and Nez Perce, complained about Indian women usurping the power of men, acting independently, and neglecting household chores. Her sister, Kate McBeth, complained that Indian women did not like the idea of men being the head of the household.[67]

If Indian women displayed this type of independence, what did male missionaries mean when they talked about removing women from subservient roles? In thinking about this question, I realized that a statement by Edwards provides a clue to understanding what he thought a "Christian" education of men and women should accomplish. Edwards wrote, "If they [Native Americans] have but one horse, the man rides; the woman walks and carries the child or bundle. Frequently, now, this order is reversed. *We then take it for granted at once that they have received the gospel* [italics added]."[68]

Obviously, Edwards' statement is not intended to imply that in the Christian family, the woman rides the horse because she is the authority figure in the family. In fact, she rides the horse because of her submissive position. In the Christian family, women are meek and weak and men are authoritative and strong. It is the role of the husband to protect the weakness and virtue of his wife. What probably bothered Edwards and other Whites about the scene of the man riding the horse with the woman walking is that it suggested equality of strength and endurance. What probably flashed through their minds was, "Look at that poor woman. Here's a strong man riding the horse while that weak woman follows behind carrying a bundle." This type of thinking evokes the image of chivalry that dates back to the Middle Ages in European society and was a favorite theme in southern antebellum literature.

Therefore, from Edwards' perspective, lifting a squaw from her debased state meant putting her on an elevated plain of virtue, where her meekness and mildness would be protected by a strong husband. Supported by the strength of the husband, the wife could focus attention on creating a Christian family and virtuous children. Similar to the Puritan idea that women knew God through their husbands, the woman would now know the public through her husband. The husband would shield her and the family from the vileness and vices of the public world. As the companion to her husband, she would temper his character with her virtue and he would worship her womanhood.[69]

In contrast to the New Hope Academy, which focused on producing domestic workers for farm households, the Wheelock Academy focused on educating women for wealthy and professional households in which the domestic work would be done by enslaved Africans or hired domestic servants. In this type of household, the wife needed to know enough to be a companion to her husband, able to act as hostess at social functions, and able to raise her children properly.

Therefore, in contrast to New Hope, which focused on the reading, writing, arithmetic, and manual training, the Wheelock Academy combined training in needlework with a curriculum consisting of arithmetic, grammar, geography, natural philosophy, astronomy, botany, chemistry, and geometry. In reporting in 1851 to the War Department about the Wheelock Academy, U.S. Indian Agent Armstrong wrote, "In reading, the teacher has not only endeavored to have her pupils read correctly but has collected such books as will lead them to think and such also as will have a moral and religious influence—[the books, include] Child's Book on Theology, History of Jonah; Natural Theology, by Gallaudet."[70] Along with religious services, this curriculum was to educate the ideal Christian woman for the ideal Christian household.

In describing the general purpose of education among the Choctaws, Edwards wrote regarding the establishment of the early missions, "The mission was commenced on the principle that there was no hope for the adults; that the only prospect of success was in taking the children in boarding schools, and making them 'English in language, civilized in manners, Christian in religion.'" It was from these boarding schools that would come the salvation, Edwards believed, of the Choctaw people.

"The English schools are important for raising up educated, native preachers and teachers, and for the temporal welfare of the people."[71]

In preparing young women for the Choctaw Nation and the Christian family, Edwards believed he was saving the tribe from extinction by teaching the superiority of Anglo-Saxon civilization and language. Women could be lifted from their lowly station as squaws, Edwards claimed, to become teachers and Christian wives, who would nurture husbands and children as they followed the path of the cross and the flag.

There was a waiting list to get into the Wheelock Academy when my great-grandfather's second wife, Carrie Gooding, attended in the 1850s. When Wright opened the institution, after receiving support under the School Act of 1842, the demand was so great that Wright could only accept half the applications. Cushman, who personally knew Wright, recalled, "So great was the desire of members of the tribe for admission of their girls . . . at first seven girls were selected from each of the three clans. . . . The list was made from twice the number of applications and only one was taken from a family."[72] A number of the graduates, including Carrie Gooding, went "to the States" to go to college.

Similar to most schools in the Nation, Wheelock fell into a state of disrepair during the Civil War and then burned to the ground in 1866. The school was rebuilt after Edwards returned in 1882. Interestingly, although the sign hung there in the 1990s proclaims Wheelock as a drug and alcohol abuse center, in the 1840s and 1850s there existed a temperance society with 300 members from the surrounding area of Wheelock.[73]

CONCLUSION: THE DARK SIDE
OF THE CHRISTIAN FAMILY

While the Methodists at the Fort Coffee and New Hope Academies were educating for a Christian family among poor and middle-income farmers, the Presbyterians at the Spencer and Wheelock Academies were educating male leaders and their educated female companions. One thing that bothered both ministries, and resulted in the closing of the Academies during the Civil War, was the issue of slavery. Goode, Benson, Wright, and Edwards believed that a true Christian family could not own other human beings. Because enslaved Africans had souls, according to Christian doctrine, the true civilizing of the tribes required the education, conversion, and freedom of enslaved Africans.

Choctaws, who themselves were constantly oppressed and exploited by Europeans, in turn oppressed Africans by passing a law making it illegal to educate enslaved Africans. I discuss this law in the next chapter, but at this point it is important to point out that the law created a quandary for the missionaries. Essentially, they asked themselves: How can we civilize Indian tribes when they refuse to allow the imparting of Christian civilization to their own enslaved Africans?

In addition, the four academies did not educate all the children of the Choctaw Nation. Shortly after removal, Presbyterians opened a number of day schools and other academies. During the post-Civil War period, the Choctaw Nation created a system of schools that was segregated by language and race. The elite mixed-bloods maintained power, destroyed traditional culture, and increased the levels of racism in the Choctaw Nation by supporting slavery, maintaining language and racial discrimination, building allegiance to Anglo-Saxon culture, and advocating conversion to Christianity.

NOTES

[1]"Indian Commissioner Crawford on Indian Policy: Extract from the *Annual Report of the Commissioner of Indian Affairs November 25, 1838*" in *Documents of United States Indian Policy Second Edition* edited by Francis Paul Prucha (Lincoln: University of Nebraska Press, 1990), p. 73.

[2]"President Jackson on Indian Removal, December 7, 1835, in Prucha, pp. 71–72.

[3]Ibid., p. 72.

[4]"Indian Commissioner Crawford...," p. 73.

[5]Ibid., p. 73.

[6]Ibid., p. 73.

[7]Ibid., p. 73.

[8]Henry C. Benson, *Life Among the Choctaw Indians and Sketches of the South-West* (Cincinnati: L. Swormstedt & A. Poe, for the Methodist Episcopal Church, 1860), pp. 56–61.

[9]Benson, p. 8.

[10]Ibid., pp. 8–9.

[11]Ibid., p. 23.

[12]William H. Goode, *Outposts of Zion, With Limnings of Mission Life* (Cincinnati, OH: Poe & Hitchcock, 1864), p. 26.

[13]Goode, p. 37.

[14]Ibid., p. 38.

[15]Ibid., p. 46.

[16]Ibid., p. 129.

[17]Benson, p. 34.

[18]Ibid., p. 34.

[19]Ibid., p. 50.

[20]Ibid., p. 187.

[21]Ibid., p. 187.

[22]Ibid., p. 188.

[23]Goode, p. 131.

[24]Ibid., pp. 130–131.

[25]Benson, pp. 194–195.

[26]See Joel Spring, *American Education, Sixth Edition*, (New York: McGraw-Hill, 1993), pp. 11–12.

[27]Goode, p. 132.

[28]Benson, p. 189.

[29]Carolyn Thomas Foreman, "New Hope Seminary 1844–1897," *Chronicles of Oklahoma* (1944)22: 273.

[30]Ibid.

[31]Benson, p. 297.

[32]Quoted in Foreman, "New Hope Seminary 1844–1897," p. 277.

[33]Ibid., p. 274.

[34]Ibid., p. 277.

[35]Ibid., p. 277.

[36]Ibid., p. 278.

[37]Ibid., p. 278.

[38]Ibid., p. 276.

[39]Ibid., pp. 292–299; Debo, pp. 95–96, 238.

[40]Foreman, "New Hope Seminary 1844–1897," pp. 283–285.

[41]Michael C. Coleman, *Presbyterian Missionary Attitudes toward American Indians, 1837–1893* (Jackson: University of Mississippi, 1985), pp. 38–42.

[42]Ibid., p. 42.

[43]Ibid., p. 17.

[44]Ibid., pp. 139–165.

[45]Ibid., p. 44.

[46]Ibid., pp. 95–96.

[47]Ibid., p. 91.

[48]Ibid., p. 17.

[49]Goode, p. 184.

[50]See W. David Baird, "Spency Academy, Choctaw Nation, 1842–1900," *Chronicles of Oklahoma* (1967)45: 25–27.

[51]Grant Foreman, *The Five Civilized Tribes* (Norman: The University of Oklahoma Press, 1934), pp. 60–61; Eloise G. Spear, *Choctaw Indian Education with Special Reference to Choctaw County, Oklahoma: An Historical Approach*, Dissertation, University of Oklahoma, Norman, 1977 (Ann Arbor, MI: University Microfilms International, 1977), p. 66; and Baird, p. 29.

[52]Foreman, *The Five Civilized Tribes*, pp. 65–67. Angie Debo, *The Rise and Fall of the Choctaw Republic* (Norman: University of Oklahoma Press, 1961), p. 110.

[53]Foreman, *The Five Civilized Tribes*, p. 67.

[54]Ibid., p. 67.

[55]Baird, p. 42.

[56]Baird, p. 42.

[57]Foreman, *The Five Civilized Tribes*, p. 66.

[58]Ibid., p. 66.

[59]Baird, p. 42.

[60]Ibid., p. 38.

[61]Edmond Gardner, "Alfred Wright-Wheelock Academy," in *McCurtain Country and Southeast Oklahoma* edited by W.A. Carter (Idabel, OK: Tribune Publishing Co., 1923), pp. 25–33; Foreman, *The five Civilized Tribes*, p. 80.

[62]Carolyn Keller Reeves, "Some Observations about the Choctaw Language of the Early Nineteenth Century," in *The Choctaw Before Removal*, pp. 17–21.

[63]John R. Swanton, "Editor's Introduction," *Chronicles of Oklahoma* (1932)10: 392.

[64]Coleman, pp. 93–95; Spring, pp. 24–32, 98–126.

[65]Coleman, p. 93.

[66]John Edwards, "The Choctaw Indians in the Middle of the Nineteenth Century," *Chronicles of Oklahoma* (1932)10: 405.

[67]Coleman, p. 96.

[68]Edwards, p.410.

[69]For the Puritan ideal of womanhood see Spring, pp. 24–28.

[70]Foreman, *The Five Civilized Tribes*, p. 78.

[71]Edwards, pp. 424–425.

[72]Foreman, *The Five Civilized Tribes*, p. 59.

[73]Ibid., p. 78.

8

"I am a slave instead of the Negroes":[1] Segregation and Language

Picking up his plate of food, my father shoved it in the Black man's face. Often, I heard this family story about the first time a Black person sat down next to my father at a lunch counter. Sometimes, racism can be the result of a historical thread running through the family and the community. In my father's family, the historical thread of racism begins in the early 19th century with the purchase of enslaved Africans. In the Choctaw community, racism was condoned by the failure of missionary educators to condemn slavery publicly and their acceptance of slave owners into houses of worship. Racism existed at the Choctaw Academy and academies in Indian Territory that used enslaved Africans to serve students. The powerful force of racism is reflected in the 1840 story, told in chapter 6, of the mixed-blood boy who killed himself after finding out his mother was an enslaved African.

The Choctaw government joined the Confederacy during the Civil War, in part, because of a desire to maintain slavery. A consequence of this decision was the death of my great grandfather, Samuel Spring, in 1863 while he served in the Confederate Army. This left my grandfather, who was born the same year, a fatherless child. Possibly, discrimination occurred when organizing two Choctaw companies for the Confederate Army at the Goodland mission. One company was comprised of full-bloods and the other company was composed of mixed-bloods under the leadership of Ben Smallwood, who would be elected Principal Chief in 1889. The mixed-blood company, according to a newspaper article, " was known as 'The Company of Three' because three brothers of the Leflore family and three of the Spring family, and three each of other families in the vicinity were members of the company."[2]

Therefore, racism gained support from the silence of missionaries, the use of slave labor in the schools, the participation in the Civil War, and the later segregation of schools. As my father lifted his plate to commit a despicable act of racial hatred, he was reenacting the historical racism of the Choctaws.

Another form of racism was denying education to enslaved Africans. "No slave or child of a slave is to be taught to read or write in or at any school," stated an 1853 law passed by the National Council of the Choctaw Nation, " by anyone connected in any capacity therewith, on pain of dismissal and expulsion from the nation."[3] The law was similar to other laws passed in southern states denying literacy to enslaved Africans. The law created a dilemma for missionary educators because they believed slavery was immoral. In addition, missionaries were concerned about a section of the law requiring school authorities to remove "any and all persons connected with the public schools or academies known to be abolitionists or who disseminate or attempt to disseminate directly or indirectly, abolition doctrines."[4]

RACISM AND THE MISSIONARIES

Missionary response to the 1853 law reveals the extent of their inaction regarding racism and slavery in Indian Territory. Missionaries were the majority of teachers prior to the Civil War, and their silence in the classroom and at the pulpit on the issue of slavery appeared to condone the practice. Implicit in the vision of the Christian family they were imparting to students was family ownership of slaves. After all, enslaved Africans were serving students as the students learned to be authoritative fathers and domesticated mothers.

Under the leadership of the old missionary stalwarts, Kingsbury and Byington, frequent meetings regarding the new law were held with other Presbyterian missionaries in 1853 and 1854. Despite the concerns of missionaries, the law had no impact on the academies or missionary day schools because, by their own admission, " The teaching of slaves in these schools has never been practiced or contemplated."[5] The law was primarily aimed at restricting instruction at Sabbath schools and in families; and it appeared that the missionaries were willing to give up these schools rather than maintain them under the conditions of the law.

In 1854, the missionaries adopted a resolution that avoided any comment on whether or not enslaved Africans should be educated. They did resolve to abandon the management of the academies if the law were enforced. Of course, this part of the resolution was meaningless because the enslaved Africans at the academies waited on the students and staff, and they were not taught in the classrooms with the other students.[6]

Also, the missionaries' resolution indicates they intended to avoid any direct confrontation with the Choctaw government over the issue of slavery. In one of those wonderful twists in theological reasoning, the resolution declared slavery to be morally wrong *as a system*, but individual slave owners were not considered guilty of an immoral act. This interesting reasoning saved the missionaries from condemning individual Choctaws for owning slaves. They compared this argument to that used to absolve the individual soldier in war of immoral actions. "While, as in war," Item Nine of the resolution states, "there can be no shedding of blood without sin somewhere attached, and yet the individual soldier may not be guilty of it; so while slavery is always sinful, *we may cannot esteem everyone who is legally a slaveholder a wrongdoer for sustaining the legal relation* [italics added]."[7]

This resolution saved the missionaries from the embarrassing situation of telling Robert M. Jones, owner of the Rose Hill Plantation and donor of money and the labor of enslaved Africans to the Spencer Academy, that he was immoral for using slaves in his cotton fields. After all, a dormitory was named after him. And, to avoid any confrontation with the Choctaw government over the issue of slavery, Item Eight of the resolutions declares, "As a missionary, he has nothing to do with political questions and agitations."[8]

The 1853 law was a major problem for the ABCFM and the Board of Foreign Missions. Along with the missionaries in the Choctaw Nation, members of these organizations believed slavery was evil. Meeting in Utica, New York in 1855, the American Board decided to send George Wood to investigate the situation in Indian missions. The Board resolved: "That Mr. Wood be requested to repair to the Choctaw Nation . . . [for] a fraternal conference with the brethren in the field in respect to the difficulties and embarrassments which have grown out of the action of the Choctaw Council."[9] While visiting the Choctaw Nation, Wood spent 3 days each at the Wheelock and Spencer Academies, and 9 days at other schools.

In Wood's report, he found the missionaries shocked by the action of the Choctaw government. "With fidelity they prosecute the great object of their high calling," Wood wrote, "and in view of the spiritual and temporal transformation taking place around them, as the result of the faithful proclamation of the gospel, we are compelled to exclaim, 'What hath God wrought!'"[10]

After investigating the schools, Wood was impressed with their achievements and wanted them to continue. He particularly stressed their importance in creating Christian families. "They are doing a good work for the nation," he wrote, "Many of the pupils become Christian wives, mothers and teachers."[11] Wood shared John Edwards' feelings regarding the importance of educating Choctaw women for the family and the school.

Besides praising missionary work, Wood supported their resolutions on the issue of slavery. Wood quoted from a variety of theological sources that agreed that,

Distinction ought to be made between the character of a *system*, and the character of the persons whom circumstances have implicated; nor would it always be just, if all the recoil and horror wherewith the former [slavery] is contemplated, were visited in the form of condemnation and moral indignancy upon the latter [slave owner].[12]

The missionaries continued teaching until the outbreak of the Civil War. They turned their backs on the issue of educating enslaved Africans and avoided any public condemnation of slavery and slave owners. What was the implicit message of their actions to their students? Did students learn that Christians avoid taking a public stand on actions they consider immoral? Did they learn that there was no conflict between Christianity and the enslavement of other humans? Did they learn that racism was okay? Did they learn that it was not immoral for a Christian home to own slaves? We will never know the exact hidden curriculum resulting from the inactions of the missionaries regarding slavery, but we do know that the Choctaws chose to fight on the side of the Confederate states.

THE CIVIL WAR AND THE CHOCTAW NATION

The Choctaw government was in a dilemma over the growing friction between the northern and southern states that eventually erupted into open warfare with the firing on Fort Sumter on April 12, 1861. Obviously, the leaders of the Choctaws sympathized with the southern states regarding slavery. On the other hand, the U.S. government owed the tribe a great deal of money for the lands purchased through treaties. What would happen to these debts if the Choctaw Nation sided with the Confederacy? Consequently, Choctaw leaders such as Peter Pitchlynn, Samuel Garland, Israel Folsom, and Peter Folsom initially supported a policy of neutrality.[13]

Two months before the outbreak of fighting at Fort Sumter, the Choctaw General Council issued a statement of regret about the political disagreement between the North and the South, because the " dissolution of the Union . . . [would disrupt] the various important relations existing . . . by treaty stipulations and international laws, and portending much injury to the Choctaw government." But the resolution also indicates the true sympathies of the slave-holding leaders: "That in the event a permanent dissolution of the American Union takes place . . . we shall be left to follow the natural affections, education, institutions, and interests of our people, which indissolubly bind us in every way to the destiny of . . . the Southern states. . . ."[14]

After hostilities began, leaders, such as Pitchlynn, continued to urge neutrality as a means of protecting Choctaw treaty rights if the U.S.

government won the war. On the other hand, large slave owners such as Jones urged an alliance with the Confederacy. A secessionist meeting was held at Doakesville on June 1, 1861, less than 2 months after the firing on Fort Sumter. Jones delivered a fiery speech supporting secession from the U.S. government. Principal Chief George Hudson appointed a committee to meet with the Confederacy and plan for the raising of a regiment for the Confederate army.[15]

On June 14, 1861, the Choctaw National Council declared the Choctaw Nation was "free and independent" of the U.S. government. The meaning of this declaration should be considered against the background of Choctaw history. Originally, the United States took over what had been a free and independent tribe and the U.S. Supreme Court had declared that Indian tribes were "dependent nations." The declaration of independence returned the Choctaw Nation to its original state of independence from other governments. For a Native American tribe to declare its independence in the middle of the 19th century was a revolutionary act.

Independence lasted a little less than 1 month. On July 12, 1861, the Choctaw Nation signed a treaty with the Confederate government. The treaty guaranteed the Choctaws a greater degree of independence than had existed under the U.S. government, and the Confederate government agreed to assume all financial obligations of the U.S. government to the Nation.[16]

The Civil War had a disastrous effect on the school system. Annuity money for support of the schools was cut off by the U.S. government. Many missionaries with abolitionist sentiments fled in fear of their lives. John Edwards abandoned the Wheelock Academy for California and did not return for 20 years. The Spencer Academy was used as a hospital and barracks for troops. Many other schools experienced a similar fate. Because of the War, the Presbyterian Church, which had played such a large role in the educational system, split, leaving the educational activities within the Nation under the control of the Southern Presbyterian Church.[17]

Interestingly, the last surrender of the Civil War took place at Fort Towson on June 23, 1865, when General Stand Watie, the famous mixed-blood Cherokee, turned over the arms of the Cherokee Confederate States Army. Historically, this is considered the last event of the Civil War.[18]

THE AFRICAN CHOCTAWS[19]

With the defeat of the Confederacy, the Choctaw Nation immediately imposed a Black Code to regulate the activities of the freed slaves. In addition, the Choctaw government tried to convince the U.S. government to remove all freed slaves from the Nation. After the signing of a preliminary treaty with the U.S. government on September 13, 1865, the Nation officially abolished slavery on October 14, 1865. The Choctaw law abolishing slavery contained a Black code that forced freed slaves into a form of wage slavery. The law required that all freed persons find an employer and sign a written wage agreement before a county judge. Those without contracts were to be arrested and their services sold to the highest bidder. The law regulated wages for eight classes of labor, and provided that working hours would be 10 hours in the summer and 9 hours in the winter, with Saturday afternoon and Sunday as holidays.[20]

Many Choctaws feared possible acts of revenge from freed Africans and formed a Vigilance Committee similar to the later Ku Klux Klan. One reason for this fear was the large number of enslaved Africans owned by the Choctaws. The census completed in 1907 revealed that African Choctaws totalled more than 20% of the population. The total population was 26,615, and the number listed as freed men was 5,994.[21]

Living in fear, and in turn wanting to instill fear in freed slaves, the Vigilance Committee was a secret organization with small groups in each locality closely communicating with each other through a system of mounted couriers. The Vigilance Committee roamed the country convicting and hanging African Choctaws whom they suspected of breaking national laws or violating an unwritten racial code. It was reported to the U.S. officials that the actions of the Vigilance Committee were creating a reign of terror in the Choctaw Nation.[22]

For almost 20 years after the abolition of slavery, the Choctaw Nation tried to convince the U.S. government to remove all freed slaves from its territory. In contrast, the policy of the U.S. government was to try and convince the Nation to adopt all freed slaves. Under the final treaty between the U.S. government and the Choctaw Nation signed on April 28, 1866, the U.S. government agreed to pay the Nation $300,000 for seceded land if the Nation would adopt their freed slaves. Otherwise, if the Nation decided on removal, the money would be used to assist the freed slaves.[23]

The majority of the Nation wanted removal, whereas Choctaw leaders such as Pitchlynn argued that freed slaves were an important source of cheap labor. In the end, the U.S. government never removed the freed slaves as promised in the treaty. Consequently, freed slaves lived in the Nation without any legal status until they were granted citizenship in 1883.

Finally, in the fall of 1880, the National Council indicated its willingness to adopt the freed slaves. On May 21, 1883, the Nation passed a law adopting all former slaves who resided in the Choctaw Nation on September 13, 1865, the date of the signing of the preliminary treaty, as well as all their descendants. The freed slaves were granted all "the rights, privileges, and immunities, including the right of suffrage of citizens of the Choctaw Nation, except in the annuities, moneys, and the public domain of the Nation."[24]

The freed slaves were given 40 acre shares in the public domain, and they were granted educational benefits equal to those of Choctaws attending neighborhood schools. Although the U.S. government never delivered on its promise of 40 acres and a mule to freed African Americans in the South, the African Choctaws did receive their promised 40 acres. In the end, the Choctaws never provided the equal educational benefits promised in the 1883 legislation.[25]

African Choctaws received a limited form of citizenship because the Choctaw Constitution required that one had Choctaw ancestry to hold public office. This constitutional provision was originally intended to exclude from public offices White men who married into the Nation. In 1890, an African Choctaw appealed to the U.S. Indian Office about the requirement, but the U.S. government ignored the petition.[26]

The National Council also passed blatantly racist marriage laws. One law denied citizenship to African Americans who married into the tribe. As I mentioned previously, Whites could gain citizenship by marrying into the tribe if they could gather signatures certifying their good moral character. Another law made it a felony for an African Choctaw and a Choctaw to marry. These two laws limited the expansion of the African Choctaw population, and kept the African and Native American populations from intermingling.[27]

The Vigilance Committee, the Black codes, early work laws, the denial of public office to African Choctaws, and the marriage laws highlighted the continuing feelings of racism among the Choctaw population. These factors, combined with segregated public schools, reinforced these patterns of racism and assured their continuation into the 20th century.

SEGREGATED SCHOOLS

During the period between 1865 and 1883, freed slaves frequently petitioned Congress to remain in the Choctaw Nation and to be provided with schools, whereas the Choctaw Nation petitioned for removal. The Choctaw government ignored all requests from the freed slaves for schools. In response to the requests from freed Africans, Congress passed legislation in 1874 that provided money for schools for the freed Africans. Contracting with the Baptist Mission Board in 1874, the U.S. government established schools for freed slaves at Boggy Depot, Fort Coffee, Doaksville, and Skullyville. The African Methodist Episcopal Church cooperated with the Baptist Mission Board to establish 13 schools by 1882.[28]

The actions of freed slaves in the Choctaw Nation followed the pattern in Southern states, where free slaves tied their hopes for freedom and independence to literacy. Having been deprived of an education under slavery, African Americans worked with church organizations or formed their own community groups to build schools. Historian Anderson argued that freed Africans throughout the South believed that education was the key to the transition from slavery to free labor for hire. In addition, he found that when civil authorities failed to provide money for schools, the freed Africans contributed their labor and money to building schoolhouses and supporting teachers.[29]

Choctaws, who were sympathetic to the actions of the Vigilance Committee, worried that the spread of education among the freed Africans would result in a loss of cheap labor and would lead to social unrest. Eventually, this antieducation sentiment resulted in the burning down of the school at Boggy Depot in the fall of 1875.[30]

After the passage of the 1883 law giving African Choctaws citizenship in the nation and guaranteed equal educational funding, the National Council began the process of creating a segregated school system that, in the end, received unequal funding. In 1885, the Council appropriated money for the establishment of "colored neighborhood schools." Under this legislation, 34 colored neighborhood schools were opened with an enrollment of 847 children.[31] But, according to a missionary from the Presbyterian Board of Missions for Freedman, Robert Flickinger, the $1 a year per student appropriated by the Council for African Choctaw children only provided for 3 months' education in areas with a concentration of freed slaves. Those living in sparsely settled neighborhoods were not appropriated enough money to maintain a school.[32]

The African Choctaw population bitterly complained about the unequal funding of educational opportunities. In reference to African Choctaw teachers, missionary Flickinger wrote, "All had personal knowledge of the existence and unusual privileges afforded the children and youth of the Choctaws at Wheelock and Spencer Academies."[33] Flickinger noted that the freed slaves believed that they were just as good at farming as their Indian neighbors, "and this fact tended to increase their desire to have a 'fair chance' and equal share in the matter of educational privileges for their children."[34]

Despite money problems, school attendance of African Choctaw children was extremely high when compared to other areas. For instance, school attendance by White children in Iowa was slightly over 71% in 1890, and the attendance of African Choctaw children was over 75%. In general, school attendance by the children of freed slaves was higher in Indian Territory than by African-American children in Mississippi. In fact, school attendance by the children of freed slaves was higher than the school attendance of Whites in Mississippi.[35]

The schools serving African Choctaws used books imported from the States. The primary emphasis was on teaching English and moral values. Missionary teachers believed it was important to instill a work ethic—similar to their attitudes toward Native Americans. Former enslaved Africans spoke a combination of English, Choctaw, and African languages. The majority of former slaves (who were enslaved Africans working for mixed-bloods) often received their commands in English, whereas those living with full-bloods learned to speak Choctaw. For instance, Jones, the largest slave owner, used only English-speaking White overseers. Some former slaves, as I mentioned earlier, were bilingual in English and Choctaw.[36]

I would hypothesize that the English language background of many African Choctaws increased the social gulf with the full-bloods. Regarding social class, the overwhelming majority of freed slaves were just as poor as many of the full-bloods. Any political and economic alliances between the two groups were made more difficult by the language barrier. Interestingly, language differences made it more likely that African Choctaws would feel closer to mixed bloods than full-bloods. Later in this chapter, I elaborate on the language issues in the schools.

In 1891, the National Council approved money to support a segregated boarding school, the Tuskaloosa Academy, to accommodate 15 boys and 15 girls. The small size of the Academy did not satisfy the African Choctaw community, and they petitioned for an expansion of the school. Ignoring the petition, the National Council did not expand the school and closed it in 1901.[37]

Therefore, the history of African Choctaw schools is one of continual demands for education from the freed slaves, and either no response or a slow response from the Choctaw government. Similar to other areas in the South, the Black community often provided its own money and labor in cooperation with religious organizations to build schools. An example of this process is the Oak Hill Industrial Academy. The school originated from a requirement of the Presbyterian Board of Missions for Freedman that African Choctaw ministers maintain schools at their churches to teach about the Bible for several months of the year.

One of the founders of the Oak Hill Church, Henry Crittenden, originally attended services conducted by Kingsbury. First, he organized a church in his cabin, then he joined with others in founding the Oak Hill Church and Sunday school. In 1876, before the Choctaw government granted citizenship to freed slaves, J. Shoals, an elder of the church, began to provide Sunday school Bible lessons for both the young and old. Two years later, Henry Crittenden convinced the Oak Hill congregation to hire a carpenter, George Dallas, to build a small frame schoolhouse. After its completion, the carpenter taught a weekday school. In 1884, the school was transferred to an old log cabin. This was the first weekday school for African Choctaws in the area.[38]

After receiving a recommendation from Edwards of the Wheelock Academy in 1886, the Presbyterian Board of Missions of Freedman sent out the first White teacher for the school, Miss Eliza Hartford of Steubenville, Ohio. She arrived on February 14, 1886 and boarded with Henry Crittenden. With regard to the condition of the old log house, Hartford recorded, "The windows are without sash or glass and the roof full of holes. The chimneys are of hewn stone, strong and massive. The house is of hewed logs, two stories in height and stands high in the midst of a fine locust groves. The well of water near it seems as famous as Jacob's well." [39]

Typical of the patterns of freed slaves throughout the South, the community banded together to repair the school. As one of the missionaries sent to the school by the Board of Missions for Freedman, Robert Flickinger, wrote, "the colored people in the vicinity, after repairing the roof and windows, cleaned, scrubbed and whitewashed the inside of this old log house, and thus prepared it for its new and noble era of usefulness."[40] While the repairs were underway, Hartford opened the school on February 16, 1886 with an enrollment of seven students. One week later, the enrollment increased to 14. On April 15, 1886, after the completion of the repairs, Hartford moved into the school and began boarding 24 pupils. After a prayer meeting, women in the congregation decided to add a kitchen. In February 1887, Hartford requested another teacher and named the school the Oak Hill Industrial School.[41]

Henry Crittenden's prayer thanking God for the new White teacher reflected the community's attitude about the importance of literacy. Ironically, the attitude was similar to that of the Cherokees' in the earlier part of the century when they welcomed missionaries to provide them with the tools to resist the aggression of Whites. In thanking God, Crittenden declared: "That the prayers of His people were answered. In their bondage they had cried unto Him and He had heard their cry. In their ignorance and darkness they had asked for light and the light had come."[42]

In April, 1887, the school added its second White teacher, Priscilla Haymaker of Newlonsburg, Pennsylvania. With the coming of Haymaker, it was decided to build a new schoolhouse and chapel. Similar to the other work at Oak Hill, the building was done mainly with contributions and labor from the community. By September 1, 1887, the school was able to accommodate 60 pupils and 36 boarders.[43]

As an industrial academy, the Oak Hill Industrial School combined the teaching of reading, writing, and arithmetic with the teaching of mechanical and domestic skills. The flavor of this domestic training and attitudes toward the education of freed slaves is captured in a letter dated March 19, 1887 from Eliza Hartford to a friend.

This has been my wash day and I will give you my experience with a girl of 15, who is very ignorant about the simplest things relating to work. It is useless to tell Elizabeth how to do any work, unless one goes with her and shows her everything. Today I had her wash her own clothes by my side, while I washed mine to show her how, and how speedily she ought to do her own work. The only way to succeed in having them work is to work with them.

These poor Freedmen have a just claim on the church. They are far below their White brothers and sisters, but they are not to be blamed for it. Slavery has made them so, and we must do something to lift them up. *This however, will not be done by sending them to expensive schools, to make ladies and gentlemen of them, but where they will learn to work thought- fully and be taught the pure religion of the Bible* [italics added].[44]

Hartford's letter contains the three goals of missionary education—literacy, moral instruction, and instilling a work ethic—that missionaries and schoolmarms brought with them to Indian Territory. And just as the Choctaws and Cherokees welcomed the early missionaries who traveled the roads of Tennessee, North Carolina, Georgia, and Mississippi and helped them erect school buildings, the African Choctaw communities welcomed government and missionary aid in providing schools.

While the missionary and government schools provided the solace of religious instruction and the potential power of literacy, the social content of instruction tended to reinforce an unequal distribution of power and wealth. The schools of the Choctaw community were clearly segregated by wealth and political power, and the African Choctaw schools were segregated from those of the Choctaw community. But, despite segregation and the emphasis on moral instruction, as I have stated before, more Choctaws and freed Africans were attending school than White children in surrounding states, Iowa, and in the former homeland of Mississippi. For oppressed people, education has the potential of providing a road to liberation.

LANGUAGE SEGREGATION

"Unlike the Indian children," Raleigh Wilson observed in his study of African American and Native American relations in Indian Territory after the Civil War, "especially the full-bloods [Choctaws] who often spoke only their native tongue, the Negro children generally had a fair command of English and, hence, could learn more readily."[45]

Wilson's observation highlights important issues regarding bilingual education. The problems resulting from the language policies of the Choctaw Nation are illuminated by the bilingual education debate of the latter part of the 20th century. As Wilson pointed out, a knowledge of

English provides an opportunity to read more material written in English. It also provides an opportunity to participate in the English-speaking society that continues to politically and economically dominate Native American tribes.

On the other hand, as it is now argued, maintenance of traditional languages also aids in the maintenance of traditional cultures. Beginning in the 1960s, the Spanish-speaking community in the United States demanded that public school instruction be given in both Spanish and English as a method for improving the achievement of students and as a means of maintaining traditional Chicano and Puerto Rican cultures. In turn, Native American tribes made the same argument for bilingual education. Ideally, bilingual education would provide the opportunity for a student to participate in the dominant English-speaking society without having to give up traditional languages and cultures. Against the background of this latter argument regarding bilingual education, one can understand the problems inherent in the language policies of the Choctaw government.[46]

Choctaw as a written language was not developed for the purpose of maintaining traditional Choctaw culture. In fact, it was developed for the purpose of destroying traditional culture and replacing it with Christian beliefs and ethics. The missionaries who developed a written Choctaw language never considered the possibility of writing down Choctaw traditions and stories in Choctaw. They only wanted to translate Christian religious works into Choctaw. Consequently, the Choctaws' learning to read the native language actually undermined traditional culture.

As I discussed in chapter 7, Cyrus Byington, Alfred Wright, and John Edwards played important roles in developing a written Choctaw language and in translating religious works into Choctaw. A recent study of these translations suggests that they reflect the basic grammar of Choctaw in the early 19th century. Using the English alphabet, Byington created a phonetic key to the Choctaw language. This allowed for the translation of English into the phonetic symbols created by Byington.[47]

After Byington arrived in Indian Territory in 1835, he continued his work on the translation of the Bible until 1839, when he sent the manuscript to Boston for publication. Wright also continued his work in Indian Territory, completing his spelling book, *Chahta Nolisso,* in 1837. In 1840, he sent the parts of the Bible he had translated off to the publisher.[48] In 1850, Cyrus Byington assembled his manuscripts and left Indian Territory for New England and New York for 3 years to arrange for the printing of his translations of a hymn book, the books of Joshua, Judges, Ruth I and II, Samuel, an abridgement of Gallaudet's *Sacred Biography*, and the *Choctaw Definer*.[49]

With a written language, the Choctaws were able to operate bilingual newspapers and issue documents in both English and Choctaw. In 1848, the first newspaper in the Choctaw Nation was published in Choctaw and English. Edited by Daniel Folsom, the newspaper was published weekly for several years. In 1850, the *Choctaw Intelligencer* was launched as a bilingual newspaper.[50]

Prior to the Civil War, most neighborhood schools were taught in Choctaw. Choctaw was the language used in "Saturday and Sunday Schools" and "neighborhood" schools established by the Choctaw Nation in the 1840s. These schools were designed to serve those children who remained at home and adults.[51] The primary purpose of the Saturday and Sunday Schools was to teach reading of the Bible and pamphlets that had been translated into Choctaw. An 1842 report indicates that 159 children and adults were in Saturday and Sunday schools learning to read in the Choctaw language.[52]

The neighborhood schools were usually taught by Choctaw teachers who were trained in missionary schools. Instruction in reading, writing, and arithmetic was in Choctaw. In a letter to the War Department, U.S. Agent Armstrong wrote about one of these schools, "Two of the teachers are young ladies of about 18 years of age, native Choctaws. They conduct the schools and deserve great credit for their ability and exertions in behalf of their people. They speak the Choctaw language and have the entire confidence of the Nation."[53]

The result was that Choctaws who became literate in Choctaw could read the Choctaw language columns in the *Choctaw Intelligencer.* This made it possible for all Choctaws to be informed of events and laws in the Choctaw Nation. It also made it possible for Choctaws to have some form of written communication between each other. On the other hand, literacy in Choctaw only limited the reader to the newspaper, a handful of religious works translated by missionaries, and government laws.

Apparently, Basil Leflore's brother, Chief Thomas Leflore, was literate in Choctaw but not in English. It was possible for him to read and understand the Choctaw language version of the Choctaw constitution and laws, but when he wanted to communicate with English-speaking individuals and groups, he had to rely upon Basil, who studied English at the Choctaw Academy. In fact, those who could only speak and read only in Choctaw had to depend on bilingual Choctaws for dealings with English-speaking society. This placed monolingual Choctaws at a serious economic and political disadvantage.

After the Choctaw Nation created the position of Principal Chief in the 1850s, as I indicated in chapter 6, all the Principal Chiefs, with one exception, were taught in English-speaking schools. This would seem to indicate a further isolation of the monolingual Choctaw from positions of power in the Choctaw Nation.

There was the possibility of overcoming this language disadvantage after the Civil War, when neighborhood schools began to teach in English only. When superintendent Forbis Leflore took office in the 1870s, the curriculum of the neighborhood schools was modeled on the public schools in the states. More full-blood children were brought into the school system with the passage of the 1884 compulsory attendance law that fined parents if their children were not in school. But similar to the African-Choctaw schools, these neighborhood schools never received as much funding as the academies. Although they were supposed to operate for 9 to 10 months, they often closed after 4 or 5 months because of lack of funds.[54]

The language policies of the neighborhood schools were not ideal for teaching English or other subject matter to non-English-speaking students. For instance, students were discouraged from speaking Choctaw in the classroom. All the textbooks came from the States, including U.S. history books, and all of them were written in English.[55] Current research on language instruction suggests that literacy in the language of the home aids in the learning of a foreign language. For instance, a person coming from an English-speaking home finds it easier to learn French or another foreign language if they first learn to read and write in English. In addition, if all the textbooks in the classroom are in a foreign language, it is difficult to keep up with other subjects while learning that foreign language. For example, an English-speaking child entering a French-speaking classroom with all the textbooks written in French will have difficulty learning arithmetic and history while simultaneously learning French. It would be much easier for the English-speaking student to be taught both in English and French and to begin studying other subjects in English before making a transition to using textbooks written only in French.[56]

In addition, the textbooks from the States must have had the same effect of deculturalization as the Choctaw language books focusing on Christianity, particularly the U.S. history books that depicted the struggle of White settlers against heathen Indians. The only thing used in the classroom that tied in directly to the Choctaw Nation was the Choctaw Constitution. But in the context of traditional culture, a written constitution was a White person's idea. Although most of the teachers in the neighborhood schools in the latter part of the 19th century were Choctaws educated at tribal schools, they were not examined for literacy in Choctaw or knowledge of Choctaw history and traditions. They were examined in common school subjects, including U.S. history and government, and in their knowledge of the Choctaw constitution.[57]

The Choctaw-speaking child was at a serious disadvantage in a neighborhood school due to the combination of inadequate funding, instruction only in English, textbooks in English, and the teachers' possible lack of knowledge of written Choctaw, Choctaw history, and Choctaw traditions. White teachers in the system even lacked a knowledge of spoken Choctaw.

CHOCTAW SCHOOLS
AND THE LIFE OF THE FULL-BLOODS

An understanding of the problems facing Choctaw-speaking students and most full-bloods in the latter part of the 19th century is available through interviews conducted in the 1930s with Native Americans who lived in Indian Territory prior to its demise. Although those interviewed are not named, their remembrances provide insights into life in neighborhood schools, social class differences, and continuing cultural traditions.

In one interview, an elderly Choctaw lamented that he barely knew how to read and write, and, because of this educational handicap, he felt, "I am a slave instead of the Negroes." He was quite aware of the social class differences in the Choctaw school system and commented that some children went to school until they could read "a book called history." From his perspective, knowledge of this book qualified them for an examination by the superintendent, which could result in their being sent to college in the States. "Just children of the better-to-do people," he said, "got to go and get an education."[58]

He clearly linked education and money: "People with money and an education lived better than we did."[59] He described those with education and money as living in nice frame houses with cook stoves, wearing store-bought clothes, and owning livestock. In contrast, he grew up in a log cabin where the cooking was done in the fireplace with pots and iron skillets. The family ate out of their cooking utensils.

Another Choctaw remembered the pressure not to speak Choctaw at the Armstrong Academy. The Armstrong Academy opened the same year as the Fort Coffee Academy. During the Civil War, the Armstrong Academy became the headquarters of the Choctaw government. Later it was reopened as an orphanage for boys. The parents of the Choctaw being interviewed died in 1903 and 1904, and his uncle took him to the Armstrong Academy. As part of the student initiation at the school, he remembers being taken by another student to a cemetery on the pretext of meeting a teacher. On arriving, he found a kangaroo court composed of students. He was immediately asked a series of questions, and, he stated, "I answered all questions in my own native tongue and was instantly told that I was not allowed to talk in my own tongue but must talk in English." He was found guilty of "talking Choctaw." He was sentenced to wrestling a series of other boys until he lost.[60]

An example of the establishment of neighborhood schools and the conditions within them is captured in an interview with a former teacher. In this particular interview, it was revealed that my grandfather rented her a house in 1900 in Goodland. My grandfather was one of the founders of the town. She recalled, "I returned to our home at Goodland, known now as Hugo, and taught the first day school for

Indians . . . I rented a vacant house from Joel Spring and converted it into a schoolhouse." She received a salary of $75 a month from the Choctaw government. The school had no desks and, consequently, the younger children sat on a long bench holding their books and slates in their laps. The older children sat around a long table. For instruction, she used "McGuffey's Latest System, cardboard style." A piece of cardboard was hung on the wall with a picture and the lesson.[61]

After 1 year in Hugo, the teacher got married and moved 5 miles west of Goodland, where her new husband built one large room for a school behind their house. She called it the Wigwam School and taught there for 3 years.

Many full-bloods felt, as indicated in the first interview, they were worse off economically and socially than African Choctaws. The significant differences in wealth and culture between poor full-bloods and wealthier mixed-bloods by the end of the 19th century is captured in another series of interviews. One Choctaw remembered their first family home to be a two-room log cabin with a stick-and-mud chimney and a fireplace used for cooking. Most of the houses, occupied by full-bloods, the person recalled, had no windows and only one door. During the summer, the chinking between the logs was knocked out to provide extra ventilation. Those houses with windows usually lacked glass and had to use shutters on cold days. Wood was gathered from the countryside and water obtained from a well.[62]

Food was a major problem. One person remembered their father traveling to Arkansas along with other Indians to obtain flour, sugar, and coffee. They raised corn and used it to make bread. His mother made a mortar for the corn out of a post of oak block that was square on each end. A bowl 7 inches deep for grinding corn was formed by burning coals in one end of the post. The mother also gathered roots for the dinner table. This Choctaw remembered, "We had a hard living in those days."[63]

In contrast, an interview with the White daughter of the housekeeper at the Rose Hill Plantation provides a portrait of living conditions of the wealthy mixed-bloods. It is interesting to note that Jones employed a White housekeeper as opposed to using an enslaved African. She remembered Rose Hill as a two-story framed house with the interior completed with material imported from France. The house had the first transoms over the door that she had ever seen. She described the first floor as having a wide hall, dividing two large front rooms with fireplaces of native stone in contrast to the stick-and-mud fireplaces of the full-bloods. The back of the hall extended to two more large rooms. According to her, by the end of the century, Jones owned 28 stores and four farms totaling 28,000 acres. His two steamboats docked at a large warehouse and store on the Red River.[64]

Many full-bloods retained traditional Choctaw beliefs. At one level, many cultural changes had occurred among the full-bloods. They were no longer polygamous, their family names were carried by the father, the clan system was gone, and traditional religious practices had given way to Christianity. In addition, the full-bloods were now living under a government with a formal system of laws and police.

Many of these cultural changes were the result of conversion to Christianity. The missionaries and circuit riders were successful. As one Choctaw stated, "It does not matter how far out in the woods one may live, he would rather live near to church where he can attend meetings. This has been the practice of the Choctaw Indian that he is not satisfied unless he attends church now and then."[65] Little log cabin churches, he said, were scattered across the country. During the summer, Choctaws simply used a brush arbor for a church.

But despite the influence of the schools and of Christianity, Choctaw superstitions and traditions are mentioned frequently in the interviews. Choctaw baseball, something missionaries hated because of the gambling and all-night dancing associated with games, continued through the 19th century. One man interviewed in the 1930s said he still had his ball sticks made of hickory with a basket on the end. Another man recalled the games as "really rough." He belonged to the Gaines County team that played against teams from other counties in the Choctaw Nation. "Any kind of rough treatment," he said, "as long as the hands alone were used, was permissible."[66]

A belief in herb doctors and witches continued into the 20th century. One man recalled that in 1907, after a frustrating day of deer hunting, he went to the home of an herb doctor and asked to become a great hunter. She told him that the treatment would make his hair permanently gray. She gathered herbs, and then she "smoked" him once a day for 4 days. According to him, his hair did turn gray and he did become a great hunter.[67]

Many full-bloods continued to rely on traditional medicine. One person claimed the herbs and teas given by medicine men were effective, although their rites were "a lot of humbug." The medicine men gave cascara made from the wahoo bush to those who felt run down. The May apple root was used as a general medicine.[68]

Apparently, one of my relatives was a witch. One person remembered, "there was an old woman named Spring who was considered a witch. . . . People said that black cats talked to her, but I never did see a black cat at her house." When his father complained of neuritis, one of Spring's sons told him to go to his mother with a gallon of lard. He remembers standing with his father while watching witch Spring boil a mixture of roots of bear foot weed and bittersweet with other herbs. The mixture was boiled down and then mixed with the lard. The father applied the mixture and was cured.[69]

When Spring's daughter became sick, Spring sought a cure from another witch named Snow. This witch announced that the illness was a result of being shot by a "witch ball." With the use of a pillow case, Snow enveloped the daughter's head in vapors from a pot of boiling roots. After about a half hour, Snow strained the liquid from the pot and found the witch ball made of human hair in the strainer.[70]

The history of Choctaw funeral practices provides a good example of the modification of cultural traditions. As the reader will recall, my great-great grandmother in the early 19th century received a traditional funeral that included placing the body on a high rack until the flesh was removed from the bones. After 6 months, a bone picker would be used to remove the final bits of flesh and the clan would gather to have a "Big Indian Cry." The "Big Indian Cry" involved wailing and other traditional signs of grief. The bones would then be placed in a special house. By the time the Choctaws arrived in Indian Territory, bone picking had ended, and bodies were typically buried near the home or under the porch. Six months later, relatives would gather for the "Big Indian Cry."

By the early 20th century, bodies were still buried near the house in a pit lined with rough hewn logs with the body placed on a feather bed. When a man lost his wife, he would go bare headed or wrap his head in a handkerchief until after the cry. Then he would be able to marry. If the husband died, the woman would remain in the house until the cry and then she would also be able to marry.[71]

One major change in this tradition was the dispensing with the "Big Indian Cry." Interviewed in the 1930s, one man said, "They don't have the Indian cries that they used to have. . . All the Indians took part in the cries, but they have quit now on account of the white people making fun at them."[72] This same full-blood Choctaw admitted that he had never been to school and could not speak or write in English. As late as the 1930s, this full-blood stated, "I can speak the Choctaw language but that is all."[73]

Missionaries, government officials, and mixed-bloods failed in their efforts to instill in many full-bloods a strong desire to acquire property. The avaricious nature of Whites was not transplanted into the character of many full-bloods. From the time of the early colonists, Whites had criticized Native Americans for sharing property and lacking a desire to work hard to accumulate wealth. Many full-bloods expressed their distaste for the avaricious nature of White society.

CONCLUSION: THE EFFECT OF SCHOOLS

By the closing days of the Nation, Choctaw society had evolved into a complex multiracial community with social class divisions determined by wealth, race, and language. It was in the context of this community that the historical thread of racism touched my father.

The Choctaw educational system contributed to establishing and maintaining these racial and language divisions. At the top of the political and economic system were bilingual mixed-bloods who created an educational system to maintain their privileged positions. Whites marrying into the tribe, although having the advantage of being English-speaking, did not have access to political positions because of the constitutional requirement that office holders have Choctaw ancestry. This constitutional requirement also kept African Choctaws out of political office.

In addition, school segregation reinforced racist feelings. Despite sharing the bottom of the social and economic ladder with poor full-bloods, many African Choctaws did have the advantage of speaking English. The Choctaw government provided full-bloods with schools that were inadequately funded and operated with language policies that made it difficult for the monolingual full-blood child to become bilingual.

For full-bloods, bilingualism was not a major disadvantage in the Choctaw republic. Common ownership of land provided the opportunity to live in contentment while maintaining small agricultural plots, hunting, and fishing. But being monolingual became a serious disadvantage for full-bloods when Indian Territory became Oklahoma. Also, with the coming of statehood, the continued disinterest in accumulating property made the full-blood vulnerable to the avaricious nature of Whites.

NOTES

[1]Comment in the 1930s by full-blood Choctaw on social and economic conditions in Oklahoma. In Theda Perdue, *Nations Remembered: an Oral History of the Cherokees, Chickasaws, Choctaws, Creeks, and Seminoles in Oklahoma, 1865–1907* (Norman: University of Oklahoma Press, 1993), p. 139.

[2]*Reflections on Goodland Volume I* edited by David Dearinger (Hugo, OK: Goodland Presbyterian Children's Home, 1992. Pages are unnumbered, but this quote can be found on the second page of chapter 3. Also see, "Joel Spring, Pioneer Hugo Citizen, Played Important Part in History," *The Hugo Daily News*, Cavalcade Edition, Section 3, August 28–29, 1941, pp. 1–2.

[3]George Wood, *Visit to Choctaw and Cherokee Missions* (Boston: Press of T.R. Martin, 1855), p. 6.

[4]Grant Foreman, *The Five Civilized Tribes* (Norman: University of Oklahoma Press, 1934), p. 83.

[5]Wood, p. 10.

[6]Ibid., p. 11.

[7]Ibid., p. 13.

[8]Ibid., p. 13.

[9]Ibid., pp. 5–6.

[10]Ibid., p. 6.

[11]Ibid., p. 10.

[12]Ibid., p. 18.

[13]Annie Heloise Abel, *The american indian as Slaveholder and Secessionist* (Lincoln: University of Nebraska Press, 1992), p. 74.

[14]This resolution is reprinted in Abel, p. 73.

[15]Angie Debo, *The Rise and Fall of the Choctaw Republic* (Norman: University of Oklahoma Press, 1961), pp. 81–82.

[16]Ibid., Abel, p. 156.

[17]Eloise Spear, *Choctaw Indian Education With Special Reference to Choctaw conty, Oklahoma* (Ann Arbor: University Microfilms International, 1977), pp. 136–148.

[18]Frances Imon, *Smoke Signals From Indian Territory* (Wolfe City, TX: Henington Publishing Company, 1976) p. 65.

[19]I am using the term *African Choctaws* because of the unusual circumstances surrounding the citizenship of freed Choctaw slaves. Originally, these enslaved Africans were owned by choctaws who were without U.S. citizenship. After the Civil War, Choctaws and freed Africans still did not have U.S. citizenship. Eventually, Choctaw citizenship was extended to these freed Africans. U.S. citizenship was granted to Choctaws and freed Africans in 1901. Therefore, I am using the term African Choctaws to indicate the citizenship of these freed Africans between the end of the Civil War and 1901.

[20]Debo, p. 99.

[21]Raleigh Archie Wilson, *Negro and Indian Relations in the Five Civilized Tribes From 1865–1907* (Dissertation: University of Iowa, 1949), p. 232.

[22]Debo, *The Rise and Fall of the Choctaw Republic*, p. 100.

[23]Ibid., pp. 89, 102–103.

[24]Ibid., pp. 104–105.

[25]Ibid.

[26]Ibid., p. 108.

[27]Ibid., pp. 105, 109.

[28]Debo, *The Rise and Fall of the Choctaw Republic*, p. 100.

[29]James D. Anderson, *The Education of Blacks in the South 1860–1935* (Chapel Hill: The University of North Carolina Press, 1988).

[30]Ibid., p. 104.

[31]Spear, p. 166.

[32]Robert Flickinger, *The Choctaw Freedman and the Story of the Oak Hill Industrial Academy* (Pittsburgh: Presbyterian Board of Missions to Freedman, 1914), p. 103.

[33]Ibid., p. 104.

[34]Ibid., p. 104.
[35]Wilson, pp. 197–199.
[36]Ibid., p. 193.
[37]Ibid., pp. 189–190.
[38]Flickinger, pp. 103–104 and Spear, p. 164.
[39]Flickinger, p. 108.
[40]Ibid., pp. 108–109.
[41]Ibid., pp. 107–109.
[42]Ibid., p. 109.
[43]Ibid., pp. 109–113.
[44]Ibid., p. 115.
[45]Wilson, p. 193.
[46]For a discussion of language policies see joel Spring, *Intersection of Cultures: Multicultural Education in the United States* (New York: McGraw-Hill, 1995), pp. 117–134.
[47]Carolyn Keller Reeves, "Some Observations about the Choctaw Language of the Early Nineteenth Century," in *The Choctaw Before Removal*, pp. 17–21.
[48]Foreman, pp. 55–56.
[49]Ibid., p. 84.
[50]Ibid., p. 70.
[51]Spear, p. 116.
[52]Ibid., p. 33.
[53]Foreman, pp. 77–78.
[54]Angie Debo, "Education in the Choctaw Country After the Civil War," *Chronicles of Oklahoma* (1932), pp. 383–91.
[55]Ibid., p. 386.
[56]Spring, pp. 117–134.
[57]Debo, "Education in the Choctaw Country...," p. 384.
[58]Theda Perdue, *Nations Remembered: An Oral History of the Cherokees, Choctaws, Creeks, and Seminoles in Oklahoma 1865–1907* (Norman: University of Oklahoma Press, 1993), p. 139.
[59]Ibid., p. 139.
[60]Ibid., p. 131.
[61]Ibid., p. 137.
[62]Ibid., p. 50.
[63]Ibid., p. 53.
[64]Ibid., pp. 45–46.
[65]Ibid., p. 126.
[66]Ibid., pp. 77–78.
[67]Ibid., p. 58.
[68]Ibid., p. 103.
[69]Ibid., p. 103.
[70]Ibid., p. 104.
[71]Ibid., p. 144.

[72]Ibid., pp. 128–129.
[73]Ibid., p. 129.

9

From Thomas Jefferson to Henry Ford: The End of the Choctaw Republic

"There is no selfishness, which is the bottom of civilization," Senator Henry L. Dawes of Massachusetts complained about the Native Americans in Indian Territory. Speaking at the third annual meeting of the Mohonk Conference in 1883, Dawes praised the achievements of the Five Civilized Tribes, but, he argued, "They have got as far as they can go, because they own their land in common . . . and under that there is no enterprise to make your home any better than that of your neighbors."[1]

This complaint—that Indians would not be civilized until they desired to improve and accumulate property—was first heard from English colonists; it was reiterated by Thomas Jefferson; it was used to justify removal to Indian Territory; and finally it was used to end the common ownership of land. It was the central maxim of the Protestant ethic that laziness was an evil that could be overcome by being acquisitive. Desire for property, it was believed, caused humans to work hard. In the end, as it had so many times in the past, it was the acquisitive desires of Whites for land that led to the demise of the Choctaw Republic.

Of course, many Choctaws did practice the art of selfishness. There was Robert M. Jones and his Rose Hill plantation, and my grandfather, who used the downfall of the Choctaw Republic as an opportunity to help found Hugo, Oklahoma and literally plaster his name across buildings in the downtown area, including a building that housed the Hugo National Bank that was still standing in the early 1990s. The story of the demise of the Choctaw Nation, my grandfather's entrepreneurship, and the breakup of my family can be traced to the Mohonk Conferences and the Dawes Commission. Therefore, I begin the story at the Mohonk Mountain House, which still stands, due to another twist in history, a few miles from my office at New Paltz College.

179

THE DAWES COMMISSION

Perched on a small mountain about 80 miles from New York City, the Mohonk Mountain House on one side overlooks a clear mountain lake and on the other side, a deep valley. In the 19th century, it was a favorite retreat for self-styled humanitarians. The group to which Senator Dawes addressed his remarks on selfishness called itself the Lake Mohonk Conference of Friends of the Indian. It held meetings from 1883 to 1916. The participation and leadership of Senator Dawes resulted in the resolutions of the Lake Mohonk Conference's having a significant impact on Congressional legislation.

At its second meeting in 1884, the Lake Mohonk Conference issued a series of resolutions regarding the "Indian problem" in the United States. The first resolution called for the abolition of Native American tribes and governments, and the second resolution dealt with the issue of common ownership of land. "Resolved, That the organization of the Indian in tribes is, and has been," the first resolution states, "one of the most serious hindrances to the advancement of the Indian toward civilization, and that every effort should be made to secure the disintegration of all tribal organizations. . . ." This radical and, certainly, arrogant view of tribal governments was followed by a second resolution: "Resolved, That to all Indians who desire to hold their land severalty allotments should be made without delay; *and that to all other Indians like allotments should be made so soon as practicable* [italics added]."[2]

As an important step in achieving the breakdown of tribal governments, the Mohonk resolutions called for the granting of U.S. citizenship to all Native Americans after they went through a process "analogous to naturalization." From the perspective of the Mohonk Conference, U.S. citizenship would undermine the loyalty of Native Americans to their Indian Nations. In 1901, the Native Americans in Indian Territory were granted U.S. citizenship 12 years before the "Indian Citizenship Act of 1924."[3]

And, echoing a century of Indian policies, the Mohonk Conference resolutions called for the education of Native Americans in farming, industrial training, language, and religion. Similar to what Jefferson and McKenney called for in the early 19th century, the Mohonk Conference proclaimed "Resolved, That education is essential to civilization. The Indian must have knowledge of the English language . . . practical industrial training to fit him to compete with others in the struggle for life . . . [and] a Christian education to enable him to perform duties of the family, the State, and the Church."[4]

To make these changes, the Mohonk Conference concluded, required legislative action. With the resolutions in hand, Senator Dawes returned to Congress to give his name to the Dawes Act of 1887. In line with the Lake Mohonk Conference resolutions, the Dawes Act gave the President

the Indian Nations. Strange as it sounds, the town was named after French author Victor Hugo because the wife of one of the town developers admired his writings.

A photograph appearing in a 1916 booklet boosting the community of Hugo captures the excitement of the early years of real estate speculation. The photograph, taken before the actual building of Hugo, shows five men in heavy coats posed in front of a large white tent set on a barren plain. The only buildings are a small, weathered, framed building with a horse tied to the side and a small warehouse or barn. The caption to the picture reads:

> Hugo, Oklahoma Before Statehood: Small investments here have grown into great fortunes. The Southwestern Land Company has been the chief factor in this development. The future growth of this most prosperous city is now assured. Would you like to share some of the profits to investors to be derived from the building of this new city?[18]

Speculation and boosterism dominated the spirit of the townsite sales. Would the new town succeed? Would a rush of White settlers cause real estate prices to skyrocket? How could the buyers of townsites boost the importance of their community so that more White settlers would be attracted to the area? The Oklahoma land rush was on. And, similar to the rush for cotton lands in Mississippi in the 1830s, the Oklahoma land rush left many full-bloods with the poorest land.[19]

The Hugo townsites went up for sale in 1901 and, despite cold weather, the first building was completed in February 1902. The rush to complete these new Oklahoma towns was captured by a 1906 newspaper article describing the rapid construction of Hugo: "Since the first nail was driven there has been about 80 working days, at least one-fourth of which were so cold that no outside work could be done. Thus the actual number of working days are reduced to about 60, and for every working day more than six new buildings have been added to the list."[20]

A key question for the land speculators was: Where would the center of town be located? This question was resolved by my grandfather's stealing the post office from his relative, Samuel Bailey Spring. The townsite plot was divided by a railroad. In 1901, Samuel Bailey Spring was appointed the first U.S. Postmaster for Hugo and located the post office in his store west of the tracks. This greatly increased the value of his lands because the post office usually served as the center of the downtown business district. In 1903, my grandfather and a business partner, R. L. Overstreet, raided the post office and moved it to an area east of the tracks that became the downtown business district.

In 1905, my grandfather completed the Hugo National Bank building that still stands on the east side of the tracks in the old downtown area of Hugo. When walking through Hugo in the early 1990s, I felt rooted in Oklahoma history to see "Joel Spring 1905" on the top corner of the building. The Palace Drug Store was built on the other side of the street a block away. In what is now a dusty and forlorn looking business section of abandoned buildings were the dreams of the Oklahoma land speculators of the early 20th century.

SCHOOLS AND THE END OF "CIVILIZING"

"Destined to be One of the Foremost Cities in the Great New State, where Huge Fortunes are Being Made on Small Investments," proclaimed a promotional pamphlet distributed in 1916 by the Southwestern Land Company of Hugo. Part of the sales pitch to investors and families, as it has been in U.S. communities throughout the 20th century, was the claim of having good schools. A photograph of a two-story brick building was proudly captioned: "$35,000 High School Hugo, Okla." And another showed "Two of the $25,000 Ward Schools, Hugo, Okla."[21]

What happened to the Choctaw school system in the rush of White settlers and the growth of small-town boosterism? By the 1890s, the major source of support of the Choctaw schools was coal revenues. The Atoka Agreement gave control over these revenues to the U.S. government. Consequently, the U.S. government assumed takeover of revenues meant takeover of the schools, and in 1899 John D. Benedict of Illinois was made superintendent of the tribal school systems.

Benedict took over a Choctaw school system which by 1893 had 189 neighborhood schools with 3,819 students enrolled; 7 boarding schools with 490 enrolled; and 40 students enrolled in colleges in the states. Figures available for 1887 indicate the Choctaw government spent $7,975 to send 13 girls and 14 boys to college. It is important to note, regarding the status of women in the tribe, that there were almost an equal number of males and females sent to college on government funds. Through the years, many of the students sent to college in the states became prominent lawyers, doctors, and politicians in the Nation.[22]

Superintendent Benedict complained about the academic emphasis in many Indian schools. He argued that Indian boys should be trained for industry and girls for the household. Also, he began to recruit new teachers that resulted, by the time he was through, in the elimination of most Native American teachers. Later, Benedict was charged with corruption and general neglect of the schools. By the time of Oklahoma's statehood in 1907, Benedict's administration resulted in an actual decline in school enrollments and most of the schools were in a state of disrepair.[23]

Of course, the tribes protested the takeover of their schools. After all, Native American-controlled education, according to the arguments of the 1820s and 1830s, was supposed to "civilize" Indians. Indians, particularly those without wealth, feared that White takeover of the schools would result in discrimination and a denial of education to Indians. One Chickasaw Indian explained, "Now, when I take a little Indian child to school the white man and the negroes will go before me to school with their children and they will put their children first and they will push mine out of school, and that is the way it will go."[24]

The Choctaw government stopped funding segregated schools after the signing of the Atoka Agreement. Under the Atoka Agreement, African Choctaws could not receive funds for mineral rights. Consequently, the Choctaws stopped funding segregated schools from coal money and refused admission of African Choctaws into Indian schools even with offers to pay tuition. This resulted in the closing of at least 34 neighborhood schools and one academy for African Choctaws. In hindsight, one could argue that the wealth of the Choctaw Nation was in part the result of exploiting slave labor and, therefore, freed slaves were entitled to part of the Nation's wealth, including its mineral resources. This was one of the final acts of racism as the curtain began to close on the Choctaw Republic.[25]

Spurred by boosterism and the desire to attract investors, the new townsites began organizing schools, as tribal schools were rapidly declining. An educational huckster opened the first school in Hugo. Advertising himself as Professor W. D. Hoffman of Pennsylvania, a person named Martin opened a subscription school in 1902. After it was discovered that he stole the diploma of a Hoffman who graduated from the Pennsylvania Normal School, Martin was run out of town.[26]

Similar to other towns created under the Atoka Agreement and the Curtis Act in Indian Territory, local boards of education were organized prior to the creation of a state system of schools. Their major concern was creating schools for White children moving into the area. After Martin (a.k.a. Professor Hoffman) was run out of town, an election was organized to create a school board. By 1904, Hugo was operating its first public school and in 1906 built a high school. This public school system was linked to a statewide school system in 1907 with the birth of Oklahoma.[27]

THE ALLOTMENT SYSTEM

On May 8, 1899, my grandfather and grandmother took their brood of six children to the post office in Goodland, Indian Territory to be registered on the Choctaw Rolls with the Dawes Commission.[28] Three years prior to registration, when the Spencer Academy burned, my grandfather was listed as a local tribal chief—Chief Joel Spring.[29] On the Dawes Commission rolls, my grandfather was given roll number

3874 and my grandmother, Winnie Spring (Gooding), was given roll number 3875. The rest of the children were given numbers ranging from 3876 to 3881. My father, Cicero Spring (for obvious reasons he took William as his first name later on in life) was born in 1903 and was placed on the Choctaw Rolls that year as a newborn and given a roll number NB-968.[30]

As if to give the appearance of fairness to the breaking of treaties, and the fraud and corruption of the allotment system, the Dawes Commission rolls were done in meticulous handwriting with neat columns indicating blood quantum and the registration dates of parents. Adding an official air to the document is the stamp of approval of the Secretary of the Interior.

Of course, the allotment rolls broke the Treaty of Dancing Rabbit Creek. With hundreds of clerks and surveyors, the Dawes Commission began its work in 1896. Many of the full-bloods did not even know what was happening and were tracked down in the backwoods. Some full-bloods refused to be listed because they rejected the whole allotment process. Redbird Smith, a full-blood Cherokee, reported to a Senate Committee in 1902 that when he refused to enroll, he was arrested and put in jail. "They kept me all night in jail," he told the committee, "and on Sunday morning the let me out, and then they took me to the commissioner's office and made me enroll against my will."[31]

The varying value of the land complicated the allotment process. Obviously, 320 acres of good farmland was worth more than 320 acres of poor farmland. Consequently, assessors for the Dawes Commission surveyed the land, attaching different values for different sections. When the final distribution of land was made, the allotment to citizens of "320 acres of average land" varied in amount from 160 to 4,165 acres and the freedman's sections of 40 acres of land varied from 20 to 521 acres. Newborns, such as my father, received 160 average acres.[32]

There was a great deal of false information given to the Dawes Commission because of the restrictions placed on the sale of allotments by Indians listed as having over 50% Choctaw blood. Consequently, many Choctaws, including my grandfather and grandmother, lied about their ancestry. Therefore, the final rolls do not indicate the true number of full-bloods. When the rolls closed on March 4, 1907, there were listed on the Choctaw rolls 7,087 full-bloods, 10,401 mixed-bloods, 1,651 Whites (with Choctaw citizenship), and 6,029 freedman. The total citizenship of the Choctaw Republic was, therefore, 25,168. It should be noted that the largest "blood group" on the roll was mixed bloods and that the number of African Choctaws almost equaled the number of full-bloods.[33]

And, of course, as Debo details in *And Still the Waters Run: The Betrayal of the Five Civilized Tribes,* it was the full-bloods and the African Choctaws who were most vulnerable to swindlers and speculators. Those full-bloods who retained their allotments lived in remote hill sections with poor farmland. An Indian receiving 4,000 acres of poor land, as opposed to 320 acres of average land, could not grow enough food to maintain a family. A 1927 Congressional investigation found full-blood Choctaws menaced by famine while living on one or two meals a day of corn bread and gravy supplemented by an Indian drink made of parched corn. The investigation found a number of deaths resulting from "undernourishment" and "diseases due to insufficient nutrition."[34]

Driven from their homes in Mississippi in the 1830s, where the rich soil and bountiful game provided a world without starvation, the full-bloods now ate the dust of the hill country of Oklahoma without the protection of the Choctaw Republic. Assuming they would always have their Nation as promised by Andrew Jackson, they had learned to function in a world where literacy only in Choctaw was required. Speaking and reading only Choctaw, many full-bloods found themselves disconnected from the English-speaking governments of the state and towns of Oklahoma. Their tribal schools controlled by the Choctaw Republic were replaced by the schools of the U.S. Bureau of Indian Affairs. It is little wonder that the poor full-bloods in the hills of Oklahoma became an embittered people.

FROM THOMAS JEFFERSON TO HENRY FORD

While many full-bloods were languishing in the hills, my grandfather rode the crest of the boom, moving his store and home from Goodland to Hugo. "Chief Joel Spring," my aunt Winnie Spring Griffith commented in a 1969 interview, "whose wife was Winnie R. Gooding, was Hugo's most outstanding citizen. In 1902, Chief Spring moved his store, the Goodland Trading Post, to Hugo, and he built a large rambling house whose spacious grounds covered a city block."[35] My grandfather's wave of fortune came crashing down with his sudden death at the age of 45 on February 21, 1907. Born in the middle of the Civil War, he experienced life in the Choctaw Republic and, similar to some other mixed-bloods, profited in its collapse. He died the same year as statehood came to Oklahoma. A 12-foot-high ornate monument rests on his grave in the Spring Chapel Cemetery south of Hugo.

My grandmother, the granddaughter of Basil Leflore, was left with five dependent children, my grandfather's debts from his speculation in real estate, and without the protection and support of the Choctaw Republic. Three of her other children were grown up and, of course, one died in the Spencer Academy fire. Winnie Gooding was born on April 27, 1867 and died at the age of 96 on November 23, 1963. Reflecting the decline in the family's economic fortunes, only a small stone marks her grave next to the monumental stones of my grandfather and uncle.

Mirroring the crumbling of the Choctaw Nation, my grandmother's family began to fall apart with the death of her husband. One of her sons killed a man after a fight in a dance hall. The man left the dance hall with my uncle's horse. My uncle killed the man with his pistol and, changing his name, fled to California. My father found him many years later.

I once asked my father at what age he learned to ride a horse. He remembered that it was sometime around the age of 3 or 4 his father was still living. When he reached school age, he said, his horse would often miss the school and end up at a fishing pond. When my father entered his early teens he went wild. My father literally became a wild Indian. One day, the story is told, he rode his horse through Hugo, shooting out store windows and pockmarking buildings. Then he started running away by riding the rails under box cars. One time, he was riding on the cow catcher of a steam engine when it hit a cow, spraying him with blood and bits of flesh and intestines. My grandmother tried to control him by sending him east to a military school. He was thrown out of the school after beating up the commander's son. My father remembered the trip to the military academy while we were standing together in Cincinnati's Fountain Square in the 1970s. "That's the corner," he recalled, "where I went for a beer around 1916 [he was thirteen at the time] when I was sent to the Academy."

One day in 1919, he rode the rails to Springfield, Missouri, where he met a Navy recruiter who convinced him to join even though my father had never seen salt water. Lying about his age, he was sent at the age of 16 to the Great Lakes Naval Training Center north of Chicago. The Navy was a secure job for a person interested in drinking, brawling, and gambling. It was particularly secure for an "Okie" with no skills during the Depression years of the 1930s.

What did my father do with his Indian allotment, the land that was the final payment for ancestral lands in Mississippi and Indian Territory? He sold the allotment in the early 1920s and used the money to buy a Model T Ford to drive over dirt and plank roads to California. My father fulfilled Jefferson's dream by selling his land for manufactured goods.

My father married and quickly divorced during the 1920s. In San Francisco in the early 1930s, he met my mother. Now, my mother's family is another story. They were true products of the White person's movement west. In passing, I will just mention that her grandmother on her mother's side—a tough-looking woman from her photograph—owned a string of brothels in San Francisco and made a small fortune providing housing to the homeless after the great San Francisco earthquake. She made my grandmother sleep in a bathtub in one of her establishments so that there would be more room for paying guests. My mother, Hazel Meachem, became Hazel Spring on May 10, 1932 in a secular ceremony before the judge of the municipal court in San Francisco. She was 20 years old at the time of the ceremony and had recently killed her boyfriend in an automobile accident.

What is interesting about their marriage certificate is Section 4, labeled "Color or Race." Nothing so clearly indicates the social construction of the meaning of race as this section on the official California marriage form of the 1930s. Using color and race as a combined category, would a person of African and European ancestry in the 1930s who had White skin be classified as white or Negro? Would a person born into the Choctaw tribe who inherited his great-grandfather's blue eyes and a ruddy complexion, and whose great-grandfather was a Principal Chief and whose father was a local Chief, be classified as White or Indian? In California, my father was classified as White.

Of course, I do not know what role my mother might have had in classifying my father as White. Like my father, she was also a racist and her racism included Indians. "Don't tell anyone your father is an Indian," she would always remind me. "Be proud that you're part German and Scottish," she advised, referring to her part of the family. "Germans are the most intelligent people." Her father was a Prussian army officer who ended up tending a train station in Milford, Utah in the early 20th century. I always wondered how the Prussian grandfather could be more intelligent than Chief Joel Spring or Principal Chief Basil Leflore.

My father continued his drinking, gambling, and womanizing until my mother divorced him near the end of World War II while he was serving in the Pacific. "All he thought about was sex," she told me when I reached an age for understanding this type of remark. Now, her remark reminds me of the early reaction of English colonists to the free sexuality of Native Americans. Of course, she was not without her sexual side. After living in a series of foster homes, I joined her as she traveled from Los Angeles to San Diego, to Florida, and back to San Francisco, and then on to Hawaii for a couple of years, and then finally back to San Diego where I graduated from Mission Bay High School in 1958. All along the route, she told me of her many lovers. After all, this was the granddaughter of the reputed "Grand Madam" of San Francisco.

In the meantime, my father drank his way through a number of marriages. At one time, I was told he married seven times. But my brother gave me a lower number and my father was unwilling to confirm any number. My father, I guess, was practicing a modern form of the traditional Choctaw practice of polygamy. Because he enlisted at the age of 16, he was able to retire at the relatively young age of 46 in 1949 after 30 years in the Navy. Buying one of the first Airstream trailers in the early 1950s, he traveled back and forth between Florida and California, pulling his "wigwam" and marrying women along the way.

While in college in 1959, I took a group of friends to visit him at a trailer camp near the Del Mar race track in California. He was still a gambler. Now, I can imagine him gambling at Choctaw ball games in the 19th century. Well, in this case, modern life provided him with race horses. I remember him draining a can of beer for breakfast my first morning in his trailer. He excused himself around noon to visit the wife of the writer of a handicapping sheet who lived in a trailer nearby. They pulled their trailer from track assignment to track assignment. While the writer was at the track studying horses, my father went to bed with his wife.

My father never forgot his Indian heritage and the harm done to the Choctaws. His stories were full of names, such as the Leflores and the Goodings. "Always remember," he told me, "that you're related to Basil Leflore." Of course, in my younger years I only thought that "Basil" as a name was pretty weird. But, in later years, I could appreciate the importance of their roles in tribal history. Occasionally, he would receive money from the tribe from funds owed by the U.S. government.

The Great Seal of the Choctaw Nation was hanging on the living room wall of my father's small one-bedroom apartment in Long Beach, California when I went to visit him shortly before his death in 1986. My father was proudly displaying his Native American heritage. A smaller version of the Great Seal adorns my office door at New Paltz College, which, as I mentioned earlier, is only a short distance from where Senator Henry Dawes proclaimed that Indians should learn to be selfish.

My father honored the Great Seal of the Choctaw Nation, which was officially adopted by the Choctaw General Council meeting in Doaksville on October 16, 1860. The tribal legislation dictated that the seal would contain "an unstrung bow, with three arrows and a pipe hatchet blended together, engraven in the center." Around the edges were the words, "The Great Seal of the Choctaw Nation." The pipe hatchet symbolized the ceremonial pipe smoked at council meetings during the deliberation of important issues. The unstrung bow represented peace, and the arrows represented the willingness of the Choctaws to defend their homes.[36]

Today, the Great Seal of the State of Oklahoma incorporates the Choctaw Seal in its upper left-hand ray. I am often startled to see something that looks like the Choctaw Seal on Oklahoma license plates. It is an odd history that this seal legislated in the small town of Doaksville in 1860 might appear on an automobile on the New York State Thruway in the 1990s.

I am surprised by the lack of knowledge by other people of the history of the Choctaws and the other Five Civilized Tribes. I remember being at a party at Maxine Green's apartment in New York City in the early 1970s. She is, of course, one of the great educational philosophers of the 20th century. Among her guests were a married couple who coauthored a book on curriculum history. While I was sitting next to them, the husband blurted out that all radicals came from middle-class Jewish homes. Being a self-styled radical of the times, I replied, "But I am Native American." He answered, "You're lying! You're Jewish."

Of course, after what happened to tribal lands and with my father exchanging his heritage for a Model T Ford, I always applied for college positions under affirmative action. One time, when I was applying for a job at the State University of New York at Albany, the affirmative action officer, who was an African-American female, said to me, "You don't seem to have been much affected by your culture. We can hire two African Americans for the cost of you." I wanted to reply that most chiefs of my tribe in the 19th century were highly educated, with many having studied Latin and Greek. And, on the other hand, I thought, "Well there may be some justice to this, given the Choctaw history regarding slavery." The hiring committee suggested I should have worn war paint and feathers to the interview. Of course, this was a suggestion that reflected their lack of knowledge about the history of the southern Indians.

When my father died in 1986 at the age of 83, the Great Seal of the Choctaw Nation was one of his fondest possessions. This part of my family heritage represents only a part of the many historical threads woven into the fabric of the United States. The history of the tribe demonstrates the complicated nature of the history of Native Americans. The history of the Choctaws also represents, as I discuss in the next section, is part of the historical heritage of the United States. This heritage provides an alternative to the Protestant ethic that dominates political life in the late 20th century.

CONCLUSION: WHITE ON THE OUTSIDE AND RED ON THE INSIDE

What have I learned from my family and tribal history extending from the French colonial army in the 18th century to a trading post and inn on the Natchez Trace, to a plantation near Doaksville, to a community at Goodland, to the boosterism in Hugo, to the Great Seal of the Choctaw Nation hanging in a lonely apartment in Long Beach, California in 1986? What did more than a century of federal civilization programs and missionary efforts accomplish? Should I conclude that these programs worked by creating "apples": Red on the outside and White on the inside? Or should I become a new type of apple: White on the outside and Red on the inside?

The breakup of the Choctaw Nation and the collapse of my grand-mother's family left my father adrift in the changing world of the 20th century. He led a wandering life void of meaning except for a few fleeting marriages and affairs and good nights at the gambling table. In turn, his life, combined with my mother's roving nature, left me rootless and adrift. Similar to Choctaws of the 19th century, I found my life being molded by the policies of the federal government. After graduating from high school in 1958, I joined the war against communism by accepting a Navy scholarship to college. After abandoning the Navy, I avoided the military draft by continuing in college. As the Viet Nam War heated up in the 1960s, I continued to avoid military service by accepting federal money under the National Defense Education Act to become a school teacher. After 1 year in the public schools, I returned to college in 1965 and completed my dissertation in 1969. These were the years of major protest against the Viet Nam War.

Similar to many people of my generation, the antiwar movement changed my political perspective. But I was not drawn to European philosophies of socialism and communism because they involved more government control and intervention. I was haunted by the feeling of being manipulated by forces outside my control. I turned my attention to the study of public schools, because they openly claimed to shape my behavior.

With regard to a political philosophy, I found the antigovernment and antiauthoritarian approach of anarchist philosophy most appealing. This led to involvement in the Libertarian Party and working for methods such as vouchers to counter the controlling aspects of schooling. I was attracted to the Libertarian position on foreign affairs, which was critical of the interventionist policies of the U.S. government. I was attracted to their support of cultural and intellectual freedom.

One thing that bothered me about libertarianism was the quickness of business groups to use libertarian arguments to justify ending federal regulations that reduced their profits. The 1980 election of Ronald Reagan brought many libertarians into government and I learned that the call for less government and more freedom simply meant allowing businesses to make more profit. While the new conservatives gave business more freedom to make money, they sought greater controls over culture and morality.

I was in a rage. The psychological and the political within me came together. I was rootless and adrift in the modern world of disintegrating families and relationships. Places of beauty I knew as a child—California and Hawaii—were now cesspools of environmental destruction. My heart cries whenever I see what has happened to the United States. Why? Why has the United States become a wasted opportunity?

And then, I returned to the history of my tribe and family. What a story! From Jefferson to Dawes, the primary concern was teaching Choctaws to be selfish, acquire wealth, and reshape nature. It is astonishing, but true. Thomas Jefferson wanted to create a desire among southern Indians for manufactured goods so that they would be willing to sell their lands. He wanted the yeoman farmer who would desire to constantly improve his lot by working harder. Thomas McKenney believed civilizing the Indians involved creating patrilineal nuclear families so that the fathers would want to acquire wealth to pass on to their children. Missionaries wanted a patrilineal families for the same reason and, in addition, they thought it would result in stricter discipline of children. The missionaries believed that the traditional Indian value of sharing should be replaced with a work ethic and desire to acquire property. And, of course, Senator Dawes believed the failure in not civilizing the Indians was a result of not teaching selfishness.

What were the results of the efforts to "civilize" Indians? One was the creation in tribes of social classes. Another was the instilling of a work ethic among some Indians, mainly mixed-bloods. Accompanying the work ethic was greed. When I think of success at instilling these values, I think of my great-great-uncle Greenwood Leflore sitting in his huge plantation house in Mississippi being waited on by slaves; or my great-great grandfather, Principal Chief Basil Leflore, living on his plantation outside of Doaksville; or my grandfather, Chief Joel Spring, welcoming the end of the Choctaw Republic as he engaged in real estate speculation in Hugo. I also think of the traditional full-bloods who were uprooted from their homes in Mississippi and later in Indian Territory to make way for the White person's greed. I remember my father during his dying days sitting in a lonely apartment in California staring at the Great Seal of the Choctaw Nation hanging on the wall.

The results of "civilizing" Indians helps me to understand the underlying problem with the American creed. The problem is the "Protestant ethic"—the very values inflicted on Indians by government leaders and the missionaries. These values were destructive of Native American values, and, I argue, of much of the joy that might be possible in American lives.

Imagine a politician who campaigned with the slogan "Less work and more enjoyment." Imagine an economist who argued, "We should focus technological development on creating jobs that are interesting and provide more free time to the worker." Imagine a set of values based on increasing human pleasure and fulfilling human desires rather than trying to deny pleasure and curb desires.

The problem with capitalism is not the free market, which never completely existed in the United States. The problem is the set of values accompanying capitalism. I always laugh when someone suggests that this country was built on capitalism. Slavery built the economy of the south, free homesteads to settlers and free land to railroads built the west, and federal investment in military technology made the United States a world power. And, of course, the conquest and breaking of treaties with Native Americans opened lands to European settlers. This is hardly capitalism.

The Protestant values underlying U.S. institutions and the economy, which are the same values that were imposed on Native Americans, are nicely articulated by Newt Gingrich in his book, *To Renew America*. Of course, Gingrich is interested in renewing these values in the United States, while I am interested in replacing them with more humane values. Correctly, I think Gingrich argues, "From the Jamestown Colony and the Pilgrims to the very founding fathers, the centrality of God and religion is unmistakable."[37]

One problem with Gingrich's statement was his failure to identify "God." The "God" of the Pilgrims, Puritans, and founding fathers was a Protestant God. Certainly, it was not the Great Spirit of the Cherokees or Choctaws. This Protestant God was interested in the value of work for work's sake, the improvement and accumulation of property, and the centrality of humans over the rest of nature. As Gingrich states, "This brings us to another American characteristic: the work ethic." And, probably to the astonishment of those who work at meaningless jobs in food service, offices, and factories, Gingrich describes: "The Spirit of Free Enterprise: Americans get up every day hoping to put in *a good day's work, create a little more wealth, provide a little better service to their customers, or invent a slightly better mousetrap for the world* [italics added]."[38]

The values of the Protestant ethic have hardly produced a utopia. It would be difficult to defend the proposition that people are any happier today than they were 100 years ago even though we are surrounded by "better mousetraps." We are confronted with a future in which most people will be working longer hours at uninteresting work, economic inequalities will be greater, and the environment will be destroyed. The traditional Protestant ethic of the American creed is supportive of this depressing future by valuing hard work, accumulation of wealth, and the domination by humans over nature.

Just as the imposition of the Protestant ethic destroyed Native Americans, it continues to have the potential for destroying human happiness. I think we need to radically change the dominant values of the Protestant ethic by incorporating Native American values into the American creed. This would result in new values directing social change: the minimization of time spent at unpleasant work; the maximization of time for pleasure and the celebration of life; the desire to share rather than accumulate property; and the placement of humans in the scared hoop of nature as opposed to assumption that nature exists for humans.

It is important for the reader to understand that these are values to guide future economic, social, and political changes. It is not a specific plan for an economy or government. These are the values we need to create a more enjoyable and humane future. These are the values we should use in making decisions about our economy, our community, and our government. We should reject the values of hard work, the curbing of desires, the accumulation of property, and the shaping of nature to meet human needs.

One could argue that the values I am proposing are not part of human nature. I remember delivering a paper on Native American values at a conference when someone in the audience asked me: "Aren't greed and self-interest part of human nature? Don't we need to build an economy around those inherent features of human nature?" I replied that the history of Native Americans seems to indicate that greed is not inherent in human nature but is learned. And, as I thought about it, I pointed out that in the history of Christianity there was some emphasis on sharing and meekness. The money changers were chased out of the temple. On the other hand, the Protestant ethic seems to have welcomed them into the temple of America.

The history of my tribe and family has changed my politics and values. Now, I feel rooted in the American past. My ancestors five generations removed were "apples" who were "White" on the inside and "Red" on the outside. Now I am a different type of "apple." I am White on the outside and Red on the inside. I want to end the reign of the Protestant ethic and replace it with values emphasizing minimum work with maximum pleasure, sharing, maximization of play and ceremonies, and the sacred hoop of nature. We need a new breed of "apples."

NOTES

[1] Quoted in Angie Debo, *And Still the Waters Run: The Betrayal of the Five Civilized Tribes* (Princeton: Princeton University Press, 1968), pp. 21–22.

[2] "Program of the Lake Mohonk Conference, September 1884," in *Documents of United States Indian Policy, Second Edition* (Lincoln: University of Nebraska Press, 1990), p. 163.

[3] Ibid., 163; on Indian citizenship acts see *Documents of United States Indian...*, pp. 199, 218.

[4] *Documents of United States Indian...*, p. 164.

[5] See "General Allotment Act (Dawes Act). February 8, 1887," *Documents of United States Indian...*, pp. 171–174.

[6] Quoted in Debo, *And Still the Waters Run...*, p. 55.

[7] See "Commission of the five Civilized Tribes (Dawes Commission) March 3, 1893," *Documents of United States Indian...*, pp. 189–190.

[8] "Report of the Dawes Commission November 20, 1894," *Documents of United States Indian...*, p. 193.

[9] Ibid., p. 192.

[10] Ibid., p. 191.

[11] Angie Debo, *The Rise and Fall of the Choctaw Republic* (Norman: University of Oklahoma Press, 1961), p. 256.

[12]"Curtis Act June 28, 1898," Documents of United States Indian...,
pp. 197–198.

[13]Photograph of Principal Chief Green mcCurtain can be found in
Debo, *The Rise and Fall of the Choctaw Republic*, p. 253.

[14]"Joel Spring, Pioneer Hugo Citizen, Played Important Part in History," The Hugo Daily News, Section 3, August 28–29, 1941, pp. 1–2.

[15]"Mrs. Griffith relates Tales of Pioneer Life Here Told Her by Her
Grandmother," *The Hugo Daily News,* Section 3, August 28–29, 1941,
pp. 4–6.

[16]"Joel Spring, Pioneer...," p. 2.

[17]Frances Imon, *Smoke Signals from Indian Territory* (Wlfe City, TX:
Hennington Publishing Company, 1976), pp. 4, 51–55.

[18]"Opportunity: Hugo Oklahoma: A City of Wonderful Resources,"
(Hugo, OK: Southswestern Land Company, 1916), pages are unnumbered. Available through the Hugo Historical Society.

[19]See Debo, *And Still the Waters Run...*, for a discussion of full-blook
losses during the land rush. I discuss this issue later in this chapter.

[20]Quoted in Imon, p. 1.

[21]"Opportunity: Hugo Oklahoma. . .," pages are unnumbered.

[22]Eloise Spear, *Choctaw Indian Education with Special Reference to
Choctaw County, Oklahoma* (Ann Arbor, MI: University Microfilms
International, 1977), p.p. 161, 167–168.

[23]Debo, *And Still the Waters Run...*, pp. 66–74.

[24]Quoted in Ibid., p. 71.

[25]Spear, pp. 166, 203.

[26]Imon, p. 3.

[27]Ibid., pp. 3.

[28]"Choctaw Nation. Choctaw Rolls," Field No. 1402, Goodland, Indian
Territory (May 8, 1899).

[29]Spear, p. 180.

[30]"New Born, Choctaw Nation, Choctaw Roll," Post Office: Hugo,
Indian Territory, Card No. 1071, April 28, 1905. As indicated on the card,
my father was born on December 23, 1903, and he was officially approved for enrollment on July 22, 1905. It should be noted that my
father's enrollment took place in the post office my grandfather "stole"
from the west side of Hugo.

[31]Debo, *And Still the Waters Run . . .*, p. 46.

[32]Ibid., p. 51.

[33]Ibid., p. 47.

[34]Ibid., p. 356.

[35]Spear, pp. 194–195.

[36]Frances Imon, *Smoke Signals from Indian Territory Volume II*
(Wolfe City, TX: Henington Publishing Company, 1977), pp. 19–21.

[37]I must admit that I did not buy Mr. Gingrich's book. I am quoting
from an excerpt from *To Renew America* published as Newt Gingrich,

"Renewing America: In his new book, Newt says stop whining," *Newsweek* (July 10, 1995), p. 26.

[38]Ibid., pp. 25–26.

10

Afterword: The Role of Schooling in Modern Society

The use of schools by the federal government to gain Indian lands in the 19th century reflected a belief in the power of the school to control the values, actions, and ideas of citizens. Also, the use of schooling as a part of general Indian policies represents growing consideration of schooling as an instrument of public policy. In a broader framework, this was the birth of schooling as means of ideological management.

One of the distinctive features of modern schooling is the use of classroom and school organization to consciously shape the social behaviors of students. The introduction of the Lancasterian method of instruction in the United States in the early 19th century represented a distinct break with previous conceptions of education. Missionary educators of the Choctaws and Cherokees in the early 19th century used the Lancasterian system of classroom management for the purpose of changing the behavior of Native American students. In the Lancasterian system, the habits of orderliness, industriousness, and obedience that students learned through the method of instruction were considered as valuable as the knowledge they gained through formal instruction and reading. Often likened to a factory system, the Lancasterian method of instruction was considered an important means of socializing children to developing methods of production and to work in business offices. Using this method of instruction, along with instruction in agriculture and domestic arts, the missionaries hoped to change the behaviors and social values of the Choctaws.

Modern schools exist to instill belief in particular economic and political systems. In the case of the Choctaws, U.S. government officials were interested in instilling economic and political values that were compatible with capitalism and representative government. Traditionally, most Native American tribes were organized around a different set of values based on a clan system of sharing and consensus government. The conversion from traditional economic and political ideas to an acceptance of capitalism and representative government was a key factor in the cultural transformation of the Choctaws.

Among Choctaws, who traditionally did not have social classes, schooling became an important means of creating and distinguishing social classes. For instance, the Spencer Academy in the Choctaw Nation served the children of elite families. Many of its graduates went on to college. The social function of the Spencer Academy was similar to other modern schools that mirror the inequalities in society and, consequently, they often reinforce those inequalities. In a society that prizes schooling, school credentials often indicate social class. Traditionally, graduation from an elite university indicates either the graduate's family is a member of the upper class or the graduate has the potential for gaining entry into that social class. Today, graduation from high school or college is directly related to potential future earnings. The individual whose education is limited to high school most often comes from a low-income family, whereas graduates of average colleges and elite colleges come from middle-income and upper-income families, respectively.

The Choctaws established a differentiated school system that selected students by social class and prepared them for different and unequal roles in the Choctaw economy. Some tribal schools provided what was considered an elite education whereas others offered manual training. In the same manner, the modern school also supports inequalities in the labor market. These inequalities require workers to believe that salaries should be differentiated on the basis of skills and education. For instance, garbage collectors perform a great deal of distasteful work. Why should their labor be worth less then that of a white collar worker? In general, separate curriculum tracks in high school divide students according to their future destination in the labor market. Often, vocational education tracks prepare students for jobs that pay less than the jobs being prepared for by students in college preparatory tracks.

Although Choctaws experienced racism from Europeans, they also practiced racism toward their own enslaved Africans. As a slave-owning and racist tribe, they helped maintain the inferior status of their freed slaves by creating segregated schools. Similar to the Choctaws, many modern schools support racist patterns of segregation that are used to create a sense of inferiority and provide justification for economic exploitation. In U.S. schools, the segregation of Native Americans, Mexican Americans, Chinese, Japanese, and African Americans at different periods of time was associated with their economic exploitation. Native Americans were exploited for their lands; Mexican Americans were exploited for their lands and labor; and Chinese, Japanese, and African Americans were exploited for their labor. Despite the fact that laws requiring racial segregation no longer exist in the United States, U.S. schools continue to be highly segregated.

Among the Choctaws, literacy became an important means of gaining political power. As tribal government changed from a system of rule by tradition and consensus to rule by written law, literacy became an important means of gaining political power. The growth of lawyers in Indian Territory reflected the transition to a government of written laws. In a similar fashion, the spread of schooling and literacy made it possible to centralize government operations and develop a bureaucracy.

Literacy became the key to tribal control of trade. European-American economic systems require literacy for understanding contracts and accounts. Some Choctaws wanted schools to prepare tribal members to function in the White economic system. Trade and the accumulation of wealth under a system of laws required literacy. If tribal members were to gain economic independence, they had to end dependence on the White frontier traders.

How do you educate Native Americans so that they accept the authority of a White-dominated government? How do you keep them from rebelling against the very government that is providing the schools? Modern systems of schooling often contain the seeds of resistance and revolution. Many tribal leaders wanted schools so that they could protect themselves from the aggression of the U.S. government. Although both groups wanted education for the Native Americans, there was a major difference between the goals of the U.S. government and the intentions of the tribe. This difference represents one of the major problems with modern systems of schooling. Schools can serve as instruments of control or they can serve as instruments of freedom. In the case of Native Americans in the 19th century, the U.S. government leaders primarily used schools to control Native Americans as a means of gaining their lands.

Index